Consuming the Environment

Consuming the Environment explores the environmental impacts of consuming everyday products and explains how we can consume more sustainably.

Written in an accessible style, this book begins with our everyday mundane experiences of consuming products – online, in the grocery store, at the mall – and shows how these practices are connected to a global system dependent upon ever increasing consumption. Drawing on the expertise of researchers in topics such as energy, food, water, land, fashion, electronics, eco-tourism, green products, and (micro)plastics, this volume unpacks the complex and largely invisible relationships that consumerism has with resource extraction and manufacturing. By focusing on a diverse range of everyday consumer products, as well as more subtle things that have been transformed into products, such as knowledge, waste, and pets, the chapters are structured around the central argument that we must re-orient ourselves as citizens rather than consumers. It is as citizens that we may help to organize our communities and hold our governments and industry accountable to planetary sustainability boundaries.

With the inclusion of summary boxes, directed discussion, assignment questions, and further reading in each chapter, this book will be an essential resource for undergraduate and postgraduate students studying courses on consumerism, sustainable consumption, and environmental sociology.

Myra J. Hird is a Full Professor, elected Fellow of the Royal Society of Canada, and Queen's National Scholar in the School of Environmental Studies, Queen's University, Canada. Hird is Director of *Waste Flows*, an interdisciplinary research project focused on waste as a global scientific-technical and socio-ethical issue. Hird has published 12 books and over 90 articles and book chapters on a diversity of topics relating to science studies. Hird's 12th book, written with Hillary Predko, is called *Extracting Reconciliation* and is published by Routledge. Hird represented Canada at the G7 Science Meeting on Plastic Pollution in Paris, France.

Routledge – SCORAI Studies in Sustainable Consumption

This series aims to advance conceptual and empirical contributions to this new and important field of study. For more information about The Sustainable Consumption Research and Action Initiative (SCORAI) and its activities please visit www.scorai.org.

Sustainable Products in the Circular Economy
Impact on Business and Society
Edited by Magdalena Wojnarowska, Marek Ćwiklicki and Carlo Ingrao

Narrating Sustainability through Storytelling
Edited by Daniel Fischer, Sonja Fücker, Hanna Selm and Anna Sundermann

The Low-Carbon Good Life
Jules Pretty

Teaching and Learning Sustainable Consumption
A Guidebook
Edited by Jen Dyer, Daniel Fischer, Jordan King, Marlyne Sahakian, and Gill Seyfang

Consuming the Environment
Edited by Myra J. Hird

For more information about this series, please visit: www.routledge.com/Routledge-SCORAI-Studies-in-Sustainable-Consumption/book-series/RSSC

Consuming the Environment

Edited by Myra J. Hird

Routledge
Taylor & Francis Group
LONDON AND NEW YORK

earthscan
from Routledge

Designed cover image: Getty images

First published 2025
by Routledge
4 Park Square, Milton Park, Abingdon, Oxon OX14 4RN

and by Routledge
605 Third Avenue, New York, NY 10158

Routledge is an imprint of the Taylor & Francis Group, an informa business

British Library Cataloguing-in-Publication Data
A catalogue record for this book is available from the British Library

ISBN: 978-1-032-53536-4 (hbk)
ISBN: 978-1-032-53537-1 (pbk)
ISBN: 978-1-003-41252-6 (ebk)

DOI: 10.4324/9781003412526

Typeset in Galliard
by Newgen Publishing UK

Contents

Contributors

Terry Beckman received his Ph.D. in Marketing from Queen's University and his M.B.A in International Business from the University of Victoria. He teaches Marketing Management, and International Business Management in an online environment. In addition to teaching and developing courses for an online university, he has also done some research in pedagogy and online learning. Prior to Athabasca University, he taught at Queen's University, The Royal Military College of Canada and the University of Victoria. His research interests are primarily in corporate social responsibility, corporate branding, international business, and marketing strategy. He has published one edited book and a variety of articles in his areas of research interest.

Patrick Brodie is an Assistant Professor and Ad Astra Fellow in the School of Information and Communication Studies at University College Dublin. His research focuses on the environmental implications of digital infrastructures, including their connections with energy, extraction, and rural geographies. He has published widely in the areas of media, communication, geography, and science and technology studies, and he is the co-editor of the *Journal of Environmental Media*.

Gabriella Dee earned a PhD in Biology, and recently completed a master's at the School of Environmental Studies, Queen's University, Canada, where she investigated the relationship between the waste hierarchy and local waste management, the pros and cons of bringing more waste services back under city control, and the importance of volunteers in reducing waste at festivals. With her move from the study of life to the study of discarding objects, Dee personifies current efforts at bridging the gap between natural and social sciences in the study of waste in society.

Romain J. Garcier is an Associate Professor of geography at Ecole Normale Supérieure de Lyon, in France. He researches and teaches energy and material issues, especially those related to the nuclear industry and critical metals.

Sonya Graci is an Associate Professor at the Ted Rogers School of Hospitality and Tourism Management at Toronto Metropolitan University. She is also the Director of the Institute of Hospitality and Tourism Research. Dr. Graci's research focuses on sustainable tourism specifically in island destinations as well as Indigenous tourism. Her passion to create sustainable livelihoods is evident in her research with communities across the globe.

Nicolas Graham is a Banting Postdoctoral Fellow in the Department of Sociology at the University of British Columbia. His research focuses on the political economy of decarbonization and energy transition and seeks to understand the forces and actors enabling and obstructing effective and just climate action.

Myra J. Hird is a Full Professor, elected Fellow of the Royal Society of Canada, and Queen's National Scholar in the School of Environmental Studies, Queen's University, Canada. Hird is Director of *Waste Flows*, an interdisciplinary research project focused on waste as a global scientific-technical and socio-ethical issue. Hird has published 11 books and over 90 articles and book chapters on a diversity of topics relating to science studies. Hird's 12th book, written with Hillary Predko, is called *Extracting Reconciliation* and is published by Routledge Press. Hird represented Canada at the G7 Science Meeting on Plastic Pollution in Paris, France.

Lara Houston is a Research Fellow at the Global Sustainability Institute, Anglia Ruskin University (Cambridge, UK). She investigates sustainability through grassroots, citizen-led practices – this has included collaborations with electronics repairers, citizen scientists and urban farmers. She specialises in using creative, inventive and participatory methods.

Priscylla Joca is a non-Indigenous researcher and an Assistant Professor at Toronto Metropolitan University's Lincoln Alexander School of Law, with a Doctorate in Law from the University of Montreal and a Master's in Constitutional Law from the Federal University of Ceará. Her research focuses on the human and environmental rights of Indigenous peoples and traditional local communities from a pluralist, international, and comparative perspective, particularly in Canada and Brazil. She is a member of the Autonomous Protocols Observatory.

Marta Massi, PhD, is Assistant Professor at Athabasca University, Canada. She was Assistant Professor at Trent University and Lecturer at McGill University. Her research focuses on consumer behavior, digital marketing and branding. She has published her research in outlets such as *Psychology & Marketing*, *Journal of Strategic Marketing* and *Journal of Business & Industrial Marketing*. Most recently, she edited the Routledge book *Digital Transformation in the Cultural and Creative Industries. Production, Consumption and Entrepreneurship in the Digital Economy and Sharing*.

Josh Milburn is a Lecturer in Political Philosophy at Loughborough University in the UK. His work addresses questions about human relationships with animals in moral, legal, and political philosophy. He is the author of *Just Fodder: The Ethics of Feeding Animals* (McGill-Queen's University Press, 2022) and *Food, Justice, and Animals: Feeding the World Respectfully* (Oxford University Press, 2023), as well as the host of the animal studies podcast Knowing Animals.

Luciana Nóbrega holds a doctorate in Sociology, a master's degree and a degree in Law. She specializes in Indigenism at Fundação Nacional dos Povos Indígenas (National Indigenous Peoples Foundation in Brazil). Her research focuses on Indigenous peoples, socio-environmental conflicts, extractivism, Indigenous cosmopolitics, and related areas. She is a member of the Autonomous Protocols Observatory.

Leiliane Jacinto Pereira, a member of the Juruna/Yudjá Indigenous People, also known as Bel Juruna, is a multifaceted professional from Muratu village. She works as a nursing technician, artisan, and farmer, and she is the secretary of the AYMIX association and a member of the Autonomous Protocols Observatory.

Emily Potter is Professor in Writing and Literature, in the School of Communication and Creative Arts, Deakin University. She researches across place-making and narrative practice, and critical environmentalism and consumption studies. She is co-author of *Plastic Water: The Social and Political Life of Bottled Water* (MIT Press), and author of *Writing Belonging at the Millennium: Notes from the Field of Settler Colonial Place* (Uni Chicago).

Elaine Power is a Professor in the School of Kinesiology & Health Studies at Queen's University, where she has taught courses on the social determinants of health and food systems. She has been researching food insecurity for more than three decades, and has become a proponent of a guaranteed liveable basic income as a more effective and just solution to food insecurity than charitable approaches that leave relations of power and inequity intact.

Jacob Riha was a Master's student in the School of Enviornmental Studies at Queen's University. He lives in Kingston, Ontario.

Laurence Rocher is Professor in urban planning at Lyon 2 University and member of the research laboratory Environnement, Ville, Société. Her research focuses on the social and spatial issues of environmental public policies (waste, climate and energy). She is particularly interested in the reconsideration of urban resources and flows with a view to the energy transition and the circular economy.

Sofi Thanhauser is the author of *Worn: A People's History of Clothing* (2022). She has received fellowships from ClimateWorks Foundation, the Calderwood Fellowship for Journalism, the Fulbright Program, MacDowell, and the Ucross Foundation. Her writing has appeared in *The Guardian, Vox, Observer Magazine, Dame, The Drift* and *MIT Technology Review*.

Tony Walker is a Professor at the School for Resource and Environmental Studies, Dalhousie University in Canada. Tony has studied impacts of plastic pollution for nearly 30 years. He helped participate in a Leaders and Experts Roundtable on Plastics and Marine Litter to help develop the Ocean Plastics Charter for Canada's 2018 G7 presidency. He participated in the Canadian Science Symposium on Plastics to inform represented Canada at the G7 Science Meeting on Plastic Pollution in Paris, France. He has published extensively on policies to reduce impacts of plastic pollution and is Associate Editor for *Marine Pollution Bulletin* and Cambridge Prisms: Plastics.

Kaitlyn Washbrook has a bachelor's in hospitality and tourism. She is actively involved in research involving consumer behaviour and sustainable tourism at Toronto Metropolitan University. Her expertise and research focus includes regenerative tourism, consumer behaviour, and Indigenous tourism.

Acknowledgements

Edited collections can be tricky: organizing contributors, chapters, revisions, and permissions is often akin to herding cats. I thank all of the contributors to this book who took up the challenge of writing thoughtful chapters, replying with grace to my incessant emails, and for staying convivial throughout the process. What we collectively produced is more than the sum of its parts. The contributors have ensured that *Consuming the Environment* helps us to think about the connections between entities that we are accustomed to thinking about in isolation: fashion and water; pet food and electronics; knowledge and land, and so on. Understanding these interconnections invites us to appreciate the complexities that consuming entails, and the urgency of addressing its environmental, human health, and social injustice consequences.

I thank Grace Harrison, Matthew Shobbrook, Rosie Anderson, and Jyotsna Gurung for editorial guidance and support throughout the editing process.

An earlier version of Chapter 14 appears in Hird, M.J. and Riha, J. 'Prepping for the [insert here] apocalypse and wasting the future', in Z. Gille and J. Lepawsky (eds) *Handbook of Waste Studies*, New York and London: Routledge, 2021, pp 305– 21 and is used with permission. I thank the Social Sciences and Humanities Research Council of Canada for funding for some of the research described in this book. I thank Gabriella Dee for her helpful conversations and support during the editing of this collection.

As always, this book, like everything else, is made better with Inis and Eshe in my life: my ground, my safe and sound, my aerials.

Introduction

Myra J. Hird

Introduction

Consuming the Environment is a book about the impact that consuming things and services has on the Earth: the place we live, and depend on for our survival. The Earth is 149.6 million kilometers from the sun. It has a surface area of 510.1 million km^2 and a land area of 148.9 million kilometers. The Earth is about 4.5 billion years old, and life in its earliest microbial forms evolved some 3.7 billion years ago. There are some 8.7 million species of plants and animals living on Earth, most of which are insects. And there are about 7.8 billion people living on the planet.

We define the environment as the natural world, which includes living organisms (from bacteria to polar bears) as well as all of the rocks, sand, water, sun and so on. The Earth involves very complex continuous interactions between physical, chemical, and biotic elements, often referred to as the **ecosystem**. Ecosystems are in fact plural, with many geographic areas where microorganisms, plants, animals, and other organisms interact with each other and the geography, including the weather and landscape of a particular area. Ecosystems may be very small, such as a small pond; or they may be larger, such as a crop of trees. We may think of the Earth as a series of interconnected ecosystems. Each element of an ecosystem affects each other; which is to say that each element depends on every other element. A change in humidity or temperature, for instance, may change the ecosystem and affect the living organisms dependent on that ecosystem. Several ecosystems may be joined together in a **biome**, which is a larger surface area, such as a forest, tundra, ocean or desert.

Throughout history, humans have constantly interacted with ecosystems and biomes. Since approximately 11,000 BCE, humans began clearing land, planting crops and raising animals. This process accelerated, producing more food, which enabled increases in human and animal populations. Now, according to the World Resources Institute, "worldwide agriculture has already cleared or converted 70 percent of grassland, 50 percent of savanna, 45 percent of the temperate deciduous forest and 27 percent of tropical forests" (in

DOI: 10.4324/9781003412526-1

Hanson and Ranganathan 2023: np). The dramatic increase in the transformation of forests and other natural land into agriculture is part of what is known as the **Great Acceleration**. The Great Acceleration refers to a period of time, starting in the mid-20th century and continuing today, during which human activity has increased dramatically. This human activity includes things like resource extraction (fossil fuels and minerals), an enormous increase in agricultural land-use, the production and consumption of products and services, and massive increases in waste and pollution. The Great Acceleration includes hydro-electric dams, agriculture (including dramatic increases in pesticides and fertilizer use), global tourism, domestic and foreign investment and trade, electronics, communication and other technologies, transportation (mainly using fossil fuels), and so on.

As the chapters in this book show, these dramatic increases in extraction, production, distribution, and consumption have, and are having, severe impacts on the environment. Scientists have identified nine global planetary environmental processes that are essential to human survival, and the limits to which these processes may be taken. Scientists call this **planetary boundaries**, and they include: climate change; stratospheric ozone depletion; atmospheric aerosol loading; ocean acidification; biogeochemical flows; novel entities; freshwater change; land-system change, and; biosphere integrity. In 2023, an international team of scientists quantified nine planetary boundaries. We had crossed three boundaries by 2009. As of 2023, we have crossed six of the nine boundaries: climate change; novel entities; biogeochemical flows; freshwater change; land system change, and; biosphere integrity (Richardson et al 2023).

Having surpassed six boundaries already, we must ensure that we do not surpass the three remaining boundaries as well as find ways to bring the six already-surpassed planetary boundaries within the Earth's capacity to function. Transgressing these boundaries, often called **Global Tipping Points**, are causing increased environmental instability, which is taking the form of increased forest fires, floods, higher regional and global temperatures, melting glaciers, water shortages and so on – events that are increasingly brought to our attention through global media reports. These increasing environmental events are triggering social consequences such as a dramatic increase in environmental refugees, financial destabilization, violent conflicts over resources, and other worrying impacts (Lenton et al 2023). These negative tipping points must be replaced with positive tipping points, such as transitioning to renewable energy, and they must happen very soon (ibid).

People around the world – and especially people with the economic resources to buy and to choose what they buy – are increasingly recognizing connections between environmental degradation and consumption. When we consider consumption alongside depleting natural resources and surpassing planetary boundaries – or what is sometimes called the Earth's carrying capacity – we may usefully think of this as **consuming the environment**.

Consumption, Consumers, and Consumerism

Simply put, **consumption** is the using of a resource. A resource may be non-renewable: once used, it cannot be re-used or renewed (ex. fossil fuels). Or a resource may be renewable: once used, it will eventually replenish as part of the Earth's natural materials cycling (ex. wind, fresh water). **Consumers** are generally defined as people who use non-renewable or renewable resources. By this broad definition, all human beings are consumers (even breast-fed babies, who consume milk produced by people who must consume food, water and other resources). The term **consumerism** gets to the heart of the relationship between consumption and the environment. Consumerism is the attainment of goods and services beyond what is required for survival.

While Roman orgies and the excesses of monarchs throughout history are famous examples of over-consumption, the daily over-consumption that characterizes modern society is a fairly recent phenomenon. Up until the mid-twentieth century, thrift was the norm. People in economically developed countries like France, the United Kingdom and the United States regularly reused, mended, refurbished, and otherwise held on to their clothes, household furnishings, food leftovers for as long as possible. Factories at this time commonly reserved some jobs for sorting through ashes, bones, and other materials leftover during the manufacturing process. Thrifting, re-using, and refurbishing – and just plain doing without – has largely been replaced in affluent nations in what is termed our "throwaway society" (Strasser 1999). Now these things – sewing clothing, knitting and combing through clothes in a used clothing store – are defined as hobbies rather than vital to household economic maintenance. But before the twentieth century, these things were normal everyday practices. As well as middle-class people trading rags and other materials to peddlers – men who went door-to-door in communities collecting these materials and then selling them to buyers – in exchange for needed items:

> ...customers practiced habits of reuse that had prevailed in agricultural communities here and abroad. Women boiled food scraps into soup or fed them to domestic animals; chickens, especially, would eat almost anything and return the favour with eggs. Durable items were passed on to people of other classes or generations, or stored in attics or basements for later use. Objects of no use to adults became playthings for children. Broken or worn-out things could be brought back to their makers, fixed by somebody handy, or taken to people who specialized in repairs. And items beyond repair might be dismantled, their parts reused or sold to junk men who sold them to manufacturers. Things that could not be used in any other way were burned; especially in the homes of the poor, trash heated rooms and cooked dinners.
>
> (ibid: 12)

A thriving popular literature concerned itself with offering advice to women as to how best to manage their households (which included slaves and servants in the United States and other colonial nations) through thrift. Books and magazines such as Christine Herrick's *Housekeeping Made Easy* and Lydia Child's *The American Frugal Housewife* extolled the moral and practical virtues of minimizing waste as much as possible and contained all sorts of varied advice from glue-making recipes to repairing broken ceramics and marble to chemical mixtures to remove stains, waterproofing fabrics and cleaning chamber pots. Serving leftovers was elevated to an art form in such books as *The Family Save-All: A System of Secondary Cookery*, with a plethora of recipes and tips for re-serving food to families. When that route was exhausted, women were advised to give food to the household livestock and to servants (who, the books and magazines warned, must be properly supervised at all times lest they steal food from their employers). Women were advised on how to patch, darn, and otherwise mend clothing. When one child outgrew a shirt or pants, it should be passed down to the next child, or taken apart and fabric added to enlarge the garment for further wear. Rags could be made into rugs and quilts to keep homes warm. Even the packaging that goods such as furniture came in was reused. First of all, the packaging was made out of fabric, wood and other much more readily reusable materials (rather than single-use plastics). And as Strasser points out, people paid for packaging (directly, and not as part of the cost of the product, as is now the case). The packaging was valuable: businesses reused this packaging. Consumers also used packaging: "the purple wrapping paper that came with sugar...could be used for dye, the brown overalls patched with flour sacks, the rugs hooked on coffee sacks, the paint-covered pickle jar" (1999: 67). As late as 1882, manuals had to actually define what a wastepaper basket was (ibid). In all of this advice, women were central to the value of stewardship; of keeping their homes, husbands and children clean and tidy. Women were to gather up any household surplus, from crockery to coats and socks, and donate them to poorer families.

As such, up until industrialization, economies were largely circular. Extensive everyday thrifting, reuse and informal collectors collecting and selling back to manufacturers who in turn used these materials in their production of new products meant that raw and manufactured materials remained for much longer periods in circulation, rather than going to waste shortly after their first consumption. This is not to say that industrialization had no negative impact on the environment: on the contrary, industrialization produced extensive land, water, and air pollution.

The manufacturing, retail, and consumption revolution temporarily dipped during World War II (although war-products such as munitions, soldier uniforms and kits and so on dramatically increased) and allied and enemy countries alike rapidly created public service campaigns to get people to gather and donate valuable materials in service to the war effort. While countries like Germany (East and West) and the United Kingdom maintained rationing for years after World War II ended, other countries – most notably the United

States – witnessed a surge in production, consumption, and waste. People were encouraged by manufacturing, retail, and waste management companies to demonstrate their social class through wasting. New products replaced old products, and products for every part of the household, from small appliances to matching living room and bedroom sets to the outfitted garage to the surge in products for leisure activities (football, windsurfing, skiing etc.) were heavily advertised. Hobbies became consumer activities and power tools, card game paraphernalia, and 'how to' books became necessary investments to optimize leisure time (ibid.). A whole industry of consumer magazines overtook the traditional Sears or other order-through-the-mail catalogues. All of this consumption was advertised to people as technologically superior, more convenient, more hygienic, and a better reflection of how well one was doing in society. As the makeup company Loréal's 1971 advertisement proclaimed 'You're worth it' (Specht and Erikson n.d.).

Companies such as the consortium of American Can companies were able to successfully replace reusable glass bottles with plastic bottles by launching heavy media campaigns to shift people's attention from the plastic waste their new product would produce, to roadside litter for which post-consumption would be blamed and held responsible. Other companies employed the same tactics to introduce a number of products – such as disposable drinking cups and sanitary products – on to the market (Strasser 1999). Not only were these new products advertised as more hygienic (and therefore safer) but much more convenient. Much more convenient and time-saving, then, for the busy housewife to serve her family dried cereal than a cooked breakfast. Women in particular were promised a greater level of freedom from household drudgery with convenience products: the cereal box and leftover cereal tossed into the trash rather than the fat leftover from breakfast painstakingly scraped into the fat jar kept cool, the other food leftovers reserved in yet more cooking, the plates and cutlery washed at the sink. Consumerism, in short, promised women in particular, freedom. Discarding things became an act of personal freedom: freedom to buy whatever we want, and freedom to toss it away when we no longer want it.

More companies are advertising more products more often. Think of how much more people are exposed to marketing via social media – TikTok, Instagram, X, Facebook etc. – compared with radio advertising before the invention of television. Advertising has not only increased in frequency; it has also become more effective in increasing consumption. There are now entire companies devoted to helping other companies increase their sales through marketing (fictionalized through such television shows as Mad Men). But advertising is not the only mechanism through which manufacturers increase consumption. **Planned obsolescence** is a policy that builds technological breakdown and aesthetic undesirability into products in order increase replacement purchasing. Planned obsolescence occurs when manufacturers advertise replacing working products (clothing, appliances, furniture, cars etc.) based on aesthetics. Replacing functioning orange or green wall-to-wall carpeting in vogue during the 1970s with short-ply carpeting is an example of consumption for aesthetic reasons. It is designed to shorten the time span between purchases, known as the 'shortening of the replacement cycle' (Slade 2007).

Analyses of planned obsolescence often identify car manufacturing as the beginning of this policy and practice. In the United States, up until the 1920s, Henry Ford had staked his claim and built his empire on reliable cars built with as few irregularities as possible from a streamlined assembly line. Ford's advertising platform was that his cars were highly dependable and designed to last. This meant that Ford car owners had little need to buy new cars. In 1924, General Motors introduced yearly changes to their cars, heavily advertising these style changes as desirable, and holding on to one's current car as undesirable. The advertising worked, General Motors sales outpaced Ford's and the planned obsolescence race to increase car sales began (Strasser 1999). In the decades since General Motors outsold Ford through constant product 'upgrading', planned obsolescence has gained enormous speed and traction, and has become an in-built feature of 'doing business' in our global capitalist society. This is not to say that, along the way, planned obsolescence critics have not objected to this policy. Design engineers were highly skeptical of obsolescence caused by built-in product failure, pointing out that this was anathema to the whole point of engineering. In his popular books, *The Hidden Persuaders* (1957), *The Status Seekers* (1959) and *The Waste Makers* (1960), Vance Packard extensively studied what he called 'obsolescence of quality' which referred to planned product failure, 'obsolescence of desirability', which referred to aesthetic changes in products designed to increase sales, and 'obsolescence of function', which referred to product modifications that increased the product's performance, such as its efficiency. Packard's books were directed toward the public, to consumers rather than academics. He demonstrated how manufacturers build in obsolescence to their products intentionally, to increase their profits. He pointed out that planned obsolescence depends on consumers not knowing how long a product can actually last. And he heavily criticized consumers for succumbing to the perpetually new 'shiny object'. According to Susan Strasser (1999), Packard's arguments were sharply criticized by business, who argued that consumers wanted constantly updated products, and that 'out-with-the-old; in-with-the-new' was intrinsic to modern business.

It is beyond question that marketing is a significant contributor to increasing consumption. As Harrison Ford's character, Allie, from *The Mosquito Coast* put it:

> We eat when we're not hungry, drink when we're not thirsty. We buy what we don't need and throw away everything that's useful. Why sell a man what he wants? Sell him what he doesn't need. Pretend he's got eight legs and two stomachs and money to burn. It's wrong.
>
> (1999)

Since the early 20th century, the list of single-use and other plastics products has exponentially increased. Swanson's *Hungry Man* (the family business that Tucker Carlson owes his fortune to) and other ready-made dinners in the 1950s (followed by ready-made lunches, breakfasts, and snacks) specifically advertised the disposability of the packaging as an asset (Strasser 1999). Today, fashion and single-use plastics epitomize what François Jarrige and Thomas Le Roux refer to as the "plastification of the world" (2020: 238). As Susan Strasser notes:

> Packaging may have been disposable, but it was hardly worthless; the costs of packaging research and development, marketing, and raw materials were often equivalent to the cost of the contents. New materials and new combinations of paper, foil, and plastic went into food packaging, ranging from coated paper boxes to the three-section foil tray and six-colour laminated box developed for the Swanson TV Dinner. These packages were fundamental to marketing prepared foods... . As the title of a 1967 American Management Association publication put it, *Packaging is Marketing*.
>
> (1999: 268, my italics)

Planned obsolescence certainly made its mark in car manufacturing, as well as numerous other businesses. Two industries, fashion and fossil fuels, are particularly acute examples of businesses' use of advanced advertising and other techniques to encourage, shame, incite and otherwise get people to buy their products.

The Uneven Distribution of Consumption and its Consequences

While all human beings consume in order to survive, some human beings consume more – and for some, much more – than they need to survive. As it turns out, about 20 percent of the world's population consumes about 80 percent of the world's resources (Acconia n.d.). In other words, a minority of people are wildly over-consuming while most people are consuming well within the Earth's carrying capacity. For decades, the non-profit organization Global Footprint Network has been comparing human consumption with the Earth's **carrying capacity**. In his book, *The Day the World Stops Shopping* (2021: 32–35), J.B. MacKinnon puts it this way. If everyone lived like the average American, we would need 5 Earths in order to sustain us. Another way of putting this: each person on Earth can use up 1.6 global hectares' worth of resources. Each American uses up 8 global hectares. We need four or more Earths to live like Swedes, South Koreans, Australians or Canadians. We need more than three planets to live like people in Germany, the Netherlands, Russia, Finland or Norway. We need about two planets to live like the average person in China. It is important to note that within any country, there may be wide differences in wealth and consumption.

Some countries consume far more than other countries, *irrespective of development.* People in Ecuador, Cuba, Sri Lanka, Armenia, the Dominican Republic, the Philippines, Jamaica, Indonesia or Egypt consume about what our planet is capable of sustaining. All of these countries have high levels of development. Indeed, people in some fifty-three countries consume at or below the one-planet level, and account for almost half of the world's population (ibid.). And yet, these consumption patterns do not positively correlate with people's happiness. Indeed, there is evidence to suggest the opposite: most highly developed consuming countries do not make the top-ten of the **Happy Planet Index**. Developed by the Wellbeing Economy Alliance, the Index measures the wellbeing of a nation's people multiplied by their life expectancy and divided by their ecological footprint (Happyplanetindex.org n.d.). Interestingly, among the top 10 countries are (in descending order) Costa Rica, Vanuatu, Colombia, Switzerland, Ecuador, Panama, Jamaica, Guatemala, Honduras, and Uruguay. Out of 152 countries, the United States ranks 122. So, all of this consumption is not making us happier. Equally true is the fact that some few millions of people are wildly overconsuming while most of the global population are not.

The environmental costs of affluent countries' overconsumption has been, up until relatively recently, kept mostly beyond the view of consumers, as are the sites of extraction and production: "the decoupling of sites of production – subjected to direct pollution – from sanitized sties of consumption rendered almost imperceptible to the public the increase in emissions of toxic substances in the environment" (Jarrige and Le Roux 2020: 237). This is changing. While people in poorer regions do not enjoy the luxury of the 'decoupling' that separates consumption from its environmental footprint, people in affluent regions are increasingly aware that waste – if it is not a local issue – is certainly a global crisis. This book contributes to the unmasking of consumption's effects on our environment.

Chapter Summaries

Some of the following chapters consider the environmental consequences of consuming things we need in our everyday lives; things like land, water, energy, food and clothing. Yet, even when we are consuming these basic necessities, the chapters reveal that there are not only wide differences in how, where, when, who and why these basic necessities are consumed, but that these differences matter when it comes to ecological consequences. For this reason, the chapters in this book consider many regions around the world, from Brazil to Australia, Ireland to the United States, China to Canada. Learning about the environmental consequences of consuming with a global perspective helps us to appreciate that 'our way' is not necessarily the 'only way' to live and to consume. It also reveals that consuming a product often involves a long chain of consuming that begins with the materials extracted to make the product, through its assembly and to its distribution for sale. This chain involves multiple transactions, labour, and resources.

Chapter 1, **Consuming Land**, considers the devastating impacts of minerals mining in Brazil, drawing attention to the often obscured relationship between the things we consume and where they come from. In Chapter 2, **Consuming Water**, we learn that cultural attachments to certain identities (in this case, the Australian 'Aussie outback' explorer, and sports and recreation) impacts consumption patterns that exceed the carrying capacity of regions or countries to increasingly produce and supply necessities such as water. Chapter 3, **Consuming Energy**, continues this analysis, detailing both the complexities of energy as a resource and also that non-renewable energy sources are not keeping up with demand from energy-intensive nations that are disproportionately consuming energy. Chapter 4, **Consuming Fossil Fuels**, takes a deep-dive into our global dependence on oil, gas, and coal to fuel our lives. The environmental consequences, of carbon and other emissions and the impacts on land and water (see the two previous chapters), is well-known, and is leading to increasing calls to shift (rapidly) to renewable energy sources (wind, solar). The chapter reveals that the very powerful oil, gas, and coal industries are deploying effective tactics in delaying this transition. Chapter 5, **Consuming Waste**, considers initiatives to consume waste as an environmentally sustainable solution to our global waste, and energy, crisis (and the ever-accelerating growth in extraction, production and consumption that has produced this crisis). The chapter analyzes how three popular concerns converge: energy demand, trust in technologies, and the global waste crisis. Burning waste to create one-time energy (electricity, heating) appears to offer a 'having our cake and eating it too' scenario whereby we are actually encouraged to consume more to 'have enough' to burn to produce energy. This capitalist promise is revisited in the book's final chapter.

Chapter 6, **Consuming Food**, challenges the prevalent claim that donating leftover food to income-insecure people is a morally and environmentally responsible way of dealing with food waste. The chapter analyzes how this 'solution' not only licences the continued over-supply of food in some regions of the world and the under-supply to other regions, but also licences the continued over-consumption of food: presenting food waste donation as an effective way of dealing with waste disincentives people from consuming less. A much more socially and environmentally just solution is the introduction of a guaranteed basic income to reelevate poverty. Chapter 7, **Consuming Pets**, considers a form of everyday consumption that falls below the radar of many discussions of consumption. Just as there are environmental consequences of people consuming food, so too are there environmental consequences to our pets eating food. This chapter considers pet vegan diets as more environmentally sustainable to the current meat-heavy diet. Chapter 8, **Consuming Plastics**, tackles plastics pollution, which ranks among the top five global environmental concerns. This chapter concentrates on the effects of plastics and microplastics on the environment and human health, as well as efforts to curb our 'plastics appetite'. The chapter considers global plastics bans (for instance, Bangladesh leading the increasingly single-use plastic bag ban in 1998) as well as other proposed alternatives to plastics.

Chapter 9, **Consuming Electronics**, considers the environmental consequences of our global dependence on electronics. Electronics consumption is consistently increasing, exponentially in the case of smart phones and other electronic products. The rare earth and other materials required to meet this increasing global consumer demand is placing significant stress on the environment, as extractive industries seek increasingly remote regions where materials are difficult to extract and require enormous infrastructure. Chapter 10, **Consuming Knowledge**, extends the analysis to argue that initiatives to reuse and repair electronics – rather than sending discards to regions of the world overwhelmed with electronics waste – is not only far more environmentally sustainable, but represents a shift in how people in affluent countries consume knowledge itself. Chapter 11, **Consuming Fashion**, considers the global manufacture, retail, consumption and wasting of clothing. Based on the author's own investigative analysis, the chapter details how the invention and wide consumption of synthetic fibres has dramatically changed the manufacturing and consumption of clothing, from durable intergenerational clothes to 'fast fashion' and its devastating consequences for the environment and human labour.

Chapter 12, **Consuming Tourism**, examines global tourism's environmental impact as part of a wider set of impacts on communities' economic, social and cultural wellbeing and sustainability. The chapter considers ecotourism as a recent attempt to forefront community wellbeing (which includes environmental sustainability as a top priority) as a future-thinking alternative to traditional tourism. Chapter 13, **Consuming Green**, examines the increasingly complicated supposition that consumers may help the environment *through* consumption: that is, by consuming products that have less negative impact on the environment, consumers may effectively lower their ecological footprint. As the final chapter makes clear, refusing to purchase has a far greater positive ecological footprint than any claims to 'green' consumption. Chapter 14, **Consuming Preparedness**, focuses on prepping as a particular response to the uncertainty of our species' survival. What most characterizes preppers is their mass consumption: preppers spend many thousands of dollars stockpiling resources like food, water, and weaponry. The chapter observes that while prepping is understood as an extreme behaviour, it is actually at the edge of a far larger continuum of over-consumption practiced by millions of people worldwide. By insulating themselves and their loved ones, consumers 'buy out' of efforts to safeguard a safe environment, protective labour conditions and other societal-level safeguards. Finally, Chapter 15, **Consuming Less**, considers the implications of all of the chapters. Taken together, the chapters analyze the environmental impacts of consumption. The final chapter explores modest to bold alternatives: the re-municipalization of goods and services, greater producer responsibility and circular economies to degrowth and the re-organization of our global society.

References

Acconia. (n.d.). 'Natural Resources Deficit'. www.activesustainability.com/environment/natural-resources-deficit/?_adin=02021864894#. Accessed 14 March 2024.

Hanson, C. and Ranganathan, J. (2023). *How to Manage the Global Land Squeeze? Produce, Protect, Reduce, Restore.* World Resources Institute, 20 July. www.wri.org/insights/manage-global-land-squeeze-produce-protect-reduce-restore#:~:text=By%20one%20estimate%2C%20"worldwide%20agriculture,have%20been%20drained%20for%20agriculture. Accessed 7 February 2024.

Happy Planet Index. https://happyplanetindex.org/wp-content/themes/hpi/public/downloads/happy-planet-index-briefing-paper.pdf Accessed 5 August 2024.

Jarrige, F. and T. Le Roux. (2020). *The Contamination of the Earth: A History of Pollutions in the Industrial Age.* Cambridge, MA: The MIT Press.

Lenton, T.M., Armstrong McKay, D.I., Loriani, S., Abrams, J.F., Lade, S.J., Donges, J.F., Milkoreit, M., Powell, T., Smith, S.R., Zimm, C., Bailey, E., Buxton, J.E., Dyke, J., Ghadiali, A., and Laybourn, L. (eds.) (2023). *The Global Tipping Points Report 2023.* Exeter, UK: University of Exeter.

MacKinnon, J.J. (2021). *The Day the World Stops Shopping.* London UK and New York, USA: Verso Press.

Packard, V. (1960). *The Waste Makers.* New York: IG Publishing.

Packard, V. (1959). *The Status Seekers.* Philadelphia, Pennsylvania, USA: David McKay Co.

Packard, V. (1957). *The Hidden Persuaders.* London, UK: Longmans, Green and Company.

Richardson, J., Steffen W., Lucht, W., Bendtsen, J., Cornell, S.E., et al. (2023). 'Earth beyond six of nine Planetary Boundaries', *Science Advances*, 9: 37.

Slade, G. (2007). *Made to Break: Technology and Obsolescence in America.* London UK: Harvard University Press.

Specht, I. and Erickson, M. (n.d.). '15: L'Oréal (1971) – Because I'm Worth It', *Creative Review.* www.creativereview.co.uk/because-im-worth-it-loreal/. Accessed 31 October 2023.

Strasser, S. (1999). *Waste and Want: A Social History of Trash.* New York: Henry Holt and Company.

Wellbeing Economy Alliance. (n.d.). *Happy Planet Index.* https://happyplanetindex.org/wp-content/themes/hpi/public/downloads/happy-planet-index-briefing-paper.pdf. Accessed 14 March 2024.

1 Consuming Land

Priscylla Joca, Luciana Nóbrega, and Leiliane Jacinto Pereira

Summary

- Mining projects have both environmental and human impacts on Indigenous and non-Indigenous people globally.
- Indigenous peoples tend to emphasize the inherent interdependence of land, water, and people.
- State and extractive industries emphasize land as a resource for economic exploitation.
- The divergence of these understandings may escalate conflicts.
- Disregarding the rights of Indigenous peoples may intensify the detrimental impacts of land consumption on Indigenous communities' health and environment.

Keywords: Consume, Lands, Waters, Indigenous Peoples, Megaprojects, Mining

Introduction

In the Brazilian Amazon region, Indigenous peoples and traditional communities cohabit, along with a profound diversity of forests, rivers, animal species, and other beings; there, lands, waters, and territories hold a considerable part of the biodiversity existing on Earth (FAO and FILAC 2021). The term "**traditional communities**" in Brazil encompasses a variety of collective identities organized into distinct communities. This includes the Quilombola, recognized as traditional communities of Afro-descendant origin, and riparian communities (Pinho and Joca 2021).

The use and consumption of these interconnected lands and waters have been the target of socio-ecological conflicts involving, on the one hand, the Brazilian state and private resource extraction companies and; on the other hand, the Indigenous and traditional communities who live with the land and waters. Various studies have indicated that such conflicts relate to different

DOI: 10.4324/9781003412526-2

understandings of development models and the use/consumption of land and other natural resources (Herculano and Pacheco 2008). However, some studies have also pointed out more vital and fundamental issues about different economic, cultural, socio-ecological, and cosmopolitical understandings regarding the land's meaning and interconnectedness with Indigenous peoples and traditional communities (Latour 2004; Blaser 2016).

This chapter questions how the perspectives of the Brazilian state and companies on land consumption differ from Indigenous cosmopolitics (Blaser 2016). Here, cosmopolitics is defined as Indigenous peoples' relationships with the land, water, and various life forms that share their territories. These relationships are not between subjects and things but rather intense negotiations with the beings that govern everything around them. They are subject-subject relationships that can only be carried out by people who are willing to do so: "Every trans-specific interaction in the Indigenous world is an international intrigue, a diplomatic negotiation, or a war operation that must be conducted with the utmost circumspection in cosmopolitics" (Danowski and de Castro 2014: 96).

This chapter also aims to unravel the main tensions and conflicts stemming from these diverse perspectives in the context of land consumption and use. The chapter focuses on a case study of the consultation process and the associated environmental impact assessment of a gold mining project, proposed by a Canadian mining company in the Brazilian Amazon region, which has affected the Juruna Indigenous people (self-named Yudjá), along with other Indigenous peoples and traditional communities. We have chosen not to name the mining company or project in this article because of recent actions by the company, which recently filed a criminal complaint against Indigenous leaders, researchers, and members of civil society organizations (Solidarity Note, 2023).

The potential impacts of the proposed gold mining megaproject are deeply articulated with an existing megaproject, the Belo Monte Hydroelectric Plant. Drawing on judicial and administrative documents, technical reports, and documents prepared by the Juruna/Yudjá, this chapter analyzes the divergent perspectives on the consumption of land by the Brazilian state, the companies, and Juruna/Yudjá cosmopolitics. These perspectives contrast a view of land as a commodity resource to be exploited with the Juruna/Yudjá perspective that understands land and water as interconnected entities that interrelate with people and other beings that cohabit in shared territories in socio-ecological relationships of interdependence.

The Hydroelectric Dam's Impact on Juruna/Yudjá Indigenous People Dynamics

The Juruna/Yudjá traditional territory is located in Pará, in the Brazilian Amazon region. Due to the displacement of Indigenous populations in Brazil, part of the Juruna/Yudjá people inhabit the Xingu Indigenous Land, that is a national park located in the state of Mato Grosso, Brazil, in a transition zone between the Amazon rainforest and the Cerrado biome. The Juruna/Yudjá also inhabit the Paquiçamba Indigenous Land, one of the smallest Indigenous lands recorded in Brazil. Yet more Juruna/Yudjá live in adjacent areas, on lands not yet demarcated by the Brazilian state. The life, culture, and identity of the Juruna/Yudjá people have been deeply connected with the Xingu River for centuries, inhabiting "land (as in 'solid ground,' and in opposition to islands), islands, and aquatic environments" (Juruna/Yudjá and Arara Indigenous Peoples 2018: 16). The way of life of the Juruna/Yudjá people interrelates with the Xingu river and its environmental changes throughout the year and over time.

The Juruna/Yudjá people have been intensely affected by the construction and operation of the Belo Monte hydroelectric dam, which crosses the Xingu River in Pará and is considered Brazil's largest **hydroelectric power** plant. The plant began operating in 2016, having affected and displaced thousands of Indigenous people, including the Juruna/Yudjá, riparian communities, and local populations. It is considered one of Brazil's most emblematic cases of disrespect for the right to prior consultation (Lacerda 2017; Monteiro 2018; Durst et al 2018; Klein 2022; Schumann 2018).

Case Study: Belo Monte

The Belo Monte case in Brazil concerns the construction of the Belo Monte dam in the Amazon region. Belo Monte has been highly controversial due to its significant environmental and social impacts and is considered an emblematic case of disregard for the right to prior consultation in Brazil. The project has been criticized for failing to adequately consult with or obtain the consent of Indigenous peoples and traditional communities whose lands and lives have been directly affected by the construction of the dam and the subsequent flooding of large areas of rainforest. Despite legal requirements and international standards mandating consultation with Indigenous peoples, critics argue that the Brazilian government has failed to meaningfully consult with them, leading to violations of their rights and exacerbating tensions over land rights and environmental conservation in the region.

Due to the diversion of the Xingu River for energy production caused by the Belo Monte Dam, the Volta Grande do Xingu (the region where the Juruna/Yudjá live) suffers from off-season droughts (Mayer et al 2021). The so-called 'reduced flow stretch' artificially reduces the river's water flow to divert and use this portion of water to form a reservoir. This has caused severe environmental changes, affecting the reproduction of flora, fauna, and fish species. It has also caused socioeconomic impacts, such as on traditional fishing activities,

Figure 1.1 Members of the Juruna Indigenous People navigate the Volta Grande of the Xingu River. Photo credits: Josiel Juruna.

and negatively affected the interrelations between the peoples and communities living in the region.

Responding to this situation, "Juruna/Yudjá and riparian researchers from Volta Grande do Xingu, alongside academics from different areas of science, proposed the Piracema Hydrogram program, which aims to present an alternative to the release of water flow to maintain life in/on the Xingu River, making it possible for fish species to reproduce again" (Roman and Matovanelli 2023). From the Juruna/Yudjá perspective, new projects – such as the mentioned gold mining project – could aggravate the negative socio-environmental impacts already experienced as a consequence of Belo Monte. As the Juruna/Yudjá consultation protocol predicted, "We do not know what the river, the animals, the forest, and even the people who live here will be like" in the face of social, economic, environmental, and food impacts that could be caused by Belo Monte associated with other projects (Juruna/Yudjá 2017: 13). It is in this context that the cited mining company is now proposing to mine gold in the same region that has been affected by Belo Monte. This proposal is generating conflicts and resistance.

Examining the Impact of the Hydroelectric Dam Experience and the Proposed Gold Mining Project

In Brazil, the right to free, prior, and informed consultation is provided by Convention 169 of the International Labor Organization (Marés et al 2022). After the Juruna/Yudjá people began to protest the Belo Monte plant in

2010, the Brazilian federal government claimed that it had both properly consulted and adequately addressed the social and environmental impacts on the affected communities. The Juruna/Yudjá people learned "hard lessons" from their experiences of inadequate and meaningful consultation in the case of Belo Monte (Garzón 2019: 32), and as a consequence decided to develop their **Consultation Protocol**, motivated in part by the experiences of other Indigenous peoples (ibid.).

A consultation protocol is an instrument elaborated by the Indigenous peoples themselves and, in the case of Brazil, also by traditional communities, in which these peoples/communities define the process, the manner, and the procedures that the state must follow to ensure the meaningful and adequate realization of the right to consultation (Joca 2020: 68). The Juruna/Yudjá protocol gained significant importance when, in December 2017, a judicial decision, for the first time in the country, stated that the consultation process should be carried out "according to the respective consultation protocol [...] by the provisions of ILO Convention 169" (Desembargador Federal Jirair Aram Meguerian 2017: 4). The Regional Federal Court of the 1st Region (acronym in Portuguese: TRF1) decision suspended the environmental license of the proposed gold mining project installation until the consultation with the Juruna/Yudjá was carried out according to their own consultation protocol.

Initially, the Brazilian state did not recognize the Juruna/Yudjá as being potentially affected by the proposed gold mining project on the basis that the community would live more than 10 km away from the ore extraction site, identified by the Study of the Indigenous Component (acronym in Portuguese: ECI), and therefore outside the mine's impact area (Chaves and Souza 2018). As such, the Brazilian state argued that the mining company did not need to consult with the Juruna/Yudjá. However, after intense disputes involving the company and federal and state government agencies, and with research studies showing that this project would be located "less than 50 km from the main dam of the HEP Belo Monte and less than 9.5 km from the [...] Paquiçamba [Indigenous land]" (AIDA 2021; Rede Xingu 2023), the potential negative impacts on the Juruna/Yudjá were acknowledged, thus legally requiring a consultation process.

In 2015, the Juruna/Yudjá requested that the National Foundation of Indigenous Peoples (acronym in Portuguese: Funai) grant them time to develop their Consultation Protocol, which would serve as a guideline for conducting the ECI. However, Garzón reports that only after the judicial decision of 2017 (noted above), which recognized the legal validity and full applicability of the Juruna/Yudjá protocol, did the mining company initiate a consultation process (Garzón 2019). At first, the mining company attempted to negotiate directly with the Juruna/Yudjá, undermining the Consultation Protocol, which establishes that consultation should be carried out by government agencies. The protocol also states that companies may or may not be invited to consultation meetings, depending on the collective decision of the Juruna/Yudjá.

This provision is built into the Protocol in order to ensure that the state does not delegate the duty to consult to private companies (Mendes and Da Silva 2019; Précoma, Braun and da Silva 2020; de Oliveira et al 2022). The Protocol specifies this in order to avoid power asymmetries between private companies and Indigenous peoples in direct consultation negotiations and to claim the protection and enforcement of Indigenous rights as the responsibility of the state (Joca 2022). Among these rights, recognized by the Brazilian constitution, is the right to traditionally occupied lands, according to Article 31 of the Federal Constitution of 1988 (Brazil's Constitution of 1988 with Amendments through 2017, [1988]). In light of these circumstances, the Juruna/Yudjá notified the TRF1, Funai, and the government of Pará, demanding to be consulted according to the Protocol (Garzón 2019). The Juruna/Yudjá also requested that the government develop a work plan to properly implement the consultation according to the Protocol.

Throughout the ensuing environmental licensing process, the mining company presented studies based on secondary data without any participation from the affected Indigenous peoples. In 2017, Funai requested that the mining company conduct a Study of the Indigenous Component (acronym in Portuguese: ECI) based on primary data with the participation of the involved Indigenous peoples, respecting their protocols (Rede Xingu 2023). In 2020, the mining company presented a new Indigenous component study (AIDA 2021). Despite having requested additional information about the impacts of the enterprise, in November 2020, Funai declared that the ECI presented by the mining company would be ready to be presented to the involved Indigenous peoples and could be altered after a meeting with them (Rede Xingu 2023). As such, Funai's decision may contradict the Juruna protocol, which requests prior and comprehensive information about socio-environmental impacts before discussing the acceptance of any proposal. Furthermore, independent reports (AIDA 2021; APIB 2023) and technical opinions (Camargo, Wahnfried and Sawakuchi 2021) indicated that, in addition to the inadequate consultation with the Juruna/Yudjá people and other peoples and communities impacted by the project, various socio-environmental impacts were not adequately considered in the environmental assessment of the project either by the Brazilian state or by the company.

For example, "[the company] announced on its website that during the 11 years predicted for the operation of the gold extraction project, 39.767 megatonnes of rock will be removed. However, the studies presented in the environmental licensing only foresee the removal of 2.78 megatonnes" (Rede Xingu 2023). In other words, the environmental licensing predicts a much smaller amount of rock to be removed than the company predicts; it indicates that the impact assessment did not consider an accurate amount of rock removal and its potential environmental impacts. Among other predicted socio-environmental impacts, the project foresee the use of cyanide in ore extraction, an extremely toxic substance for soil and water resources (Rede Xingu 2023; Freitas and Horta 2023). In addition, "the environmental studies of the project foresee the risk of the dam breaking during the operation and closure phases as high risk" (Rede Xingu 2023). According to Steven H. Emerman, in his independent report about the "Evaluation of the Tailings Dam, Cyanide Use and Water Consumption at the Proposed Volta Grande Gold Project, Pará, Northern Brazil", "The dam has not been designed with any seismic safety criterion and with no study of local or regional seismicity. In the most likely failure scenario, the initial runout of tailings would cover 41 kilometers with significant impact on the Arara de Volta Grande do Xingu indigenous land" (2020:1)

In 2020, Funai indicated that the company could present the report of the Indigenous component study online due to the COVID-19 pandemic (Mantovanelli et al 2021). The Juruna/Yudjá requested not to be consulted online (Rede Xingu 2023). As stated in their Protocol, consultation meetings should occur in their territory to enable the broad participation of all population segments. Also, for the consultation to be participatory, "[c]onsultations must be carried out with the participation of as many people as possible.... There can be no consultations with villages separately nor individual consultations" (Juruna/Yudjá 2017:24). The Juruna/Yudjá explain that consulting small groups outside their traditional territories makes more involvement by all people more difficult, especially women, children, youth, and older people (ibid). Everyone should collectively participate in decision-making that affects their "present and future" and "development priorities," as the Juruna/Yudjá Protocol states (Juruna/Yudjá 2017: 15).

Finally, in light of Funai's approval in 2021 of the new study of the impact on Indigenous communities, indicating its agreement with the environmental agency responsible for issuing the preliminary license, the Federal Prosecution Service presented to the TRF1 in February 2022 a technical opinion prepared by the Autonomous Protocols Observatory on the violation of the right to free, prior, and informed consultation in this case (Rede Xingu 2023; Marés et al 2022). The Federal Prosecution Service is an autonomous state body responsible for the defense of social and individual fundamental rights, **Indigenous rights**, and the defense of the legal system and the democratic regime in Brazil. The Observatory is "a network of researchers, representatives of traditional peoples and civil society organizations that proposes to monitor cases of threats and violations [against] the right to consultation and prior, free and informed consent in Brazil and other countries in Latin America and Africa" (Observatory, 2024). In April 2022, the TRF1 "upheld the 2017 decision that suspended the installation license in its complete terms" (Rede Xingu 2023). At the time of writing this chapter, the consultation process with the Juruna/Yudjá people is ongoing.

Conclusions: Deciphering the Nuances of Yudjá Cosmopolitics

The Juruna/Yudjá's understanding of the potential synergistic and cumulative impacts of the hydroelectric and gold mining projects on their lives and territory, and their strategies of resistance, demonstrate how their cosmopolitical understandings are structured and articulated around ontological and epistemic paradigms. The relationship between humans and nonhumans emphasizes care and reciprocity in their relationships with the land, water, and all beings that coexist in Juruna/Yudjá traditional territory. However, the consultation and environmental licensing processes carried out in the case of these two projects have not yet created space for the recognition of Juruna/Yudjá cosmopolitics.

In the case analyzed in this chapter, the state, allied with the mining company, competes with Indigenous peoples for the same geographic area. However, the conflict is not limited to this territorial dimension or to its main "natural resources", lands, waters, and minerals. We are not debating between a use that leads to depletion and exhaustion, or between a more sustainable use of water and territories that would allow the renewal of natural cycles.

In fact, it is a conflict about how to understand land and waters, and how they relate or do not relate to humans. In this sense, the basis or root of this conflict is, first and foremost, ontological (Escobar, 2014) and cosmopolitical (Blaser, 2016). Thus, we are not in the field of disputes between beliefs or between different cultural contributions, which would be to treat Indigenous understandings and, in this case, Juruna/Yudjá, not as the result of profound reflections on how reality is structured. There is a deeper debate here.

Overcoming nature-culture dichotomies in the context of the relational ontologies of many Indigenous peoples, for example, rivers are considered sensitive and sentient beings endowed with agencies and capacities to act, resist, and operate in the so-called "cultural" world. For these peoples, such beings are alive and capable of performance, including political actions and mobilizations. Thus, the interrelationships between Indigenous peoples and other beings are experienced in their diverse views of the cosmos and their political interrelations with the worlds and beings that co-inhabit their (shared) territories, understood as vital space-times.

In the Juruna/Yudjá cosmopolitics context, aspects of their relational ontology stand out, such as considering the Xingu River a living and pulsating being and entity. Yudjá cosmopolitics also emphasizes aspects related to epistemology, reflecting on the process of knowing itself and what can and should be known or what is known and accessible only to some people. Hence, it is not enough for others to speak for the Yudjá; they must speak for themselves as stewards and guardians of the Xingu River.

The resistance of the Juruna/Yudjá people in the cases described here has made their knowledge, epistemology, ontology, and cosmopolitics more explicit to the Brazilian state. Although the consultation and licensing processes were not carried out based on the norms, principles, and procedures of consultation, decision-making and consent as indicated in the Juruna/Yudjá Consultation Protocol, the Juruna/Yudjá, through their struggles and legal-political actions and strategies, have created space for what follows. Today, they make their arguments clearer to the Brazilian state and companies to promote consent-based decision-making processes that would recognize and respect their cosmopolitics. They have also done so by using and contesting the meaning of the tools provided by Western law: written, persuasive norms recognized by the Brazilian judiciary. The Juruna/Yudjá Consultation Protocol, written and validated by the Juruna/Yudjá, was thus also recognized as a document of a compelling character, and enforceable.

By opening up this fissure in the field of state law and expressing that Indigenous people are also creators/interpreters of legal norms, the Juruna/Yudjá are expanding the possibilities for legal-political disputes and tensions. These consultation and environmental licensing processes may present themselves as "minefields" where procedural debates, for example, about the distance of Juruna/Yudjá lands from the project, may conceal substantive issues that integrate the background of these disputes (Garavito 2010: 1). Namely, there are different understandings of the environment and what it means for private resource extraction companies, public authorities, and the Juruna/Yudjá to consume this environment. In the words of Juruna/Yudjá researchers and riparian communities, when referring to processes related to Belo Monte:

> These collectives do not passively accept living in arid conditions, which Bel Juruna[/Yudjá] defines as the main impact of the company, but fight for better living conditions for the Xingu River, the fish and aquatic plants, and their families. Neglected in this process of a war of papers and technical opinions in the environmental licensing of the company, the ecosystemic knowledge of these groups associated with their ways of life reveals sophisticated modes of species management of procedures for co-creation and proliferation of life. The ecosystemic knowledge of these collectives also denounces chains of impacts that continue to be ignored in environmental licensing, being repeatedly underestimated. The decisions on the impact matrix of the hydroelectric company and the criteria for the operation of the plant do not consider these people's knowledge.
>
> (Sawakuchi 2022: 2)

The Juruna/Yudjá people, like several other Indigenous peoples in Brazil, have communicated their socio-ecological and ontological knowledge and science to non-Indigenous people through public speeches, resistance, claims, consultation protocols, territorial and environmental management plans, proposals such as the Piracema Hydrogram, and various other means. In this way, the Juruna/Yudjá are articulating ways to make their cosmopolitics known and to demand respect in their collective struggles for existence as a people.

Nevertheless, large resource extraction projects continued to be proposed and implemented without meaningful and adequate free, prior, and informed consultation. They are also carried out without considering traditional Indigenous science and knowledge in environmental assessments. They disregard the self-determination, territorial rights and right to free, prior and informed consent of Indigenous peoples. At times, these enterprises promise job creation and income, development, and wealth without taking into account agroecological practices, ecologically adapted dwellings, and other forms of cultural, political, and ecological organization of local peoples that configure the space they live in and their relationship to their territories.

This is the case for the Juruna/Yudjá people, whose territory is rich in socio-biodiversity and whose traditional knowledge is adapted to the water cycles that sustain life in the Volta Grande do Xingu. These people's way of life has shaped the territory, which includes lands, forests and the Xingu River, interacting harmoniously with other beings that share this part of the planet with them. Their ancestral work of building, configuring, and shaping the living space, based on their relationships of complementarity, coexistence and belonging, is threatened by the association of hydroelectric and mining companies, which exploit the same territory.

Understanding the cosmopolitical relations of the Juruna/Yudjá people requires us to make an effort to decolonize the hegemonic concepts of the environment as a natural resource to be exploited and of land, water, and territory as environments to be necessarily explored by extractive projects. Yudjá cosmopolitics, centred on the physical and cultural reproduction of their collective life and constitution as a people, involves interconnectedness, interrelation, care, and reciprocity between humans and other beings. It is also a proposal for new epistemes and ontologies. By contrast, Ailton Krenak reflects on a mode of human existence that is hyper-focused on the extractive consumption of land:

> [...] [It] does not tolerate so much pleasure or enjoyment of life. So, they preach the end of the world as a way to make us give up our dreams. And my provocation to postpone the end of the world is always to be able to tell another story. If we can do that, we will postpone the end of the world.
> (Krenak 2020: 26–27)

Indigenous peoples and communities have fought to continue to exist collectively against socio-ecological violence and, in more dramatic cases, ecocides and genocides (Milanez 2019: 120). For them, their struggles are also cosmopolitical struggles to prevent the end of their worlds, where land and water coexist with them.

Questions for Consideration

1. How do the perspectives of the Brazilian state and companies on land consumption differ from Indigenous cosmopolitics?
2. In what way did the secondary research, through document analysis, contribute to the understanding of different perspectives on land consumption?
3. What are the main tensions and conflicts identified between these perspectives in relation to land consumption?

Further Reading

Mongabay featured a story showing how the operationalization of the Belo Monte Dam has dried up stretches of the Xingu River, causing severe impacts on the Juruna/ Yudjá Indigenous people, traditional fishing communities, and various species of fish and aquatic plants (Belo Monte dam dries up Xingu river's Big Bend, Indigenous communities and residents say [2021]). This video with English subtitles is available at: www.youtube.com/watch?v=GmLjTpix4Uw&t=3s

Helena Palmquist, "Belo Monte: peoples of the Volta Grande region call on Ibama to release the Xingu River", (2023), online: *Sumaúma* https://sumauma.com/en/belo-monte-povos-da-volta-grande-reivindicam-que-o-ibama-liberte-o-xingu/.

Solidarity note for social movements, organizations, and rights advocates who are victims of criminalization attempts by the company Belo Sun Mineração Ltda., (2023), online: https://docs.google.com/forms/d/e/1FAIpQLSd3NtHQPucyV5aX_nHg_qv2Qfy6p8GfvoLj0pAsEGtZpnL-0A/viewform.

Autonomous Protocols Observatory, (2024), online: *Observatory* https://observatorio.direitosocioambiental.org/#.

References

Acórdão 00025057020134013903, [2017] Desembargador Federal Jirair Aram Meguerian.

AIDA, *Análise do Projeto Volta Grande do Xingu, da Empresa Belo Sun. Anexo das Boas Práticas Globais para Avaliação de Impacto Ambiental.*, by AIDA (Associación Interamericana para la Defensa del Ambiente (AIDA), 2021).

APIB, *Mina de Sangue Relatório sobre o Projeto da Mineradora Belo Sun*, by APIB (Articulação dos Povos Indígenas do Brasil (APIB), 2023).

Belo Monte dam dries up Xingu river's Big Bend, Indigenous communities and residents say (2021).

Brazil's Constitution of 1988 with Amendments through 2017, (1988).

Blaser, Mario, "Is Another Cosmopolitics Possible?" (2016) 31:4 *Cultural Anthropology* 545–570.

Camargo, Marcelo, Ingo Wahnfried & André Sawakuchi, *Análise crítica do Estudo de Impacto Ambiental – Componente Indígena (EIA-CI) do Projeto de Ouro Volta Grande quanto à qualidade d'água e risco de contaminação em drenagens impactadas por Belo Sun*, by Marcelo Camargo, Ingo Wahnfried & André Sawakuchi (USP; UFAM, 2021).

Chaves, Kena Azevedo & Angelita Matos Souza, *De Belo Monte a Belo Sun, o Pará como espaço de espoliação & exceção: o caso da resistência Yudjá* (Barcelona: Universitat de Barcelona, 2018).

Danowski, Deborah & Eduardo Viveiros de Castro, *Há mundo por vir? Ensaio sobre os medos e os fins* (Florianópolis: Instituto Socioambiental, 2014).

Durst, Jason et al, "Contested development: the Belo Monte Dam, Brazil" in Larry A Swatuk & Lars Wirkus, eds, *Water, Climate Change and the Boomerang Effect Unintentional Consequences for Resource Insecurity* (New York: Routledge, 2018) 66.

Emerman, S. H. *Evaluation of the Tailings Dam, Cyanide Use and Water Consumption at the Proposed Volta Grande Gold Project* (Pará, Northern Brazil, Amazon Watch, 2020).

Escobar, A. *Sentipensar con la tierra. Nuevas lecturas sobre desarrollo, territorio y diferencia.* (Medellín: Ediciones UNAULA, 2014).

FAO & FILAC. *Forest Governance by Indigenous and Tribal People. An Opportunity for Climate Action in Latin America and the Caribbean*, by FAO & FILAC (Santiago: Food and Agriculture Organization (FAO), 2021).

Freitas, Juliana & Daniela Horta, "Impacts of cyanide in gold mining and cyanide removal methodologies in liquid waste from gold processing" (2023) 59 (3) *Revista de Metalurgia* 1–8.

Garavito, C. R., "Ethnicity.gov: Global Governance, Indigenous Peoples, and the Right to Prior Consultation in Social Minefields" (2010) 18 *Indiana Journal of Global Legal Studies* 1.

Garzón, Biviany Rojas, "The Juruna/Yudjá (Yudjá) People's Protocol: A Response to a Hard-Learned Lesson" in Cathal Doyle, Andy Whitmore & Helen Tugendhat, eds, *Free Prior Informed Consent Protocols as Instruments of Autonomy: Laying Foundations for Rights based Engagement* (Köln: InstitutfürÖkologie und Aktions-Ethnologie (INFOE) e. V., 2019) 32.

Herculano, Selene & Tania Pacheco, "Building Environmental Justice in Brazil: A Preliminary Discussion of Environmental Racism" in Jan Marie Fritz, ed, *International Clinic Sociology* (New York: Springer, 2008) 244.

Joca, Priscylla, *Consultation and Consent Protocols and Self-Determination: "We Have the Right to Establish Our Own Way of Being Consulted"* Université de Montréal, 2022) [unpublished].

Joca, Priscylla, "Protocolos Indígenas de Consulta e Consentimento no Brasil [Consultation and Consent Protocols of Indigenous Peoples in Brazil]" in Salvador Milaleo Hernández, ed, *Protocolos Autonómicos de Consulta Previa Indígena en América Latina: Estudios de casos en Bolivia, Brasil, Chile, Colombia, Honduras, México, Perú* (IWGIA, 2020) 68.

Juruna/Yudjá and Arara Indigenous Peoples, "Plano de Gestão Territorial e Ambiental da Volta Grande do Xingu. Terras indígenas Paquiçamba, Arara da Volta Grande do Xingu e Área" (2018).

Klein, Peter, *Flooded: Development, Democracy, and Brazil's Belo Monte Dam*, Nature, Society, and Culture (New Brunswick, New Jersey, United States: Rutgers University Press, 2022).

Krenak, Ailton, *Ideias para Adiar o Fim do Mundo*, 2nd ed (Companhia das Letras, 2020).

Lacerda, Lidia, *"Vocês Fazem Isso Porque Tem Medo De Nos Ouvir": Análise dos Discursos do Estado quanto aos Direitos Indígenas diante da Usina Belo Monte* Universidade Federal de Goiás, 2017) [unpublished].

Latour, Bruno, "Whose Cosmos, Which Cosmopolitics? Comments on the Peace Terms of Ulrich Beck" (2004) 10:3 Common Knowledge 450–462.

Mantovanelli, Thais et al, *Brazil: The dangers of rolling back social and environmental safeguards for indigenous and forest peoples during COVID-19: An Analysis of the Consequences of Measures Taken During COVID-19 in Brazil*, by Thais Mantovanelli et al (Manaus, Brazil: Instituto Socioambiental and Forest Peoples Programme, 2021).

Marés, Carlos et al, *Parecer sobre o processo de consulta prévia do Projeto Volta Grande*, by Carlos Marés et al (Curitiba: Observatório de Protocolos & CEPEDIS, 2022).

Mayer, Adam et al, "Is hydropower worth it? Exploring amazonian resettlement, human development and environmental costs with the Belo Monte project in Brazil" (2021) 78 Energy Research & Social Science 1–12.

Mendes, Geovan & Liana Amin Lima da Silva, *Protocolo Juruna/Yudjá de Consulta Prévia Frente aos Empreendimentos Hidrelétrico e Minerário na Amazônia: caso Belo Monte e Belo Sun* (Universidade de São Paulo – São Paulo: USP, 2019).

Milanez, Felipe, "Colonialism, Extractivism, and Re-Existence in the Brazilian Amazon" in Ekaterina Chertkovskaya, Alexander Paulsson & Stefania Barca, eds, *Towards a Political Economy of Degrowth* (London: Rowman & Littlefield International, 2019) 120.

Monteiro, Roberta Amanajás, *"Qual desenvolvimento? o deles ou o nosso?": a UHE de Belo Monte e seus impactos nos direitos humanos dos povos indígenas* Universidade de Brasilia, 2018) [unpublished].

Oliveira, Rodrigo Magalhães de et al, *Violações ao direito à consulta e ao consentimento prévio de indígenas e ribeirinhos: o caso de um empreendimento minerário na Volta Grande do Xingu*, Jusdiversidade e Autodeterminação 2 (Curitiba: Letra da Lei, 2022).

Pinho, Claudia & Priscylla Joca, "Défis juridico-politiques des communautés Pantaneira pensant la pandémie: le cas de la voie navigable Paraguay-Parana" (2021) 35:1 Caminando: Brisons le silence en temps de pandémie 54–57.

Povo Juruna/Yudjá, *Protocolo de Consulta Juruna/Yudjá (Yudjá) da Terra Indígena Paquiçamba da Volta Grande do Rio Xingu* (Pará, Brasil: Povo Juruna/Yudjá da TI Paquiçamba, 2017).

Précoma, Adriele, Adriano Braun & Liana Amin Lima da Silva, "Direito de Existência e Autodeterminação dos Povos Indígenas diante das Ameaças do Complexo de Hidrelétricas na Bacia do Juruena: O Caso do Projeto da Usina Castanheira" (2020) 9:18 Monções: Revista de Relações Internacionais da UFGD 373–403.

Rede Xingu +, "Volta Grande Mining (Belo Sun)", (2023), online: *Xingu Mais* www.xingumais.org.br/obra/volta-grande-mining-belo-sun?id=16731.

Roman, Clara & Thais Mantovanelli, "Pulse, Xingu! The way to relive Volta Grande after Belo Monte", (2023), online: *Socioambiental* www.socioambiental.org/en/socio-environmental-news/pulsa-xingu-the-way-to-relive-big-turn-after-beautiful-mount.

Sawakuchi, André Oliveira et al, *Hidrograma Piracema: o Monitoramento Ambiental Territorial Independente da Volta Grande do Xingu e os critérios ecossistêmicos para manutenção da vida*, by André Oliveira Sawakuchi et al (Pará: Monitoramento Ambiental Territorial Independente da Volta Grande do Xingu (MATI-VGX), 2022).

Schumann, Charlotte, *Framing Prior Consultation in Brazil Ethnographic Perspectives on Limits of Participation and Multicultural Politics*, by Culture and Social Practice (Transcript-Verlag, 2018).

2 Consuming Water

Emily Potter

Summary

- The global north practices unsustainable water consumption.
- Australia's dominant water practices are unsustainable and invested in certain settler-colonial imaginaries and narratives that support capitalist-colonial dominance.
- Drawing on Val Plumwood's notion of 'shadow places', three examples are presented of the shadow waters that lie behind (and flow into) key signifiers of contemporary Australian life: agricultural markets, mobility and adventure, and urban living.
- By contrast, First Nations' water understandings and practices point to alternative ways of knowing and living with water.
- These ways recognize our relationship to shadow water, and to the places elsewhere that sustain us, as a step towards more ethical water practices.

Keywords: Water Consumption, Australia, Colonization, Shadow Places, Shadow Waters

Introduction

Australia is a water-challenged place. It is the driest inhabited continent in the world, with 70 percent of its land mass classified as either arid or semi-arid. At the same time, it is an island surrounded by water, and with the majority of its population of 26 million living along its coastline in the nation's eight capital cities. These oceans mark the beginnings of Australia as we understand it today: they were the gateway for the first British colonizers to travel to the other side of the earth, land on its shores, and lay illegitimate claim to these already inhabited lands. Prior to 1788, hundreds of First Nations groups had lived here with water in its many forms – oceans, rivers, wetlands, humidity, snow – for tens of thousands of years. Colonization was enacted through

DOI: 10.4324/9781003412526-3

environmental as well as human control, and the alteration of Indigenous waterways, and impacts of colonization on water access and quality, brings a layer of complexity to the story of water in Australia. Water and power are intimately connected.

This chapter considers water consumption in contemporary Australia as a manifestation of unsustainable water practices across the global north that are born from capitalist-colonial logics of environmental extraction and water's utility for economic growth and privatized benefit. While there is a commonality to this context, there is also specificity in the particular paradox of Australia's relationship with water, where both water's presence and absence play into the nation's (unstable) identity – what Catriona Elder calls its 'stories of being Australian' (2008: 239) – as well as its material and cultural life. This dynamic of presence and absence is well explicated through the concept of 'shadow waters' (McLean et al 2018), drawn from Australian feminist philosopher Val Plumwood's influential concept of '**shadow places**' (2008). In Plumwood's explication, shadow places are sites and environments that bear the burden of capitalist consumption, the 'disregarded places of economic and ecological support' (2008: 139) that are the underside of our habitable spaces in the affluent west, the places we frequent for leisure, pleasure or respite. They are places, and within these, more than human communities, that sustain the lives of abundance that consumerism requires.

Exploring shadow waters through three examples of water use and consumption in contemporary Australia – water extraction for agriculture, bottled water, and urban life – this chapter will consider how multiple daily practices are caught up with water in not always visible ways. It will focus on practices that are common signifiers of Australian identity to argue that a problematic connection exists between how we imagine ourselves collectively and how we live with water. This critical link offers possibilities as much as it illuminates troubling histories and contemporary relations between humans and the more-than-human world in the dominant Australian settler-colonial imaginary. While particular kinds of water, as well as its forms of access and consumption are privileged in prevailing settler colonial culture (McLean at al 615), shadow water's material insistence, its refusal to be fully absented, means that alternative ways of living in a water-challenged land are alive and active, and continue to be practiced. It will conclude with the discussion of a recent art collaboration that brings shadow water poetically and strategically to light to affirm our entanglement with it.

Water in Australia

Australians are caught up with water everyday: this includes the water we see and consume, and the water we don't see, and still consume, nonetheless. Water sustains our bodies, but also our economy, the infrastructures and materials of our daily lives, and our sociality, our practices of living together. How we live with water is also very much connected to social and cultural values and ideals (Lindsay and Supski 2017). A dynamic of absence and presence, or visibility and invisibility, characterizes this entanglement: Australia's water resources are vast, but they are significantly hidden and under pressure. **'Consumptive water use'** is defined by Ridout et al as 'the removal of water from a local hydrological system, thereby rendering it unavailable for further use' (2010: 1714). This 'removal of water' occurs through multiple practices and processes that intersect with various waters, characterized in hydrological studies as blue (surface and groundwater) and green (natural rainfall) water. Both water sources are seriously challenged in Australia due to the confluence of climate change and drought related impacts and endemic practices of water use across domestic and commercial consumers.

Renewable freshwater resources in this country more than halved in the fifty plus years between 1962 and 2014, dropping from 45,802 m3 to 20,971 m3 per capita (Tariq et al 2020: 4). At the same time, as Tariq et al outline:

> Australia has the fourth largest domestic water footprint globally. It uses more water domestically than could be considered "essential" and may not be utilizing its water resources efficiently in the industrial sector [20,28]... [The] largest consumer of freshwater resources is the agriculture sector (59%), followed by industry (29%) and then domestic (12%) sectors'.
>
> (2020: 3)

This consumption sits in a context of intensified pressures on water resources as a consequence of reduced rainfall, related to drought and climate change. The Millennium drought (2001–2009), which particularly impacted south eastern Australia, saw the lowest ever recorded flows in the country's longest river, the River Murray, as well as salinity levels in agricultural land reach record highs (Environment SA 2024). Significant water reserves (such as reservoirs) declined during these years (Tariq et al 2020: 3), while the nation's largest capital city, Melbourne, experienced a 14 percent drop in rainfall compared to the previous three decades (Lindsay and Supski 2017: 51).

Behind these statistics, however, and interacting with the environmental and technical forces implicated in water shortage and vulnerability, are a complex set of socio-cultural values and practices which come into play in material and imaginary ways. The levels of consumptive water use in Australia suggest a water abundance, which the metric realities of declining rainfall and falling river levels do not. This dissonance, where scarcity and abundance (or water's absence and presence) are simultaneously realized, is a result of capitalist-colonial logics of water as an extractable resource, and is sustained by a wealth of narratives and practices, including settler-colonial Australia's investment in agricultural identity, the making of bottled water markets, and urban life. But this dissonance is also the outcome of shadow waters, and the extraction that sustains global economies and affluent populations like Australia's. McLean et al.'s (2018) concept of shadow water can illuminate the hidden waters that sustain dominant representations and ways of living with water in this country.

McLean's et al argue that our most visible water – surface water – feeds Australian settler-colonial self-imagining: the rivers, creeks, rainfall, and water from our taps that have a strong visual presence in our lives. In their definition, "shadow waters centers attention on the cultures that privilege certain waters while rendering other waters invisible and marginalized" (2018: 615). Groundwater such as aquifers, largely invisible and exploited, exemplifies this shadowing, as well as a dynamic between the seen and the unseen. In Australia, groundwater extraction has intensified as available surface water has declined. This is far from a 'natural' problem. The recent State of the Environment Report produced by the Australian Government states that "groundwater levels have generally been in decline for the past 40 years due to decreasing rainfall, coupled with increasing groundwater demand" (DCCEEW 2022). In some industries, such as mining and agriculture, there is a long history of exploiting groundwater, connected to its paradoxical invisibility and availability to extraction, without adequate controls or oversight from the traditional owners whose water "values, knowledges and practices" have sustained water sources in Australia for millennia (McLean et al 2018: 616). As McLean et al describe, "[i]n Australia, exploitation of groundwaters as a resource frontier is largely being pursued by companies and governments in ignorance of the interconnections between surface and groundwaters" (ibid.: 625). It serves prevailing settler-colonial water practices and imaginaries to keep surface and groundwaters disconnected in this way.

Water Practices and Imaginaries

The immigrant foundations of settler-colonial Australia have lent themselves to a particular narrative of ocean attachment. As influential Australian novelist David Malouf wrote in 1998, "if [Indigenous Australians] are a land-dreaming people, what we latecomers share is a sea-dreaming" (Boyer Lectures 1998): journeying to the island continent from elsewhere, and always, at least partially, looking back. This is perhaps why, as Stephen Muecke states over twenty-five years later, "along with the 'outback' the beach is the most mythologized and romanticized space in Australian culture" (in Norman et al 2024: np). Yet the First Australians were also coastal dwellers, and while attachment to the earth of Country deeply informs Indigenous ontology and epistemology (Kwaymullina 2005), this doesn't excise water, which is an entangled part of it. The dichotomy that Malouf rehearses between land and water reflects an influential western viewpoint of separable ecological components that can be classified, extracted, and understood as valuable or useful in discrete ways.

In contrast to this, water is an inextricable part of **Country** for Indigenous Australians, and is therefore sentient, relational and "deeply storied" (Goodall 2017: 34). Writes Palyku scholar Ambellin Kwaymullina:

> [C]ountry is much more than a place. Rock, tree, river, hill, animal, human – all were formed of the same substance by the Ancestors who continue to live in land, water, sky. Country is filled with relations speaking language and following Law, no matter whether the shape of that relation is human, rock, crow, wattle.... Country is family, culture, identity. Country is self.
>
> (2005, np)

Rivers were vital sources of sustenance prior to colonization; as well as providing water and food, they were a means of moving through Country, enabling trade and seasonal movements; accessing vital materials such as reeds for rope and basket making, (Conroy et al 2019: 174–5); and carried knowledge and stories of language and culture. The River Murray alone was home to more than 40 First Nations language groups prior to colonization (Mesikämmen et al 2021: 370). Water "thus has an interestingly plural existence"; it is "its own self... a participant in the webs of life... [and] the source of living things in their present lives and in their future prospects" (Rose 2007: 18). It is profoundly entangled in existence – "a type of kin", as Deborah Bird Rose puts it (2007: 9–10). However, the control of water was a critical strategy of colonization (Gibbs 2009), displacing Indigenous people from their life sources, 'opening up' the frontier, seeding industry and (like First Nations people before them) facilitating trade and travel.

Whereas pre-colonial water practices embraced the plurality that Rose describes and integrated ecological, economic and cultural values, underscored by ontological perspectives rooted in human-non-human relationality, settler-colonial water practices post-colonization reproduced modern western approaches to the environment, considering it passive, separate, and ready for human use. This fueled the "long sought" desire of settler-colonial Australians "to transform Australia's landscapes" (Gibbs 2009: 2967) into recognizably manageable, predictable and productivist environments. It reflected the economic and psychic investments in industrialization that had enabled colonization in the first place. Gibbs writes that the "late 19th century brought water-management tools of irrigation, river diversion, and bore drilling, making it possible to bring water to dry landscape. Transplanting water from one place to another", she continues, "separates water, physically and conceptually, from its constituent parts (land and plant and animal life) and from its context (place, lives, meanings and institutions)" (ibid.: 2967).

Contemporary settler-colonial Australia's "consumptive water use' (practices) and ways of narrating and framing water in how we think and speak about water (imaginaries) commonly reiterate early colonial water logics. They continue to position water as something to control and manage, something to access at will, and – paradoxically – something that defines the non-indigenous 'struggle' against the land in a colonized place" (2019: 18). It does this through a range of arrangements between bodies and non-human materiality in which water oscillates between presence and absence. The first of these that I will explore is agricultural water.

Agricultural Water

Drawing on Plumwood, Cameron Muir argues that "sites of agricultural production are the world's primary 'shadow places'" (2014: 5). In Australia, this has manifested in swathes of damaged environments, inherently unsuited to the kinds of farming practices taken to them over many decades, and a host of economic and social challenges resulting from – what Muir terms – "the broken promise of agricultural progress" (ibid.). Agriculture played a key role in the colonization of Australia, reflecting its settler-colonial foundations and the intentions of the colonizers to generate wealth in place through extraction, rather than to simply extract and leave. More than economic intentions lay behind agricultural expansion and the nation-building project that it sustained, however. Agriculture was deeply embedded in settler-colonial Australian self-understanding and identification. Agriculture fed particular stories about (settler-colonial) Australians, who they were and where they were headed. These had roots in elevated narratives about a land that needed 'taming' by industrious and hard-working individuals – embodied in the figure of the farmer – who ultimately triumphed and "cultivated a nation" (Mayes 2019: 1).

It is this embedding in social imaginaries that gives the "mythos of the Australian farmer" (Mayes 2019: 2) such an enduring status, despite the majority urban population. Where once agricultural production was Australia's "dominant industry" (Baker 2015: 193), it comprised just 11.6% of goods and services exports in Australia in 2021–2022 (DAFF 2024), while the percentage of land dedicated to agriculture in Australia remains significant at 58% (Tariq et al 2014: 8). This imaginary and material investment in settler-colonial identity comes at a huge environmental toll, however. Muir explains:

> The promise of scientific, industrialized, globally traded agriculture was that it would save the land and feed the world. We are still waiting for that promise to be fulfilled… Our agricultural activities have been one of the primary causes of species loss and… continue to be 'perhaps that single greatest threat to biodiversity'.
>
> (2014: 7)

Case Study: Murray Darling Basin

The twentieth largest catchment in the world, and Australia's largest river system covering 77,000 kilometers of waterways, the Murray Darling Basin (MDB) provides water to 70 percent of Australia's agriculture, one third of Australia's food and fiber crops, and contributes AU$30 billion to the economy each year (MDBA 2023), including $8 billion from tourism (Mesikämmen et al 2021: 371). These pressures on the system have come at an extreme cost, however. Since 1902, 76 percent of the MDB wetlands have been lost, with many native species of fish, birds, and frogs now endangered (Conroy et al 2019: 170). Twenty-one of the basin's 23 catchments have been assessed as being in either "poor" or "very poor" ecological health' (ABARES Insight 2). Unsustainable levels of water withdrawal from the MDB have resulted in reduced water flow, algal blooms, and increased salinity at the lower end of the system, and related human costs: "At the mouth of the River Murray, [the Traditional Owners] Ngarrindjeri measure the results of agriculture, irrigation, tourism and development in their decreasing well-being" (Hattam, Rigney, and Hemming 2007: 112).

Things are not much better upstream. Between December 2018 and January 2019, an estimated one million fish died in a 40-kilometer stretch of the Darling River. While competing claims were made over the cause of the fish deaths, the Murray Darling Basin Authority, who oversees the catchment's management, acknowledged that the 'over allocation' of water from the system was a critical factor (MDBA 2023). The language of allocation reflects dominant western colonial logic that structures water management in the Basin, and renders water a commodity to be traded and sold. In this logic, the environment is considered one stakeholder amongst many in a complex system of water entitlements. Unlike other stakeholders, however, it has no voice of its own: "farmers can speak directly to news outlets", while "trees, fish, floodplains and water birds require others to speak for them" (Kosovac 2024: 1).

Mobile Water

Virtual water disconnects water from its source – it renders it placeless. This is a key issue in western water culture, and one that feeds a mistaken sense of abundance. If the source of water is forgotten or obscured, then it becomes harder to account for, and to make visible specific practices that do harm to particular places and their life worlds. Shadow waters are also the hidden, exploited sources of water that travels. Ridoutt et al call for attention to local water resources in discussions of water precarity at a national or regional level. This is because "resource depletion is … experienced at the local watershed level", despite the virtual or "distant" nature of much water exploitation (2010: 1720). For Ridout et al, "the local character of a product's virtual water content must be made more transparent through the supply chain in order to better understand the impacts of distant consumption on local water resources" (ibid). Bottled water illustrates this disconnection, both through its visible and virtual water content. While bottled water is consumed widely around the world, with specific cultural histories informing these various markets, in Australia the marketing of bottled water aligns with particular narratives of self-identity linked to settler-colonial imaginaries of mobility and outdoor endeavor.

Bottled water has become a significant player in the non-carbonated beverage market, which has exponentially grown alongside consumer awareness of the health impacts of sugar-laden soft drinks (Hawkins et al. 2015: 195). The bottled water market is currently worth $747.7 million in Australia (Ibis 2024). Towie points out that the bottled water market's share of extracted water in Australia each year is relatively small: "just 0.5% of water extraction was for bottling, with 220 megaliters a year taken for bottling compared with more than 43,000 megaliters a year for landholders, commercial and farming uses" (Towie 2019: np). However, as a very visual signifier of water accessibility and convenience, bottled water performs a register of abundance. It makes water conceptually and practically available – for a price. It also performs **'placelessness'** as part of its mobility. The number one bottled water in Australia, Mount Franklin, is a case in point. While there are several geographical places called 'Mount Franklin' in Australia, the same branded water does not come from any of these. Instead, the Mount Franklin website declares, it is "sourced from specially selected springs around Australia: Only those water springs that meet our strict requirements for water quality and environmental sustainability are considered suitable… They might come from many places, but they all have one thing in common: the clear, lip-wetting taste of Australia" (Mount Franklin 2024: np).

Evident here, too, is Mount Franklin's appeal to Australian identity, as well as versions of 'Australian-ness' associated with settler colonialism. Its current slogan is 'the nation's hydration' (ibid.). Other brands make related moves. Frantelle brand is marketed as the 'perfect traveler' while pump brand goes by 'Ready Set Pump', referencing both mobility and action/adventure. Reinforcing this, in 2023 Cool Ridge bottled water ran a 'Win a "Back to Nature" Trip' competition. These associations sit against a 'shadow reality' (Hawkins et al 2015: 149) of water extraction, virtual water loss, petrochemical industries, and plastic pollution, including nearly 15 billion single-use PET bottles consumed in Australia each year, representing 250ml of oil and 3 liters of virtual oil each (Sustainability Victoria 2024).

Urban Water

Bottled water is ubiquitous in Australian cities, too, despite the prevalence of taps. The convenience and portability of the PET bottle means it is a common traveler in backpacks and handbags as people move about their day: this is water 'on the go' (Hawkins et al 2015: 67), always at the ready. There are other modes by which water appears abundant in the Australian city, least of all through their founding colonial designs which oriented them around coasts and rivers and towards the trade routes which stoked the fires of empire. These capitalist-colonial origins of Australian urbanism connect into the modern global city as the "engine of the Anthropocene" (Thrift 2015), resource intensive, carbon polluting and producing prevailing structures of economic and political power (Harvey 2008). These include capitalist logics of resource centralization, the spatialized production of economic inequities and social exclusions, an urban design focused on mobility, and a forward-looking ethos that pays little attention to the long and multiple histories of place (Potter 2020). Already, 72 percent of Australia's population live in its major cities, and this is only predicted to grow (AIHW 2023). Recent studies (Webb and Hennessy 2015) confirm that most Australian cities are already experiencing temperature increases as well as increases in the frequency of extreme heat events, rising sea levels, declining rainfall – and increased water scarcity (Thompson and Newman 2018; Lindsay and Supski 2017).

The shadow waters of Australian cities are vast and extend to what was erased (and yet may return) in their making, and what water from elsewhere sustained, and continues to sustain, the material and imaginary life of Australian urban places. Rod Giblett has written extensively on the destruction of wetland ecologies in the making of Australian cities. Wetlands, he argues, have held an abject place in modern western culture, "coded as bad and impure" in contrast to "flowing" water, associated with vitality and life (Giblett 2007: 31). These associations helped justify the widespread destruction of wetlands in the making of Australian cities, in ignorance – initially at least – of the critical ecological role wetlands play in riparian areas. Yet this destruction also gave shape to cities; wetlands remain a ghostly trace, a hidden water that might one day return (Giblett 2020: 10). Indeed, in some parts of Melbourne this is already happening. This was a city that "took the place of wetlands", draining and claiming its "swamps" as solid ground (ibid.). However, a recent initiative saw five 'floating' recreated wetlands launched onto Melbourne's Yarra River. These would cultivate hundreds of indigenous plants, with the intention to return lost plant and animal species to the river (Rees 2022).

Conclusions: New Water Imaginaries

On the other side of the country, in Perth, where domestic water consumption rates are some of the highest in Australia, despite a notably drying climate (Lindsay and Supski 2017), Melbourne-based artist Linda Tegg and Balladong Whadjuk woman and expert in medicinal plants, Vivienne Hansen, have also returned wetlands to where they have been erased. The art installation *Wetland* (2024) is situated in the abandoned food court of a 1980s era shopping complex, ear-marked for demolition in 2025. Amidst eerily empty service counters and signs promoting pizza and Mexican food is a living wetland that has been recreated where once hungry shoppers gathered and ate and, in the deeper past, where native wetlands once flourished: a "food court of a different kind… a sprawling… source of nourishment for (Traditional Owners, the) Noongar people" (Brennan 2024: 2). Growing in the wetland are native plants that thrived before colonization, "such as marda (bloodroot), whose red-coloured bulbous roots were a food staples; and bibool (saltwater paperbark), which was used to make a sweet tea called mangite or mungite" (ibid: 5). Extending Tegg's established practice of cultivating lost native environments and re-placing them in evocative contexts (see *Repair* 2018 (with Baracco + Wright) and *Grasslands* (2014)), *Wetland* brings the shadow waters of modern consumer culture back into sight. It makes visible the erasures that the capitalist-colonial project relies upon and seeks to hide.

In doing so, *Wetland* also refuses the self-affirming stories of settler-colonial Australia that would seek to separate past from present, human from non-human, and to compartmentalize and disconnect ecological elements. It visualizes the entanglements of living in a colonized country, where despite efforts to the contrary, the 'resilience of Indigenous water cultures in an entrenched settler colonial landscape' (McLean et al. 618) remains and offers a model for cross-cultural engagement in our water practices and futures. Importantly, *Wetland* draws attention to *this* place, the site of Carrillon City Shopping Centre in suburban Perth, as multilayered, ancient and alive with a complex ecology that extends from the past to the now, even if we can't see it. This is the power of shadow waters: to keep the local in view, and to insist

Figure 2.1 Linda Tegg with Vivienne Hansen, Wetland 2024, Water, Wetland Plants of Boorloo, Architectural Interventions, Supporting Structures. Installation View in Carillon City, Perth. Originally commissioned by Perth Festival 2024 with the support of Wesfarmers Arts. Photograph courtesy of the Artist.

on our ethical relations with it, while also asking that we think of places elsewhere – all the places that we consume everyday – and that we begin to act in their interests too.

Questions for Consideration

- How can we ethically re-engage with shadow waters?
- Is there a cost to this? Can shadows be strategic?
- What new imaginaries and narratives will we need, alongside practices, to renew our relationship with water in sustainable ways?

Further Reading

Hawkins, Gay, Emily Potter and Kane Race, 2015, *Plastic Water: The Social and Material Life of Bottled Water*, Cambridge, MA: MIT Press.

McLean, Jessica, Aleshia Lonsdale, Laura Hammersley, Emily O'Gorman and Fiona Miller, 2018, 'Shadow Waters: Making Australian Water Cultures Visible', *Transactions of the Institute of British Geographers*, 43.4, 615–629.

Muir, Cameron, 2014, *The Broken Promise of Agricultural Progress: An Environmental History*, Abingdon, Oxon and New York: Routledge.

Potter, Emily, Fiona Miller, Eva Lövbrand, Donna Houston, Jessica McLean, Emily O'Gorman, Clifton Evers and Gina Ziervogel, 'A Manifesto for Shadow Places: Re-Imagining and Co-Producing Connections for Justice in an Era of Climate Change', *Environment and Planning E: Nature and Space*, 5.1, 272–292.

References

Australian Institute of Health and Welfare (AIHW), 2023, 'Profile of Australia's Population', 6 June. www.aihw.gov.au/reports/australias-health/profile-of-australias-population, accessed 24/2/24.

Baker, Claire, 2015, 'From Nation Building to Neoliberalism: Agriculture, Change and the Social Imaginary in Australia', Proceedings from The Australian Sociological Association, Cairns, 191–197. www.TASA-2015-Conference-proceedings.pdf.

Brennan, Rosamund, 2024, '"Nature Will Have Her Way": How a Desolate Perth Shopping Mall Has Been Transformed into a Sprawling Wetland', *The Guardian*, 22 February, www.theguardian.com/culture/2024/feb/22/perth-festival-carillon-city-shopping-centre-wetland, accessed 24/2/24.

Conroy, Catherine, Alexandra R. Knight, Skye Wassens, and Catherine Allan, 2019, 'Consequences of Changed Water Management for Aboriginal Australians in the Murrumbidgee Catchment, NSW', *Australian Geographer*, 50. 2, 169–184.

Department of Agriculture, Fisheries and Forestry (DAFF), 2024, 'Snapshot of Australian Agriculture 2024', March, www.agriculture.gov.au/abares/products/insights/snapshot-of-australian-agriculture, accessed 24/2/24.

Department of Climate Change, Energy, the Environment and Water (DCCEEW), 2022, 'State of the Environment Report', https://soe.dcceew.gov.au/, accessed 24/2/24.

Elder, Catriona, 2008, *Being Australian: Narratives of National Identity*, London and New York: Routledge.

Environment SA, 2024, 'Millennium Drought', www.environment.sa.gov.au/topics/river-murray/dry-conditions/millennium-drought, accessed 24/2/24.

Gibblett, Rod, 2007, 'Black and White Water', 0in *Fresh Water: New Perspectives on Water in Australia*, eds Emily Potter, Alison McKinnon, Stephen McKenzie, and Jennifer McKay, Carlton: Melbourne University Press, 31–43.

———. 2020, *Modern Melbourne: City and Site of Nature and Culture*, Bristol and Chicago: Intellect/University of Chicago.

Gibbs, Leah M., 2009, 'Just Add Water: Colonisation, Water Governance, and the Australian Inland', *Environment and Planning A*, 41, 2964–2983.

Goodall, Heather, 2017, 'Rivers, Memory, and Migrancy: Everyday Place-Making in Changing Environments', in *Telling Environmental Histories: Intersections of Memory, Narrative and Environment*, eds Katie Holmes and Heather Goodall, Switzerland: Palgrave Macmillan, 31–50.

Harvey, David, 2008, 'The Right to the City', *New Left Review*, 53, 23–40.

Hattam, Robert, Daryle Rigney, and Steve Hemming, 2007, 'Reconciliation? Culture, Nature and the Murray River', in *Fresh Water: New Perspectives on Water in Australia*, eds Emily Potter, Alison McKinnon, Stephen McKenzie, and Jennifer McKay, Carlton: Melbourne University Press, 105–122.

Hawkins, Gay, Emily Potter and Kane Race, 2015, *Plastic Water: The Social and Material Life of Bottled Water*, Cambridge, MA: MIT Press.

Ibis World, 2024, 'Bottled Water Manufacturing in Australia – Market Size, Industry Analysis, Trends and Forecasts (2024-2029)', www.ibisworld.com/au/industry/bottled-water-manufacturing/1860/, accessed 24/2/24.

Kosovac, Anna, Alex Shermon, Erin O'Donnell, Avril Home, Emma Mesikämmen, 2024, 'Water Courses and Discourses: A Media Content Analysis of Environmental Water Reporting in Australia', *Environmental Science and Policy*, 154, 1–14. https://doi.org/10.1016/j.envsci.2024.103703.

Kwaymullina, Ambellin, 2005, 'Seeing the Light: Aboriginal Law, Learning and Sustainable Living in Country', *Indigenous Law Bulletin*, 27, classic.austlii.edu.au/au/journals/IndigLawB/2005/27.html, accessed 24/2/24.

Lindsay, Jo and Sian Supski, 2017, 'Changing Household Water Consumption Practices After Drought in Three Australian Cities', *Geoforum*, 84, 51–58.

McLean, Jessica, Aleshia Lonsdale, Laura Hammersley, Emily O'Gorman, and Fiona Miller, 2018, 'Shadow Waters: Making Australian Water Cultures Visible', *Transactions of the Institute of British Geographers*, 43.4, 615–629.

Malouf, David, 1998, 'A Spirit of Play: Boyer Lectures', *ABC Radio*. 15 November. Republished in www.mascarareview.com/issue-17-april-2015/george-michelsen-foy/page/74/, accessed 24/2/24.

Mayes, Christopher, 2019, 'Cultivating a Nation: Why the Mythos of the Australian Farmer is Problematic', *The Conversation*, 11 January, https://theconversation.com/cultivating-a-nation-why-the-mythos-of-the-australian-farmer-is-problematic-106517, accessed 24/2/24.

Mesikämmen, Emma, Lisa Waller, Brian Burkett, 2021, 'Water Wars: A "Critical Listening In" to Rural Radio Discourse on a River System in Trouble', *Environmental Communication*, 15.3, 369–385.

Mount Franklin, 2024, www.mountfranklinwater.com.au/, accessed 24/2/24.

Muir, Cameron, 2014, *The Broken Promise of Agricultural Progress: An Environmental History*, Abingdon, Oxon and New York: Routledge.

Murray-Darling Basin Authority, 2023, 'Menindee Fish Deaths', 18 December, www.mdba.gov.au/climate-and-river-health/water-quality/fish-deaths/menindee-fish-deaths, accessed 24/2/24.

Norman, Jana, Emily Potter, Lee Harrop, Mandy Treagus, Prudence Black, and Stephen Muecke, 2024 (26 August 2024), 'Mapping Shadows of the Bight: A Road Trip Residency', *Continuum*, 1–23, https://doi.org/10.1080/10304312.2024.2394960.

Plumwood, Val, 2008, 'Shadow Places and the Politics of Dwelling', *Australian Humanities Review*, 44, https://australianhumanitiesreview.org/2008/03/01/shadow-places-and-the-politics-of-dwelling/, accessed 24/2/24.

Potter, Emily, 2019, *Writing Belonging at the Millennium: Notes from the Field of Settler Colonial Place*, Bristol and Chicago: Intellect/University of Chicago Press.

———. 2020, 'Contesting Imaginaries in the Australian City: Urban Planning, Public Storytelling and the Implications for Climate Change', *Urban Studies*, 57.7, 1536–1552.

Rees, Brendan, 2022, '"Floating Wetlands" Set to Transform the Yarra River in Docklands', *Docklands News*, 14 December, www.docklandsnews.com.au/floating-wetlands-set-to-transform-the-yarra-river-in-docklands/, accessed 24/2/24.

Ridoutt, B.R., P. Juliano, P. Sanguansri, J. Sellahewa, 2010, 'The Water Footprint of Food Waste: Case Study of Fresh Mango in Australia', *Journal of Cleaner Production*, 18, 1714–1721.

Rose, Deborah Bird, 2007, 'Justice and Longing', in *Fresh Water: New Perspectives on Water in Australia*, eds Emily Potter, Alison McKinnon, Stephen McKenzie, and Jennifer McKay, Carlton: Melbourne University Press, 8–20.

Sustainability Victoria, 2024, 'Eco-friendly Alternatives to Plastic Water Bottles', 2 February, www.sustainability.vic.gov.au/recycling-and-reducing-waste/at-home/avoid-waste/minimise-single-use-items/plastic-water-bottles, accessed 24/2/24.

Tariq, Muhammad Atiq Ur Rehman, Riley Raymond Damnics, Zohreh Rajabi, Muhammad Laiq Ur Rahman Shahid, 2020, 'Identification of Major Inefficient Water Consumption Areas Considering Water Consumption, Efficiencies, and Footprints in Australia', *Applied Sciences*, 10, 6156, doi:10.3390/app10186156, 1–17.

Tegg, Linda, 2014, *Grasslands*, Melbourne International Arts Festival, www.lindategg.com/grasslands.html, accessed 24/2/24.

Tegg, Linda, Mauro Barocco and Louise Wright, 2018, *Repair*, Australian Pavilion, Venice Biennale, www.lindategg.com/repair.html, accessed 24/2/24.

Thompson, Giles and Peter Newman, 2018, 'Cities and the Anthropocene: Urban Governance for the New Era of Regenerative Cities', *Urban Studies*, 57.7, 1502–1519.

Thrift, Nigel, 2015, 'Cities in the Anthropocene'. Lecture. www.youtube.com/watch?v=ePA3e0NuqGs, accessed 24/2/24.

Towie, Narelle, 2019, 'Greed Took Over: The Farmers Fighting Bottled Water Giants for Their Water', *The Guardian*, 1 May, www.theguardian.com/environment/2019/may/01/greed-took-over-the-farmers-fighting-bottled-water-giants-for-their-water, accessed 24/2/24.

Webb, L.B. and Hennessy, K. 2015, 'Projections for Selected Australian Cities', CSIRO and Bureau of Meteorology, Australia, www.climatechangeinaustralia.gov.au/media/ccia/2.2/cms_page_media/176/CCIA_Australian_cities_1.pdf, accessed 24/2/24.

3 Consuming Energy

Romain J. Garcier

Summary

- Primary energy consumption has risen more than 6-fold since 1950, twice as fast as the increase in the world population.
- Energy production and consumption are major contributors to climate change.
- Energy is intrinsically linked to our modes of production and consumption, without us even realizing it.
- Influencing energy consumption through the energy transition is very difficult, as it implies radically changing the way we consume the environment.

Keywords: Grey Energy; Energy Transition; Great Acceleration; Consumption; Social Practices

Introduction

Since the 1950s, there has been a radical change in the human footprint on the planet, a change that environmental historians call the **'Great Acceleration'** (Steffen et al. 2015; McNeill 2016). The Great Acceleration resulted in an exponential increase in the number of humans: since 1950, the global population has multiplied by 3.2. At the same time, the Great Acceleration is leading to a very rapid increase in the use of natural resources, due to the contemporary model of production and consumption. Between 1970 and 2010, the extraction of material resources (ores, biomass, fossil fuels) tripled (Schandl et al. 2018; OECD 2018). In 2020, it exceeded 100 billion tonnes per year for the first time. It fuels economic growth: since 1959, global GNP has multiplied by more than 9 in constant dollars.

The data for energy consumption are equally impressive. Between 1950 and today, primary energy consumption has increased more than 6-fold, from

DOI: 10.4324/9781003412526-4

28.564 TWh to 178.899 TWh (Our World in Data 2024, https://ourworldindata.org/energy-production-consumption). It has therefore grown twice as fast as the population. But the status of energy consumption is not the same as that of other resources, because energy is a multiplier of possibilities: without abundant energy, resource extraction is not possible. It is the availability of energy that enables economic growth and makes the Great Acceleration possible.

The world we live in today is one in which, thanks to fossil fuels, energy is cheap and easy to circulate. All our economic structures, lifestyles and ways of inhabiting the Earth are based on this equation, which is the promise of modernity: unlimited economic growth thanks to unfettered energy consumption. The problem, of course, is that rising energy consumption is the main cause of the global environmental changes that make up the Anthropocene, and which jeopardize the sustainability of future societies. If greenhouse gases are choking the atmosphere, it's because coal, gas, and oil are being burned to extract energy. So how do we think about the relationship between energy consumption and the shape of human life in an increasingly precarious future? Energy consumption is full of paradoxes. In this chapter, I analyze some of them, which explain why reducing energy consumption is so difficult, even in the face of the dangers of global climate change.

The Nature of Energy and Its Units of Measurement

The first paradox about energy consumption is that in physical terms, energy can never be consumed. Energy is not a thing: it's a concept that designates material transformations in the world. Energy is the capacity of a body or system to produce mechanical work or its equivalent; that is, to induce a material change (e.g. altering the composition, speed or physical state of a body). Energy can take six different forms: mechanical energy, radiant energy, thermal energy, electrical energy, nuclear energy, and chemical energy, all of which can be converted into one another. For example, a plant converts the sun's radiant energy into chemical energy, and an internal combustion engine converts the chemical energy of oil into mechanical energy to power a car. The notion of conversion is crucial because no energy can be created or destroyed: the physical law of conservation of energy postulates that there are only phenomena that convert one form of energy into another. It is therefore a misnomer to speak of energy "production" or "consumption": it confuses the concepts of energy and energy sources; that is, certain energy-dense materials that can easily release it and which we certainly consume.

Like work in the physical sense, energy is measured in Joules (J), a "derived unit" in the international system. In everyday life, it is measured in other units, depending on the type of energy and the context of use (for ex. kilowatt-hour, kWh, for electricity: one kWh is worth 3600 Joules). The multiplicity of units, concepts, and objects makes it difficult to get an idea of the magnitudes involved in energy production or consumption: mastery of orders of magnitude is therefore essential in debates on energy futures, including the use of energy resources (Blain and Jancovici 2024). An important variable when discussing energy sources is their "energy density"; that is, the amount of energy they are capable of releasing per unit of mass or volume. Uranium, for example, is a dense energy source: one kilogram of uranium-235 contains 160,000 times more energy than one kilogram of coal.

Societies use energy by converting so-called **primary energy** (contained in crude oil, coal from mines, solar radiation, the force of water or wind, uranium or the heat of the Earth) into **secondary energy** (gasoline, electricity, etc.), at the cost of significant conversion and transport losses. Secondary energy is made available to consumers in the form of **final energy** (e.g. gasoline at a service station). Eventually, the use of final energy produces "useful energy" (the movement imparted to the car by the engine's operation, for example). Between these different stages, some energy is always lost, and only a fraction of the primary energy extracted produces socially useful energy. Reducing conversion and transport losses increases what is known as "energy efficiency" (ex. the output that can be produced with a given input of energy).

Energy statistics generally focus on primary energy. Why choose to express consumption in terms of primary energy (i.e. the energy that enters the economic system) rather than final energy (the energy supplied to consumers)? There are several reasons. Firstly, primary energy is easier to quantify than final energy, and there are well-established adjustment methods (the substitution method, for example) for comparing the primary energy of fossil fuels with the secondary energy produced by photovoltaics or wind power. Second, focusing on primary energy makes it possible to integrate all forms of energy mobilized by the use of a resource – including conversion losses, such as heat. But in doing so, it doesn't tell us what forms of energy are used by individuals and societies.

Energy Consumption in Late Modernity

This brings us to a second paradox. Although reining in energy consumption is often depicted as a political goal in the Anthropocene, energy has never been so cheap and abundant and demand is still growing (at about 2% per year).

In modern society, energy abundance is a major condition for improving living conditions. In the past, energy was scarce and expensive, limiting domestic use to essential needs (heating, lighting and cooking). It was mainly derived from biomass (wood, peat, cow dung, vegetable and animal fats). Humans and domestic animals provided the main source of mechanical work, along with wind and water (mills). With the revolution in fossil fuels (coal, then oil) at the end of the 18th century, and the development of electrification from the 1860s onwards, human societies entered an era of energy abundance, enabling them to multiply their activities. Energy has ceased to be a limiting factor in human activity: it is now possible to take a plane to spend a weekend thousands of kilometres away from home, for a modest cost but at the price of very high energy expenditure. Except for occasional and limited slumps in consumption (2008 financial crisis, 2020 COVID-19 crisis), energy

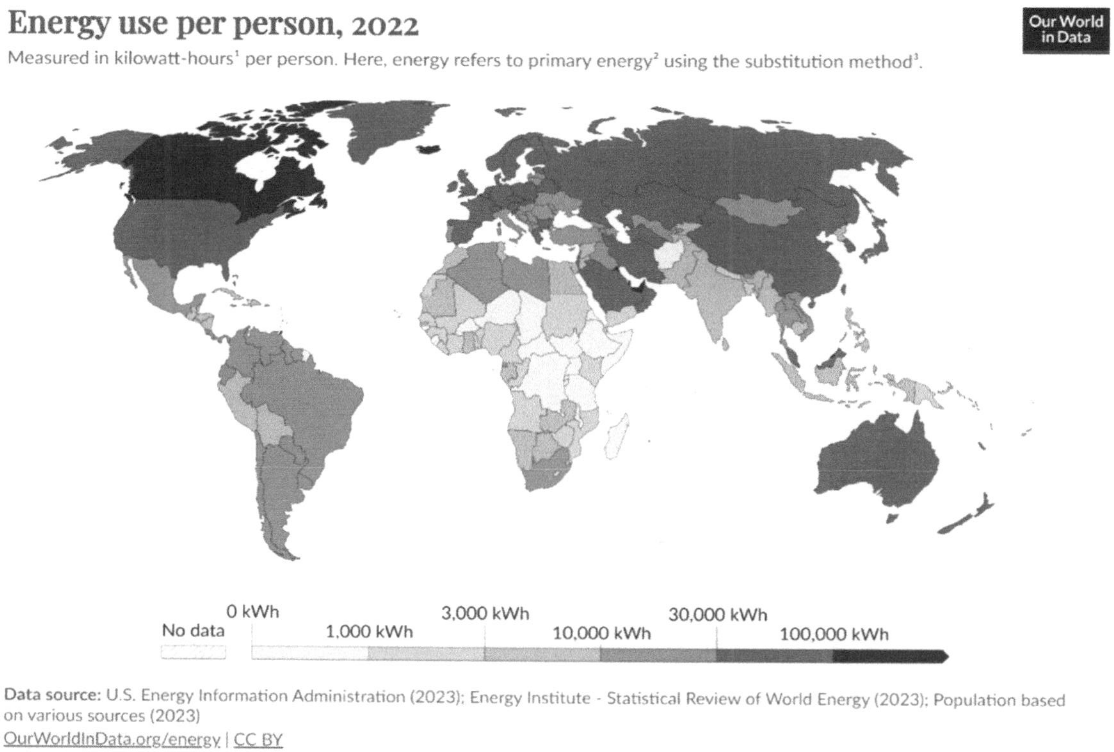

Figure 3.1 Energy Use per Person per Year.

Source: Our World in Data, CC BY License.

consumption is growing apace and the International Energy Agency forecasts that primary energy consumption will likely grow in the future at a rate of 1–2% per year.

Energy consumption remains uneven across the planet. While the average person on Earth consumes around 22,000 kWh of primary energy every year, there are major geographical disparities in energy consumption. The highest energy consumers (over 50,000 kWh/capita/year and up to over 100,000 kWh) live in countries characterized by: (1) the presence of high-consumption industries; (2) cheap energy that they often produce themselves; (3) high energy demand for heating and cooling, and; (4) high living standards. The category of high-energy consumption countries includes northern Europe (Iceland, Norway, Sweden and Finland), small oil-producing countries in the Middle East and Southeast Asia (United Arab Emirates, Qatar, Kuwait, Bahrain, Brunei) and North America (Canada and USA). A significant fringe of countries have intermediate consumption levels (between 15,000 and 45,000 kWh/year), while the poorest countries, which are also often the most deprived of industry, consume little energy per capita. This is the case in a significant proportion of sub-Saharan Africa, for example, where energy consumption is very low (less than 1000 kWh/capita). In these countries, energy is often derived from low-density sources, such as biomass (wood and dried animal dung).

Of course, the quantitative assessment of primary energy consumption doesn't tell the whole story: for individuals, it's final energy consumption that matters, since this is what enables useful uses of energy. To understand these uses, it is useful to think qualitatively about the relationship between energy consumption and all the possibilities it offers. For example, it has been established that there is a positive correlation between electricity consumption and literacy (Riva et al. 2018). There are several reasons for this. Teachers, who often belong to the educated rungs of the population, are reluctant to settle in very rural areas, where infrastructure is sketchy and electricity is lacking. For example, until 2021, a third of India's public schools had no electricity: since then, the Indian government's policy of equipping schools has remedied the situation (Bhatia 2023). Domestic electrification extends the learning day for pupils, enabling them to read or do homework after dark (Gurtoo and Lahiri 2012). While over 99% of Indian households now have access to electricity, the stability and reliability of supply remains questionable in some regions.

Understanding Direct and Indirect Energy Consumption

The third paradox in energy consumption relates to how inconspicuously energy is consumed. The most conspicuous form of consumption is **direct consumption** (electricity in the home or petrol at the gas station), which we often take for granted. However, this represents only a fraction of overall energy consumption, a very significant part of which is indirect (energy embedded in manufactured products).

Direct energy consumption depends on energy supply infrastructures that are critical to meet energy demand. These often take the form of networks operating on several scales: continental (oil and gas pipelines, electricity interconnections), national and local (commercial gas and electricity distribution networks). Networks are used to transport energy from production sites to consumption sites, which are often separate. In the absence of transmission and distribution infrastructure, energy cannot be consumed because demand cannot be met. The complex assemblages through which energy is provided are often invisible and enter public consciousness only when they fail (Bennett 2005; Abi Ghanem 2018) or when the cost of energy increases.

Energy supply often takes the form of a commercial service: except in very rural areas, it is rare for consumers to individually collect the energy sources they are going to use. Far more often, energy is purchased, and the more modest the household, the greater the share of the household budget. Social science literature has taken up these issues through the concepts of "energy poverty" (González-Eguino 2015) or "energy burden" (Graff et al. 2021). **Energy poverty** refers to the impossibility or difficulty of meeting basic energy needs. It takes many forms: whether it's the impossibility of heating one's home, putting petrol in one's car tank or having reliable access to electricity.

The proportion of the household budget devoted to energy purchases varies according to energy prices: in France, for example, depending on the year, households spend on average between 8% and 12% of their income on energy purchases for lighting and heating their homes, specific uses and fuel for their vehicles (Commissariat général au développement durable 2023). In France, households spending more than 10% of their income on energy are considered to be in a situation of fuel poverty. Some of the poorest households can spend up to 15% of their budget on energy, at the expense of other items. In India, some very modest households spend more than 10% of their budget just on kerosene for domestic lighting (Gurtoo and Lahiri 2012).

In many countries, the marketing of energy is regulated, and its price is not free. Depending on national policies, there may be taxes on energy products (for example, taxes on gasoline make up 65% to 80% of its price in the member states of the European Union); or, on the contrary, forms of **consumption subsidies** (price caps or regulated tariffs), which vary according to the type of consumption (industrial or domestic). In Egypt, for example, before a plan to reform energy subsidies came into force in 2015, the Egyptian state devoted 22% of its budget to them (i.e. 7% of GNP). Under the influence of the IMF, these subsidies virtually disappeared in Egypt in 2019: as elsewhere, they benefited proportionally more than the wealthier social classes, who consume more energy and in more elaborate forms (gas more than wood, for example). Such is the case in Argentina, which started distributing energy and transport subsidies after 2001. The subsidies grew steadily after 2006 and in 2023, consumers typically paid only 15% of their energy costs, the rest being covered by the government (for an amount of over US$ 12 Bn). On a global level, consumer subsidies mainly concern fossil fuels: in 2022, the amount of these subsidies stood at over 7,000 billion US$ and has risen sharply since 2020 (Diab 2023).

Final energy consumption by consumers, whether households or the productive sector, is just one facet of the energy issue: in addition to *direct* energy consumption, we need to add *indirect* energy consumption, linked to the manufacture of the objects we consume or which serve as inputs in production processes. This energy is called "**embodied energy**" or "grey energy". It is a measure used in life-cycle analysis studies of objects, to quantify and reduce the resources required for their manufacture. It is often underestimated, even though it can be very significant. The ICE database, originally developed at the University of Bath in the UK (Hammond and Jones 2011) indicates, for example, that one kilogram of building brick contains 3 MJ of embodied energy, while one kilogram of aluminum (whose manufacture is very energy-intensive) contains 155 MJ. A study by the US Department of Agriculture (USDA) showed that on American farms, energy consumption accounted for between 20% and 30% of expenses, depending on farm size, but that in all cases, indirect energy consumption (in the form of fertilizers and pesticides) was on average 50% higher than direct energy consumption (Beckman, Borchers, and Jones 2013). This is coherent with studies conducted elsewhere: in the EU open-field agriculture, for example, about a third of energy consumption comes from diesel fuel, and 55% comes from indirect sources (Paris et al. 2022).

One of the reasons that global energy consumption has been increasing is that modern technological innovations add new uses every year, both in households and in production activities. For example, individual mobility has been transformed by the availability of energy: in North American families (and to a lesser extent in Europe and the rest of the Globalized North), it is common to own several motorized vehicles. In advanced economies, transportation can account for more than 30% of all consumed energy. Numerous so-called "specific" uses of energy are appearing every year – for example, the electricity used to power the robots and appliances with which we have populated our daily lives. This process is not yet complete. Machines powered by energies drawn from the environment enable today's material profusion. For example, the annual installation of new industrial robots (powered by electricity) has tripled in the space of a decade: today, more than 500,000 industrial robots are installed worldwide every year, mainly in Asia, compared with just 150,000 in 2012 (World Robotics 2023).

Case Study: How much energy does an iPhone 15 require?

Apple has said that it wants to make its product range carbon-neutral by 2030. This means reducing energy and resource consumption at the manufacturing stage, switching energy consumption to low-carbon sources for manufacture and transport, and enhancing the energy efficiency of products at the use stage (through eco-design).

Since 2015, the manufacturer has been making progress on those fronts and between 2015 and 2023, the carbon footprint of iPhones has been reduced by 28%. Overall, the manufacture and use of an iPhone 15 today emits 66 to 75 kg of CO2e. The manufacturing stage accounts for 83% of all emissions – and although detailed figures are not available, an iPhone likely requires about five to six times more energy for its manufacture than for its operations over its life cycle. The end-of-life phase currently requires very little energy or resources (less than 1% of the total). Considering these figures, the most virtuous action one can undertake, energy-wise, is to extend the life of their iPhone beyond the standard two or three years of use (2/3 of smartphones get changed within four years) and get it repaired rather than replaced or recycled (Chen 2022). This strategy is of course not one favoured by phone manufacturers since manufacturing concentrates the bulk of profits.

It is difficult to assess if the energy embedded in the iPhones has been reduced on par with emissions since Apple does not communicate on those aspects. They simply insist that they are using 100% renewable electricity for manufacture. Interestingly, this means that energy consumption reduction is not a goal per se for Apple: the most relevant metric for the company is GHG emissions, not final energy use. Source: (Apple 2023)

Energy Demand and Energy Transitions

Today's situation shows a fourth paradox: the problem with energy is not that it is lacking – it is too abundant. The use of fossil fuels has such an impact on the climate that it would be necessary to restrict their use, despite the plethora of coal reserves, for example. IPCC reports have documented that action on energy consumption is an integral component of transitional climate policies. In the policy literature, such action can take three main forms.

The first form is an improvement in **energy efficiency**: for the same energy service, consumption is lower. This is what happens, for example, when we change an appliance for a newer one or opt for eco-design strategies. More efficient appliances consume less energy. Improving energy efficiency can produce decoupling effects: the increase in production is then decorrelated from the increase in energy or material consumption. In practice, improvements in energy efficiency often fall victim to the "rebound effect", identified in 1865 by the British economist William Stanley Jevons: as the individual energy efficiency of appliances improves, more of them are used. The result is an increase in energy consumption, rather than a decrease.

The second form relies on a range of price **incentives** (in the form of taxes or subsidies, for example) to steer energy consumption in a direction deemed beneficial, and if possible, avoid consumption. This may involve, for example, raising the cost of energy. It can also mean substituting electricity from renewable sources for petroleum products. Here, it is not so much the volume of consumption that is affected as the nature of what is consumed (i.e., the quality of consumption): subsidies for the purchase of electric vehicles, for example, which are found in many countries, fall into this category.

The third one would be a **structural reduction of energy demand** – that is, bringing people to change the social practices that result in energy being consumed. The difficulty is that energy demand (i.e. potential consumption) is still very poorly studied: many studies isolate energy consumption from social functioning (for example, by refusing to look at the destination of energy). They assume that rising energy consumption is a natural process, following an increase in the standard of living. They ignore the major difficulties created by certain macroeconomic interventions for populations who have no alternative to energy consumption to satisfy some of their demands or social practices. Elizabeth Shove and her team at Lancaster University (UK) have shown how energy demand is the translation of social practices that are not strictly energy-related. In fact:

> energy supply and demand are realized through artifacts and infrastructures that constitute and that are in turn woven into bundles and complexes of social practice. From this point of view, the relation between energy and society is not defined by external factors and driving forces. Instead, it is best understood as part of the ongoing reproduction and transformation of society itself.
>
> (Shove and Walker 2014: 41)

Reducing demand therefore goes far beyond one-off interventions (such as the adoption of more energy-efficient appliances): it requires a profound reconfiguration of the social uses of energy, which must nonetheless remain socially acceptable. For example, it might mean reducing the use of individual cars (whether petrol- or electricity-based) while ensuring the continuity of mobility services.

Numerous attempts have been made to envision what a world of reduced energy consumption might look like while preserving end-use services (Barrett et al. 2022; Kuhnhenn et al. 2020; Negawatt 2022). These scenarios recognize that it is possible to reduce energy consumption by around 50%, while at the same time decarbonizing it, at the price of fundamental adaptations to social uses and practices. However, the complexity of energy provision systems and their integration into the fabric of life and capitalist profits make change slow and difficult.

Conclusions

In the wake of the Great Acceleration since the mid-20th century, humanity has witnessed an unprecedented surge in population growth and resource consumption, particularly in terms of energy. This exponential increase, fueled by the abundant use of fossil fuels, has underpinned remarkable economic expansion but has also precipitated environmental degradation and climate change on a global scale. As we navigate the complexities of the modern energy landscape, it becomes increasingly apparent that the relationship between energy consumption, economic development, and sustainability is fraught with paradoxes and challenges.

On the future trajectory of energy consumption, envisioning sustainable pathways requires multifaceted approaches, that account for the complexity of energy provision in contemporary societies. Technical and economic solutions (improving energy efficiency, implementing price incentives) are not enough before they do not recognize the social underpinning of energy demand and consumption. To structurally reduce energy demand, we need far-ranging changes to how societies are organized: this goes far beyond the individual consumer's remit. It requires a paradigm shift in corporate and government attitudes towards energy consumption and a concerted effort to reconfigure energy systems in a sustainable manner.

In conclusion, addressing the challenges of energy consumption requires a holistic approach that integrates technological innovation, policy interventions, and societal changes, under renewed forms of energy literacy. By recognizing the paradoxes inherent in energy consumption, societies can work towards a more equitable and environmentally conscious future.

Questions for Consideration

- Who should do the most to reduce energy consumption?
- How can we de-carbonize energy production?
- How does energy consumption impact economic growth and sustainability?
- How can energy literacy contribute to sustainable energy consumption?

Further Reading

Blain, Christophe, and Jean-Marc Jancovici. 2024. *World Without End: An Illustrated Guide to the Climate Crisis.* New York: Zando.

Hancock Kathleen J. and Juliann Emmons Allison (eds.) 2018. *The Oxford Handbook of Energy Politics.* Oxford: Oxford University Press. https://doi.org/10.1093/oxfordhb/9780190861360.001.0001.

Shove, Elizabeth, and Gordon Walker. 2014. "What Is Energy For? Social Practice and Energy Demand." *Theory, Culture & Society* 31 (5): 41–58. https://doi.org/10.1177/0263276414536746.

Valentine, S. V., Brown, M. A., and Sovacool, B. K. 2019. *Empowering the Great Energy Transition: Policy for a Low-Carbon Future.* Columbia University Press. https://doi.org/10.7312/vale18596

References

Abi Ghanem, Dana. 2018. "Energy, the City and Everyday Life: Living with Power Outages in Post-War Lebanon." *Energy Research & Social Science*, Spatial Adventures in Energy Studies 36 (February): 36–43. https://doi.org/10.1016/j.erss.2017.11.012.

Apple. 2023. *Product Environmental Report: iPhone 15 Pro and iPhone 15 Pro Max.* Cuppertino, CA.

Barrett, John, Steve Pye, Sam Betts-Davies, Oliver Broad, James Price, Nick Eyre, Jillian Anable, et al. 2022. "Energy Demand Reduction Options for Meeting National Zero-Emission Targets in the United Kingdom." *Nature Energy* 7 (8): 726–35. https://doi.org/10.1038/s41560-022-01057-y.

Beckman, Jayson, Allison Borchers, and Carol Adaire Jones. 2013. "Agriculture's Supply and Demand for Energy and Energy Products." USDA. www.ssrn.com/abstract=2267323.

Bennett, Jane. 2005. "The Agency of Assemblages and the North American Blackout." *Public Culture* 17 (3): 445–66. https://doi.org/10.1215/08992363-17-3-445.

Bhatia, Parth. 2023. "India's State-Led Electricity Transition: A Review of Techno-Economic, Socio-Technical and Political Perspectives." *Energy Research & Social Science* 102 (August): 103184. https://doi.org/10.1016/j.erss.2023.103184.

Chen, Brian X. 2022. "Smartphones Are Like Cars. So Why Don't We Maintain Them?" *The New York Times*, November 9, 2022, sec. Technology. www.nytimes.com/2022/11/09/technology/personaltech/smartphone-repair.html.

Commissariat général au développement durable. 2023. *Chiffres clés de l'énergie – édition 2023.* Paris. www.statistiques.developpement-durable.gouv.fr/edition-numerique/chiffres-cles-energie-2023/.

Diab, Osama. 2023. "The IMF and Ending Energy Subsidies in Egypt." Transnational Institute. December 19, 2023. www.tni.org/en/article/the-imf-and-ending-energy-subsidies-in-egypt.

González-Eguino, Mikel. 2015. "Energy Poverty: An Overview." *Renewable and Sustainable Energy Reviews* 47 (July): 377–85. https://doi.org/10.1016/j.rser.2015.03.013.

Graff, Michelle, Sanya Carley, David M. Konisky, and Trevor Memmott. 2021. "Which Households Are Energy Insecure? An Empirical Analysis of Race, Housing Conditions, and Energy Burdens in the United States." *Energy Research & Social Science* 79 (September): 102144. https://doi.org/10.1016/j.erss.2021.102144.

Gurtoo, Anjula, and D Lahiri. 2012. "Empowering Bihar: Policy Pathway for Energy Access." Greenpeace India.

Hammond, Geoffrey, and Craig Jones. 2011. *Embodied Carbon – The Inventory of Carbon and Energy (ICE).* Bracknell, Berkshire: BSRIA.

Kuhnhenn, Kai, Luis Costa, Eva Mahnke, Linda Schneider, and Steffen Lange. 2020. "A Societal Transformation Scenario for Staying Below 1.5°C." 23. Publication Series Economic & Social Issues. Berlin: Heinrich Böll Stiftung. www.boell.de/en/2020/12/09/societal-transformation-scenario-staying-below-15degc.

McNeill, Professor J. R. 2016. *The Great Acceleration: An Environmental History of the Anthropocene since 1945.* Cambridge, Massachusetts: Harvard University Press.
Negawatt. 2022. *Scénario négaWatt 2022.* Paris: Association Negawatt.
OECD. 2018. *Global Material Resources Outlook to 2060: Economic Drivers and Environmental Consequences.* Paris: OECD Publishing. www.oecd.org/env/global-material-resources-outlook-to-2060-9789264307452-en.htm.
Paris, Bas, Foteini Vandorou, Athanasios T. Balafoutis, Konstantinos Vaiopoulos, George Kyriakarakos, Dimitris Manolakos, and George Papadakis. 2022. "Energy Use in Open-Field Agriculture in the EU: A Critical Review Recommending Energy Efficiency Measures and Renewable Energy Sources Adoption." *Renewable and Sustainable Energy Reviews* 158 (April): 112098. https://doi.org/10.1016/j.rser.2022.112098.
Riva, Fabio, Helene Ahlborg, Elias Hartvigsson, Shonali Pachauri, and Emanuela Colombo. 2018. "Electricity Access and Rural Development: Review of Complex Socio-Economic Dynamics and Causal Diagrams for More Appropriate Energy Modelling." *Energy for Sustainable Development* 43. https://doi.org/10.1016/j.esd.2018.02.003.
Schandl, H., M. Fischer-Kowalski, J. West, S. Giljum, M. Dittrich, N. Eisenmenger, A. Geschke, et al. 2018. "Global Material Flows and Resource Productivity Forty Years of Evidence." *Journal of Industrial Ecology* 22 (4): 827–38. https://doi.org/10.1111/jiec.12626.
Shove, Elizabeth, and Gordon Walker. 2014. "What Is Energy For? Social Practice and Energy Demand." *Theory, Culture & Society* 31 (5): 41–58. https://doi.org/10.1177/0263276414536746.
Steffen, Will, Wendy Broadgate, Lisa Deutsch, Owen Gaffney, and Cornelia Ludwig. 2015. "The Trajectory of the Anthropocene: The Great Acceleration." *Anthropocene Review* 2 (1): 81–98. https://doi.org/10.1177/2053019614564785.

4 Consuming Fossil Fuels

Nicolas Graham

Summary

- Fossil fuels became deeply embedded in systems of production, beginning with the Industrial Revolution and their consumption has accelerated since, particularly in the post-war period and via neoliberal globalization.
- As fossil fuels serve as both an energy source and as a raw material in production, the consumption of various goods and commodities is bound up with the consumption of fossil fuels.
- Parallelling the growth in fossil fuel use is a steady increase in carbon dioxide and other greenhouse gas emissions, producing climate change.
- Phasing out fossil fuels and transitioning to renewable energy sources is an urgent necessity in the face of the climate crisis.
- Despite the narrowing time frame for effective action, we witness a push to expand fossil fuel production and use, which includes Canada.
- Citizen pressure and social movements are vital in advancing energy transition, which must confront and overcome industry efforts to maintain carbon dependence and delay decisive decarbonization.

Keywords: Fossil Capitalism; Industrial Revolution; Carbon Emissions; Decarbonization; Energy Transition

Introduction

Fossil fuels, namely coal, oil, and natural gas are central to global capitalism's energy system, 80 percent of which remains carbon-based (Energy Institute 2023). Oil and gas are also used as raw materials or feedstocks in the manufacturing of various products like plastics, synthetic fertilizers, and other petrochemicals, which can be considered "fossil fuels in another form" (Drugmand et al. 2022: 4).

DOI: 10.4324/9781003412526-5

Employing the lens of **fossil capitalism**, this chapter first outlines the exponential growth in the production and consumption of fossil fuels in different historical periods beginning with the **Industrial Revolution**, followed by the post-war period, and more recently via processes of neoliberal globalization. Across each of these periods, we examine how growing fossil fuel use both supports and is driven by economic growth and profit imperatives, or the process of capital accumulation.

The chapter then offers a brief overview of Canadian fossil capitalism. This provides a further window into the contemporary dynamics of fossil fuel production and consumption, including the process of extracting, refining, and transporting fossil fuels and the role of the carbon extractive industries to that relationship. As fossil fuels are the main driver of the deepening climate crisis, we conclude by discussing the urgent necessity and challenge of **decarbonization** and **energy transition**. As the overview of Canada shows, such a transition must confront and overcome industry efforts to maintain carbon dependence and delay decarbonization.

Fossil Fuels, the Carbon Cycle and Climate Change

Fossil fuels formed millions of years ago from the remains of animals and plants, as they decomposed and were compressed and heated underground. For most of human history, fossil deposits were left largely untouched, locked out of the **carbon cycle**, which is the natural movement of carbon between the land, atmosphere, and ocean (see Riebeek 2011). Yet when fossil fuels are extracted and burned, the stored carbon and other greenhouse gases, such as methane (an especially potent greenhouse gas), are released into the atmosphere, overwhelming the ability of the climate system to absorb the additional gases, leading to climate change. Indeed, fossil fuel use accounts for approximately 75 percent of current total **greenhouse gas** (GHG) emissions and 90 percent of **carbon dioxide** (CO2) emissions (United Nations 2023).

The consequences of climate change are felt today, as global warming contributes to sea level rise, ocean acidification, biodiversity loss, and the increased frequency, intensity, duration or impacts of extreme weather (hurricanes, heavy precipitation, heat waves, and droughts) (Intergovernmental Panel on Climate Change 2023). Moreover, the time frame for decisive climate action is narrowing. In 2018, the Intergovernmental Panel on Climate Change (IPCC) released its influential *Special Report on Global Warming of 1.5°C* which declared that carbon dioxide emissions need to drop by 45 percent by 2030 and reach zero net emissions by 2050 to avoid a dangerous 1.5 °C increase in global average temperature (2018). This was followed, in 2023, by the IPCC's latest summary of the impacts of climate change, which declared that "the science is unequivocal: Any further delay in concerted anticipatory global action on adaptation and mitigation will miss a brief and rapidly closing window of opportunity to secure a livable and sustainable future for all (very high confidence)" (Intergovernmental Panel on Climate Change 2023: 55).

In the following section, we explore the origins and rise of **fossil capitalism**, which names "an economy of self-sustaining growth predicated on the growing consumption of fossil fuels and therefore generating a sustained growth in emissions of carbon dioxide" (Malm 2016: 11). As we find, fossil fuels came to be mobilized only under specific historical circumstances and through particular social (class) relations.

The Industrial Revolution and the Origins of Fossil Capitalism

At the center of the Industrial Revolution (IR) is a transition from human and animal power to industrial machinery powered by inanimate energy sources. From the late eighteenth to early nineteenth century, this industrialization, which first began in Britain and later spread to western Europe and the United States, was fueled primarily by waterpower (harnessed by a waterwheel) (Viollet 2017).

The transition from muscle power to fossil-fueled machinery was consolidated only in a later or second phase of the IR, in the mid nineteenth century. Andreas Malm (2016), who provides a close historical analysis of the eclipse of water by coal-steam power in this period, challenges a common assumption that nineteenth-century mill owners switched from waterpower to coal-steam power simply because coal was cheaper, more reliable, or more abundant. Instead, Malm's examination shows that the transition was pursued primarily because it offered the ability to relocate production to settings that would guarantee greater profits. In contrast to mills powered by water, the great advantage of coal in this period surrounded its ability to be stored and transported, meaning that industrial capitalists could locate production in areas with cheap labor, thereby using this mobility to lower or level down wages. In nineteenth-century England, this meant relocating to urban centers, which following earlier processes of land enclosure and agriculture transformation, had witnessed huge population growth and high unemployment.

In addition to the ability to (re)locate production in search of cheap labor, the switch to coal power subsequently enabled the acceleration of the pace and productivity of production. Indeed, the growing use of coal power in the later stages of the IR is bound up with the effort to increase labor productivity—reduce the worktime necessary to produce commodities—another key source of profit in an environment of market competition (Marx 1976:643–54). In turn, the acceleration of commodity production hastened the emergence of fossil powered transportation (Huber 2009). While prior to the IR, commodities were transported primarily by horse-drawn vehicles and by waterways (rivers, lakes, sail boats), coal-powered steam ships and locomotives radically reduced the amount of time required for transporting commodities and allowed for the expansion of truly global markets. The shift towards coal did not only transform societies within Europe, but was intimately associated with processes of colonial conquest that forcibly incorporated regions into an expanding world-system (Podobnik 2005).

Fossil capitalism thus names the "union of economic expansion and fossil energy consumption" (Malm 2016:12) that was first established and entrenched in the Industrial Revolution. As a result of this union, the production and consumption of various commodities became bound up with the combustion of fossil fuels.

While much of the literature is concerned with the emergence of the fossil economy, the "making" of fossil capitalism of course did not end in the 19th century. As discussed below, the post-war period, particularly in the United States, is characterized by a greatly accelerated consumption of oil and natural gas, which became embedded in everyday processes of social reproduction and in host of new fossil-derived commodities.

Post-War Fossil Capitalism

The groundwork for the post-war acceleration of fossil fuel consumption, and the growing importance of oil and natural gas in particular, was laid in early 20th century, as new methods of organizing production and dramatic increases in labor productivity were made possible through the growing electrification of industrial production (Podobnik 2005). This transformation ushered in a transition away from the heavy machinery of the nineteenth century (e.g., steam engines powered by coal) to the compact power of electric motors and assembly-line production. Total electricity generation in the United States accelerated greatly in the opening decades of the twentieth century, while fuel for the generation of electric power came from multiple sources—especially coal, oil, natural gas, and hydroelectricity (Huber 2013).

Oil also became more deeply embedded in everyday life, including via automobility, which exploded before the First World War to 1929 (Baran and Sweezy 1966). Likewise, in the 1930s, entirely new products made from by-products of oil and coal refining, or that required the high levels of energy that only oil could provide, such as chlorofluorocarbons for refrigeration, air conditioning, aerosol sprays, and a host of electrical appliances for the home, were introduced by giant manufacturers like General Motors and General Electric (Angus 2016).

In the decades following World War II, these shifts were consolidated and fossil fuel production and consumption, especially oil, skyrocketed. In *Lifeblood* Huber (2013) analyzes how in this period, oil consumption became fundamental to the growth of the "American way of life" for a specific stratum of the population, based on privatized social reproduction, including automobility and suburban consumerism.

Likewise, Angus (2016) examines how post-war capital accumulation was driven significantly by a "petrochemical revolution", which embedded oil and natural gas, often in less visible ways, in various products from plastics to pesticides to synthetic nitrogen fertilizer. The latter was an important development as it has led to the food system's dependence on fossil inputs, especially natural gas. Indeed, fossil-based fertilizers and other agrochemicals proliferated as a result of the **Green Revolution** in the 1960s, which encouraged farmers in both the Global North and South to rely on heavy synthetic fertilizer applications to raise crop yields (Wittman 2009). Subsequently, the global production and use of nitrogen fertilizers has grown from 12.9 million tons in 1961 to more than 123 million tons in 2020, while since 1960, the value of global pesticide exports increased by 15,000 percent (Drugmand et al. 2022). The food system's dependence on fossil inputs adds to the significant climate impacts from land-use change, deforestation, and industrial livestock production (see Chapter 5 of this volume).

Neoliberal Globalization and Expanding Fossil Fuel Consumption

The acceleration of fossil fuel consumption that began in the post-war period has largely been maintained into the present. Indeed, long term emissions trends show hockey stick-like upturns beginning in about 1950. Yet, the enhanced globalization of production and consumption that has accompanied neoliberal capitalism since the 1980s, has come about with the development of increasingly energy and emissions intensive systems of production and transport (Altvater 2007).

A key feature of neoliberal globalization is the diffusion of strategies of export-led development and trade liberalization (Teeple 2000). Subsequently, production-consumption chains increasingly function in a cross-border environment based on transnational corporations and are accompanied by the further growth of long-distance trade and transport. In this process, international divisions of labor have also been transformed, as some parts of the Global South became centers of industrial value production, while economies of the Global North became increasingly focused rent extraction through finance, real estate and insurance, and regimes of intellectual property rights (Harvey 2014).

Recently industrializing countries have thereby added to the consumption of fossil fuels—especially coal, whose combustion produces more greenhouse gases than other fossil fuels—with China and India now ranking as the second and third largest consumers of fossil fuels, respectively (International Energy Agency 2018). While this industrialization produces goods that sometimes serve domestic consumption, in the case of both China and India much of this development has taken place through foreign direct investment by transnational corporations and has a strong export-orientation, such that most of the commodities produced in the host countries are consumed elsewhere (Minx et al. 2011). This "offshoring" of production from high income to low-income countries, motivated significantly by the search for cheap labor, requires the establishment of new carbon (especially coal) infrastructure, and it leads to more extended and dispersed supply chains. Such elongated supply chains and a growing production-consumption "disconnect" that accompanies fully-fledged globalization beginning in the last decades of the 20th century, has contributed to the accelerated consumption of fossil fuels, causing yet more oil to be burnt in trucks, trains and supertankers.

Figure 4.1 Sunsetting the Fossil Fuel Industry.

Stalled Decarbonization and Energy Transition

In little more than two centuries, fossil fuels have become embedded in the entire economic structure, from industrial production and commodity transport to the food system, and in everyday practices of consumption and mobility. The system of fossilized production and reproduction carries steep environmental costs, ensuring the degradation of natural processes, especially the carbon cycle.

In the face of overwhelming scientific evidence, alongside the lived impacts of climate change, more and more governments and even large-industrial emitters have committed to accelerated **decarbonization**—a reduction of emissions from fossil fuels by transitioning to renewable energy such as wind, solar and hydro and via environmental efficiencies, which reduce (fossil) energy demand and intensity. While decarbonization commitments and plans sometimes avoid explicitly discussing eliminating fossil fuels, it is increasingly clear that meeting a 1.5 °C target requires the 'end of the fossil fuel age' and a process of concerted fossil fuel phase-out (Paterson 2020). Still, to date energy transition has been slow and non-fossil fuel sources have been added to the global energy system only incrementally and on top of an expansion in the consumption of fossil fuels (York and McGee 2017). Likewise, efforts to phasedown and phaseout fossil fuel fertilizers and other petrochemicals have only just begun to materialize.

In the following section, we turn to a brief overview of fossil capitalism in Canada. Moving to this context produces a subtle shift in focus, for while fossil capitalism literature discussed so far focuses on the role of fossil fuels in the production of other goods, prior to being combusted or used as a feedstock, fossil fuels must first be extracted, refined, and transported. This carries significant environmental and climactic costs additional to those from their combustion or final consumption. Moreover, in this process, hydrocarbons are themselves produced as commodities with the goal of profit making. Subsequently, the interests tied to their use, from corporations that profit from their production to governments and states that are reliant on revenue streams from their development, are an important force resisting and delaying decarbonization (Graham 2021).

Canadian Fossil Capitalism

While fossil fuel development has a long history in Canada, following a boom in production beginning in the mid 2000s, Canada has become a major global fossil fuel producer (Adkin 2016; Carter 2020). Canada is also home to a large and growing petrochemical industry. Fossil fuel development here centers on **unconventional** fossil fuel sources—oil and gas from non-traditional deposits and extraction methods—especially "tar sands" bitumen in Alberta, offshore oil in Newfoundland and fracked shale gas and oil in British Columbia and Saskatchewan. The development of these deposits is highly export oriented, and most of the Canada's extracted oil and gas is transported to and consumed in the United States (US).

While fossil fuel production has been a source of employment for workers and of revenues for governments, especially in Alberta, Saskatchewan, and Newfoundland and Labrador (Carter 2020), the expansion of the industry is plainly at odds with Canada's climate commitments (see Carter and Dordi 2021; Hughes 2021).

Below, we provide a closer examination of oil and natural gas development, alongside Canada's petrochemical industry, highlighting the consumption of natural resources (especially energy and water) required for their production and their environmental and climate costs. These costs are ignored and obscured in industry and government efforts to push fossil fuels to market while they still hold value. Indeed, this push is accompanied by dubious efforts to present fossil fuels and the fossil fuel industry as part of the solution to climate change.

Oil Sands Expansion

Most oil production in Canada (nearly 80 percent) occurs in the province of Alberta, and secondarily in Saskatchewan, Newfoundland, and Labrador. Most of the oil produced in Alberta comes from its "tar sands"—an enormous unconventional petroleum deposit containing a tar-like mixture of sand, clay and water saturated with a dense and extremely viscous form of petroleum—bitumen—found under Alberta's boreal forest and wetlands, in a region that is larger than Florida. Most bitumen production takes place in open-pit mines, some as large as three miles wide and 200 feet deep. Only a fraction of the established reserves is close enough to the surface to be mined in this way, while the bulk of them are deeper and must be extracted by an energy intensive process of 'steam assisted gravity drainage' (SAGD).

Reflecting the enormous resource requirements of bitumen production, Alberta's oil sands operations account for more than a quarter of Canadian natural gas demand (National Energy Board 2017). At the oil sands, natural gas is used both as an energy source to fuel the mining of bitumen via SAGD, and natural gas is used to dilute bitumen (create dilbit) so that it can flow through pipelines.

The bulk of Canadian bitumen subsequently flows south to the US. Indeed, approximately 70 percent of oil produced in Canada is exported, 98 percent of which goes to the US, especially the Mid-West (Natural Resources Canada 2017). Oil and gas pipelines continue to be built for consumption in the United States and we have recently witnessed a growth of transport lines that connect Canadian crude to refineries in the US Gulf. The latter is home to the world's largest concentration of complex refineries that have coking units to break down heavy crude into lighter refined products. Increasingly, however, the expansion of infrastructure for tar sands is justified as a means of getting bitumen from inland regions to new markets (especially China) via pipelines to "tidewater" in British Columbia where it would be loaded onto tankers for export. This follows from a US fossil fuel glut, alongside decisions to halt some pipelines heading south, such as the Keystone XL pipeline (Laxer 2015).

Given the energy intensive extraction process and the extensive processing, upgrading and refining required to transform bitumen into commodified energy, recent studies have found that the **lifecycle emissions** (the full scope of emissions from extraction, upgrading, transport, refining, and use) of bitumen from the tar sands range from 18 to 25 percent higher than conventional oil (Cai et al. 2015). As a result, tar sands are the fastest growing source of greenhouse gas emissions in Canada.

Growing Natural Gas

Currently, nearly two thirds of Canada's gas production take place in Alberta with a further 30 percent occurring in British Columbia (BC) (Hughes 2021). With declining conventional reserves, efforts to expand gas production are trained on developing shale gas in these regions. Gas in shale rock basins is accessible only through hydraulic **fracking**—the injection of large quantities of sand, water, and chemicals at high pressure to shatter rock and release gases. In addition to high emissions (discussed below), there are serious concerns surrounding drinking water contamination, water depletion, and carcinogens from fracking and shale gas development (Parfitt 2010).

Alongside the consumption of natural gas from oil sands production, an additional 50 percent of Canada's gas production goes to the US, where major consumers include the petrochemical industry and other energy-intensive industries that use natural gas for heat and power (US Energy Information Administration, 2016).

Facing a North American gas glut, the natural gas industry has pursued the development of liquefied natural gas (LNG) facilities on British Columbia's west coast, aimed at reaching Asian markets. Corporations and some governments have characterized natural gas as a low carbon and "bridge" fuel capable of aiding in the process of energy transition (see Graham 2017). In BC, because Asian countries are the intended target, industry proponents argue that exporting LNG will enable reductions in coal use, contributing to global emissions reductions.

However, the purported climatic merits of natural gas are based on emissions from its combustion, while the lifecycle GHG emissions of natural gas are significantly greater. The fracking process releases large amounts of methane, and in the case of BC-based LNG, best estimates find that the liquefaction, transport, and regasification process would consume close to 20 percent of the total extracted gas (Hughes 2015). Studies suggest that if methane emissions are minimized and the energy intensity of transport is reduced, the lifecycle emissions of LNG are marginally lower than those of coal (Council of Canadian Academies 2014). Nevertheless, such marginal emissions benefits over coal are no grounds for "clean energy" or "transition fuel" claims (Graham 2017; Hughes 2015).

Alongside LNG, the latest area of envisioned expansion in natural gas surrounds hydrogen, as industry and government proponents see Alberta as having the potential to be a major natural gas-derived hydrogen production hub (Government of Alberta 2020; CAPP 2021). While hydrogen production here is again being lauded as a means to reduce global warming, there is little evidence that fossil-derived hydrogen production can make a meaningful contribution to achieving a zero emissions economy (Howarth and Jacobson 2021). Instead, fossil fuel-based hydrogen development, like LNG, would likely help to lock the status quo in place and stall the transformations required for real change.

Case Study: The Potential and Role of Hydrogen in Energy Transition

Hydrogen power is increasingly being promoted to address climate change, because its combustion does not produce emissions. But since pure hydrogen does not occur in sufficient quantities in nature, it must be produced. Hydrogen can be generated by electrolysis of water and when such electricity is produced by renewable sources, such as hydro, wind, or solar, the hydrogen is often termed **green hydrogen**. Green hydrogen may be a component of energy transition, serving especially as an energy carrier for sectors of the economy that are hard to decarbonize, such as long-distance transport and cement and steel production (Oliveira, Beswick, and Yan 2021).

However, the vast majority of hydrogen produced in Canada and globally is generated from fossil fuels, particularly from natural gas. This is often referred to as **grey hydrogen**. The production of grey hydrogen releases large amounts of GHGs into the atmosphere.

A third category—**blue hydrogen**—is also created using natural gas, with the difference that carbon capture and storage (CCS) technology is applied in its production to help capture carbon emissions and later store them underground. So-called blue hydrogen is being promoted as a clean fuel by industry and some governments, including in Canada.

Yet due to high emissions from natural gas production and the limitations of CCS technology (see also Garcia Freites and Jones 2021), current research finds that the lifecycle greenhouse gas emissions from blue hydrogen are in fact greater than using either natural gas or coal directly for heat (Howarth and Jacobson 2021). Based on these findings, Howarth and Jacobson conclude that "blue hydrogen is best viewed as a distraction, something that may delay needed action to truly decarbonize the global energy economy" (2021:1685).

Thus, while hydrogen is being presented as a climate panacea, that is not the case if its production continues to be powered from fossil fuels rather than renewable energy. Concerningly, the development of hydrogen, in a manner like LNG, is allowing fossil fuel producers to misleadingly present themselves as part of the solution to the climate crisis, while delaying the necessary phaseout of fossil fuels.

Petrochemicals

Canada is also home to a large petrochemical industry. While the industry is distinctive from the fossil fuel sector, petrochemicals, as we have seen, are a core part of the fossil fuel order. Moreover, expanding petrochemical production is serving to sustain and create new demand for fossil fuels.

The industry in Canada is comprised of regional hubs centered in Ontario, Quebec and especially Alberta. In Ontario, Sarnia's "Chemical Valley" is a complex of refineries and petrochemical plants which developed around the earliest oil discoveries in Canada. While petrochemical activity in Sarnia has been in decline since the 1980s, the Sarnia-Lambton Petrochemical and Refining Complex has numerous petrochemical plants that continue to produce products made from oil and natural gas brought in via pipeline. In addition to carbon emissions, these facilities produce air pollution that has seriously undermined the quality of the community's air, including the Aamjiwnaang First Nation (MacDonald 2019).

Because a high percentage of fossil-derived chemicals are produced from natural gas, many of Canada's petrochemical facilities are located near to natural gas production, especially in Alberta, which is home to the country's largest refining and petrochemical manufacturing cluster. The region northeast of Edmonton, often referred to as "Alberta's Industrial Heartland," is home to more than forty industrial facilities, mostly hydrocarbon related, including numerous petrochemical plants (Turner 2017). Most domestic fertilizer production also occurs in Western Canada, as production of the key feedstock, ammonia, is again located near the region's natural gas supplies.

In 2020, Canada's chemical and fertilizer industry was by far the largest emitter of heavy industries, outside of the fossil fuel sector, and nearly on par with steel and cement combined (Sheldrick 2023). Rather than working to decarbonize the industry, proponents are pushing to expand petrochemical production in the region, particularly products derived from natural-gas, and envision Alberta and Canada becoming a "global top 10" petrochemical producer (See Government of Alberta 2020).

Conclusions

While energy use can support well-being and expand possibilities, accompanying the system of fossilized production and reproduction is a concentrated production of waste and pollution, most concerningly, a sustained growth in emissions of carbon dioxide and other greenhouse gases, producing climate change.

A fossil capitalism lens focuses on the close relation between capitalist growth imperatives and the growing consumption of fossil fuels, which has pushed emissions up the present. Whether economic growth and carbon emissions can be absolutely **decoupled** (via efficiency enhancements and renewable energy deployment), and at a rate rapid enough to prevent 1.5°C warming, remains an open question. Addressing the climate crisis may require the wealthiest countries to significantly reduce aggregate energy and material use, at a speed faster that what efficiency improvements alone could deliver (Hickel and Kallis 2020).

What is clearer is that confronting climate change will require us to remake the infrastructures and arrangements of the entire global economy, from energy and transport systems to the fertilizers and methods we need to make food, to built environments. In contrast to the previous energy transition that began with the Industrial Revolution, today's transition must be much more rapid and decisive, and it must be driven primarily by a concern for ecological restoration and sustainability.

As the overview of Canadian fossil capitalism suggests, a concerted phase out of fossil fuels and comprehensive energy transition will be fiercely resisted by the fossil fuel industry and other vested interests. This includes ongoing efforts to (re)position fossil fuels and the fossil fuel industry as part of the solution to climate change. A head-on confrontation with the fossil-fuel system requires robust social movements and citizen engagement to help to organize communities, shape the strategic priorities of state actors and institutions and hold governments accountable.

Questions for Consideration

- In what key ways does the energy transition that began with the Industrial Revolution differ from today's energy transition?
- Energy transition and decarbonization require technological changes. Yet, the literature on fossil capitalism points also to the need for social, political, and economic transformation. How so? What might these entail?
- What are the potentials and limitations of changes in individual behavioral and consumption for catalyzing energy transition and decarbonization? In what other ways can people become engaged in and help advance climate action?

Further Reading

Carter, A. V. (2020). *Fossilized: Environmental Policy in Canada's Petro-Provinces.* UBC Press.

Graham, N. (2021). *Forces of Production, Climate Change and Canadian Fossil Capitalism.* Brill Academic Publishing.

Malm, A. (2016). *Fossil Capital: The Rise of Steam Power and the Roots of Global Warming.* Verso.

References

Adkin, L. (Ed.). (2016). *First World Petro-Politics: The Political Ecology and Governance of Alberta.* University of Toronto Press.

Altvater, E. (2007). The Social and Natural Environment of Fossil Capitalism. *Socialist Register, 43*(1), 37–59.

Angus, I. (2016). *Facing the Anthropocene: Fossil Capitalism and the Crisis of the Earth System.* Monthly Review Press.

Baran, P., & Sweezy, P. (1966). *Monopoly Capital.* Monthly Review Press.

Cai, H., Brandt, A. R., Yeh, S., Englander, J. G., Han, J., Elgowainy, A., & Wang, M. Q. (2015). Well-to-Wheels Greenhouse Gas Emissions of Canadian Oil Sands Products: Implications for U.S. Petroleum Fuels. *Environmental Science & Technology, 49*(13), 8219–8227. https://doi.org/10.1021/acs.est.5b01255

Canadian Association of Petroleum Producers. (2021, January 27). Oil & Gas 101: Hydrogen. Context Magazine by CAPP. Retrieved from https://context.capp.ca/energy-matters/2021/og101-blue-hydrogen/

Carter, A., & Dordi, T. (2021). *Correcting Canada's "One Eye Shut" Climate Policy* (pp. 1–26). Cascade Institute. Retrieved from https://cascadeinstitute.org/wp-content/uploads/2021/04/Carter-Dordi-Canadas-one-eye-shut-climate-policy-1.1-April-16.pdf

Carter, A. V. (2020). *Fossilized: Environmental Policy in Canada's Petro-Provinces.* UBC Press.

Drugmand, D., Feit, S., Fuhr, L., & Muffett, C. (2022). *Fossils, Fertilizers, and False Solutions* (pp. 1–67). Center for International Environmental Law. Retrieved from www.ciel.org/reports/fossil-fertilizers/

Council of Canadian Academies. (2014). *Environmental Impacts of Shale Gas Extraction in Canada* (pp. 1–292). Council of Canadian Academies. Retrieved from https://cca-reports.ca/reports/environmental-impacts-of-shale-gas-extraction-in-canada/

Energy Institute. (2023). *Statistical Review of World Energy* (pp. 1–223). Energy Institute. Retrieved from www.energyinst.org/statistical-review/resources-and-data-downloads

Garcia Freites, S., & C. Jones. 2021. *A Review of the Role of Fossil Fuel-Based Carbon Capture and Storage in the Energy System.* Tyndall Centre. Retrieved from https://pure.manchester.ac.uk/ws/portalfiles/portal/184755890/CCS_REPORT_FINAL_v2_UPLOAD.pdf

Government of Alberta. (2020). *Getting Alberta Back to Work: Natural Gas Vision and Strategy* (pp. 1–26). Government of Alberta. Retrieved from https://open.alberta.ca/dataset/988ed6c1-1f17-40b4-ac15-ce5460ba19e2/resource/a7846ac0-a43b-465a-99a5-a5db172286ae/download/energy-getting-alberta-back-to-work-natural-gas-vision-and-strategy-2020.pdf

Graham, N. (2017). State-Capital Nexus and the Making of BC Shale and Liquefied Natural Gas. *BC Studies: The British Columbian Quarterly*, *194*, 11–38. https://doi.org/10.14288/bcs.v0i194.188618

Harvey, D. (2014). *Seventeen Contradictions and the End of Capitalism.* Oxford University Press.

Hickel, J., & Kallis, G. (2020). Is Green Growth Possible? *New Political Economy*, *25*(4), 469–486. Retrieved from https://doi.org/10.1080/13563467.2019.1598964

Howarth, R. W., & Jacobson, M. Z. (2021). How Green is Blue Hydrogen? *Energy Science & Engineering*, *9*(10), 1676–1687. Retrieved from https://doi.org/10.1002/ese3.956

Huber, M. (2009). Energizing Historical Materialism: Fossil Fuels, Space and the Capitalist Mode of Production. *Geoforum*, *40*(1), 105–115. Retrieved from https://doi.org/10.1016/j.geoforum.2008.08.004

Huber, M. T. (2013). *Lifeblood: Oil, Freedom, and the Forces of Capital.* University of Minnesota Press.

Hughes, D. (2015). *A Clear Look at BC LNG* (pp. 1–50). Canadian Centre for Policy Alternatives. Retrieved from www.policyalternatives.ca/publications/reports/clear-look-bc-lng

Hughes, D. (2021). *Canada's Energy Sector* (pp. 1–60). Canadian Centre for Policy Alternatives. Retrieved from https://policyalternatives.ca/publications/reports/canada%E2%80%99s-energy-sector

Intergovernmental Panel on Climate Change. (2018). *Global Warming of 1.5 °C: Summary for Policymakers* (pp. 1–24). Intergovernmental Panel on Climate Change. Retrieved from www.ipcc.ch/sr15/chapter/spm/

Intergovernmental Panel on Climate Change. (2023). *Synthesis of the IPCC Sixth Assessment Report* (pp. 1–83). Intergovernmental Panel on Climate Change. Retrieved from https://report.ipcc.ch/ar6syr/

International Energy Agency. (2018). *World Energy Outlook 2018.* International Energy Agency. Retrieved from www.iea.org/weo2018/

Laxer, G. (2015). *After the Sands: Energy and Ecological Security for Canadians.* Douglas and McIntyre.

MacDonald, E. (2019). *Return to Chemical Valley 2019* (pp. 1–28). Ecojustice.

Malm, A. (2016). *Fossil Capital: The Rise of Steam Power and the Roots of Global Warming.* Verso.

Marx, K. (1976). *Capital: Volume 1: A Critique of Political Economy* (B. Fowkes, Trans.; Reprint edition). Vintage Books.

Minx, J. C., Baiocchi, G., Peters, G. P., Weber, C. L., Guan, D., & Hubacek, K. (2011). A "Carbonizing Dragon": China's Fast Growing CO2 Emissions Revisited. *Environmental Science & Technology, 45*(21), 9144–9153. Retrieved from https://doi.org/10.1021/es201497m

National Energy Board. (2017, April 19). *NEB – Market Snapshot: Natural Gas Plays an Important Role in Alberta's Oil Sands.* National Energy Board. Retrieved from www.cer-rec.gc.ca/en/data-analysis/energy-markets/market-snapshots/2017/market-snapshot-natural-gas-plays-important-role-in-albertas-oil-sands.html

Natural Resources Canada. (2017, October 6). *Crude Oil Facts.* Natural Resources Canada. Retrieved from www.nrcan.gc.ca/energy/facts/crude-oil/20064

Oliveira, A. M., Beswick, R. R., & Yan, Y. (2021). A Green Hydrogen Economy for a Renewable Energy Society. *Current Opinion in Chemical Engineering, 33*, 1–7. Retrieved from https://doi.org/10.1016/j.coche.2021.100701

Parfitt, B. (2010). *Fracture Lines: Will Canada's Water be Protected in the Rush to Develop Shale Gas?* (pp. 1–56). Munk School of Global Affairs. Retrieved from www.ledevoir.com/documents/pdf/etudegazdeschiste.pdf

Paterson, M. (2020). 'The End of the Fossil Fuel Age'? Discourse Politics and Climate Change Political Economy. *New Political Economy, 26*(6), 923–936. Retrieved from https://doi.org/10.1080/13563467.2020.1810218

Podobnik, B. (2005). *Global Energy Shifts: Fostering Sustainability in a Turbulent Age.* Temple University Press.

Riebeek, H. (2011, June 16). *The Carbon Cycle* [Text.Article]. NASA Earth Observatory; NASA Earth Observatory. Retrieved from https://earthobservatory.nasa.gov/features/CarbonCycle

Sheldrick, O. (2023). *Decarbonizing the Canadian Chemical and Fertilizer Industry* (pp. 1–30). Clean Energy Canada. Retrieved from https://cleanenergycanada.org/wp-content/uploads/2023/03/Whitepaper-Chemicalsandfertilizers-Final.pdf

Teeple, G. (2000). *Globalization and the Decline of Social Reform: Into the Twenty-first Century.* University of Toronto Press.

Turner, C. (2017). *The Patch: The People, Pipelines, and Politics of the Oil Sands.* Simon & Schuster.

United Nations. (2023). *Causes and Effects of Climate Change.* United Nations. Retrieved from www.un.org/en/climatechange/science/causes-effects-climate-change

U.S. Energy Information Administration. (2016). *Annual Energy Outlook 2017 With Projections to 2050* (p. 64). U.S. Energy Information Administration. Retrieved from www.eia.gov/outlooks/aeo/pdf/0383(2017).pdf

Viollet, P.-L. (2017). From the Water Wheel to Turbines and Hydroelectricity. Technological evolution and revolutions. *Comptes Rendus Mécanique, 345*(8), 570–580. Retrieved from https://doi.org/10.1016/j.crme.2017.05.016

Wittman, H. (2009). Reworking the Metabolic Rift: La Vía Campesina, Agrarian Citizenship, and Food Sovereignty. *The Journal of Peasant Studies*, *36*(4), 805–826. Retrieved from https://doi.org/10.1080/03066150903353991

York, R., & McGee, J. A. (2017). Does Renewable Energy Development Decouple Economic Growth from CO2 Emissions? *Socius*, *3*, 2378023116689098. Retrieved from https://doi.org/10.1177/2378023116689098

5 Consuming Waste

Laurence Rocher

Summary

- Waste-to-energy issues have been moving to the forefront of waste management with unprecedented strength since the early 1990s.
- Heat, electricity, and gas are energy outputs resulting of waste treatment processes, encouraged by incentive policies to power energy supply systems
- Energy recovery solutions are positioned in the European Waste Hierarchy framework.
- Energy-centric market devices overwhelmingly tend to design waste policy.
- Waste counts as a (debatable) renewable energy.
- In cities, waste-to-energy often result in infrastructural lock-in.
- By turning waste into a resource, energy production tends to become a means of absorbing (i.e. consuming) waste.

Keywords: Waste-to-Energy; Energy Transition; End-of-Pipe; Circular Economy; Disposal Mode; Diversion Mode; Waste Hierarchy

Introduction

In many European cities, part of the residential buildings and public facilities are heated using waste. Commonly referred to as **waste-to-energy**, the utilization, as an alternative to fossil fuels, of energy generated by waste treatment processes is meeting unprecedented interest. Although incineration remains the most widespread waste-to-energy technology, other waste treatment solutions generate either heat or electricity –or both – from waste. In the wake of climate and energy policies, set at European and national levels, waste-to-energy solutions have been encouraged by means of a combination of legal frameworks, public support and incentives, to such an extent that waste management can be considered to be partly driven by climate and energy concerns.

DOI: 10.4324/9781003412526-6

The setting of an energy recovery policy, as a result of climate and waste converging agendas in the early 1990s, has evolved towards Circular Economy (CE) discourses. Rather than having a straightforward evolution, waste-to-energy has shown an ontological shift, from a recovery logic to the designation of waste as an energy source. By turning waste into a resource, energy production seems to be becoming a means of absorbing, and consuming, waste. In this chapter we question the setting of a waste-to-energy regime by paying attention to what made waste and energy connect, when these connections occurred, as well as what kind of reframing they entailed, namely the ability of energy to reset waste policy frameworks. In other words, how has waste become an energy issue, and to what extend is energy seen as a means of absorbing waste, in the name of circular economy?

Recovering Energy from Waste: New Perspectives from Old Ideas

The willingness to make waste a resource was part of the early evolution of waste collection services and disposal techniques. At the end of the 19th century, municipalities and industries, which first engaged in waste treatment for hygienic considerations, tried to avoid or postpone disposal through efforts intended to benefit from discarded items and materials (Barles 2005). Primarily, industrial incineration techniques were configured as recovery systems, producing electricity and steam (Brunner and Rechberger 2015). But soon, incineration (without energy recovery) and landfill dominated, as did the *sinks* (i.e. garbage dumps) that cities were in search of (Tarr 1984). These disposal modes, relying on **end-of-pipe** infrastructures (Melosi, 2005), carried on being developed throughout the 20th century to absorb increasing volumes of refuse. Even though evolving in terms of volume and nature, the aim was to dispose of waste, resulting from unquestioned production and consumption patterns, at great cost. These early infrastructural choices deeply established a linear approach to dealing with waste, long before it was identified as an environmental matter requiring designated public policies.

In the 1970s, waste policies were set in most Western countries. At that time, the oil crisis was generating disquiet, with threats of shortages and rising prices. It was concern over the energy supply that favored the link between waste and energy. The early 20th century "resource concern" came back into focus after the environmental shifts during the 1970s and the adoption of the dedicated waste management policies that followed the first European Waste Directive in 1975. Primary legislation on waste adopted in both Europe and France, in 1975, mentioned energy recovery and material recycling as (equal) waste treatment modes to be fostered. However, since this legislation was not linked with any compulsory or quantified objectives, it had no tangible effect (Bertolini 1992), with waste production increasing dramatically and requiring more and more disposal facilities. Both the oil crisis and subsequent energy stresses favored energy recovery from waste, mainly implemented by means of incineration, which gained new momentum in the 1980s and 1990s as landfilling met opposition, disincentive taxation and legal restrictions. The early 1990s were a turning point in France and Europe, when recovery and recycling gained effective support prior to elimination. The landfill ban (enacted into law in 1992 in France, and through the 1999 EU Landfill Directive) gave fresh impetus to waste policies, enacting the replacement of a then dominant **disposal mode** with a **diversion mode**, which "served to provide a new underlying objective for waste management (the diversion of waste from landfill), to solidify a new governmental rationality based on the notion of sustainability, and to provide new governing technologies" (Bulkeley et al. 2007). Diversion away from landfill was implemented in France by means of legal and fiscal incentives, consisting of restricting landfill access to purely non-valuable waste and of increasing taxes. These new regulatory choices acted as a boost for incineration – and, consequently, for incineration with energy recovery – resulting in the opening of new "energy recovery units" during the 1990s.

Growing climate concerns started being incorporated into the waste agenda, generating an unprecedented boost for energy recovery from waste (Rocher, 2020). The current energy shaping of waste originates from the climate-energy policies of the early 1990s. Climate and waste agendas have gradually been converging since then through the promotion of energy recovery from waste, and more broadly through a climate rationale incorporated into assessments and decision-making relating to waste policymaking and management. This was not without tension or contradiction when issues appeared to be competing, e.g. between energy recovery and material recycling. The 2008 EU Waste Framework Directive ranks energy recovery along the **Waste Hierarchy** as a response to the fear that energy recovery would compete with material recycling efforts and cause intensifying controversies over incineration (see also Chapter 15). Although this clarified the situation by ranking energy recovery amongst other recovery and disposal modes, it did not end the debate once and for all. In January 2017, the European Commission published a communication aimed at (re)placing energy recovery along the hierarchy by means of a refined definition of energy recovery, taking into account the variety of recovery processes and making these compatible with the CE, which now stands as a dominant narrative regarding waste matters. Indeed, the last ten years have been marked by the proliferation of energy-from-waste operations (including waste-derived biogas), by the strengthened promotion of renewable energy, and by the intensification of the principle of the CE.

The now widespread CE motto potentially deeply renews waste theory and practice by breaking with a linear approach that has long been dominant. However, such an ambition, though rather consensual, needs to be confronted with how materials circulate and are put into circulation by public policies, institutional and social rules and everyday practices. Advocating the need for "critical engagement" with the CE, "recited as an ideal" Gregson et al. insist on the necessity of "examining not just the idea of the circular economy but also the messy world of circular economies, and examining which wastes are being recovered as resources, and where" (2015: 219). This material and moral engagement functions to disentangle the specific flows constituting waste streams, notably the "downstream flows" generated by various modes of waste processing, whether they be valuable (e.g. secondary materials resulting from recycling activities, scrap metals, energy) or waste products likely to cause pollution (e.g. off gas, fly and bottom ash, leakage). We argue that energy flows generated by waste treatment (mainly by incineration, but also by other processes such as landfill or anaerobic digestion) are worth examining carefully. This is because of the prominence they are gaining, and because they are likely to displace boundaries between recovery, recycling, and elimination, as is the case with many categories framed and ranked using the notion of hierarchy. Far from being an end-of-pipe by-product, which happens to be opportunistically recovered, energy seems to be taking the lead in waste matters. By instituting waste as a resource in such an overwhelming way, energy is likely to force a new ontology of waste (Hawkins 2006).

Seven hundred and seventy-six million tons of waste excluding major mineral waste were generated in 2020 in Europe. Two hundred and twenty-four million (mainly composed of household waste) were taken in charge in municipal facilities (Fig. 1). Energy recovery rose from thirty-five million tons in 2007 to fifty-eight million in 2022. France (thirty-five million tons of municipal waste) has one of the highest incineration with energy recovery rates (around 30 percent), which equates to landfilling (30 percent), and recycling (15 percent material recycling and 15 percent composting).

Waste: A Renewable Energy?

Formally launched in 1992, with the United Nations Framework Convention on Climate Change (UNFCCC), the objective of cutting GHG emissions has led to mitigation policies to be implemented at the national level. GHG inventories had to be carried out in several designated sectors, including waste management, highlighted as a sector not only responsible for emitting a substantial amount of GHGs, but also capable of decarbonizing energy. From the early 1990s and onwards, climate change concerns and their associated targets for cutting GHG emissions entailed a re-examination of waste treatment options. Accounting exercises required by GHG reporting, in addition to climate action plans that were being set at many levels, designated waste treatment as a substantial contributor to climate change due to its emissions of carbon dioxide (CO2), methane (CH4), and nitrous oxide (N2O). One of the first challenges was to agree on shared methods of how to estimate waste sector contributions. The IPCC played a crucial role in the setting of calculating conventions, published in its *Guidelines for GHG Inventories* (IPCC 1996; IPCC 2006). These IPCC calculating conventions established metrological methodologies for waste-related GHG emissions, which were soon included in waste policies. In France, this resulted in the waste sector being responsible for 2 percent of the GHGs emitted by that country in 2007 (ADEME 2009; Record 2008). These accountancy methods played their part in designating

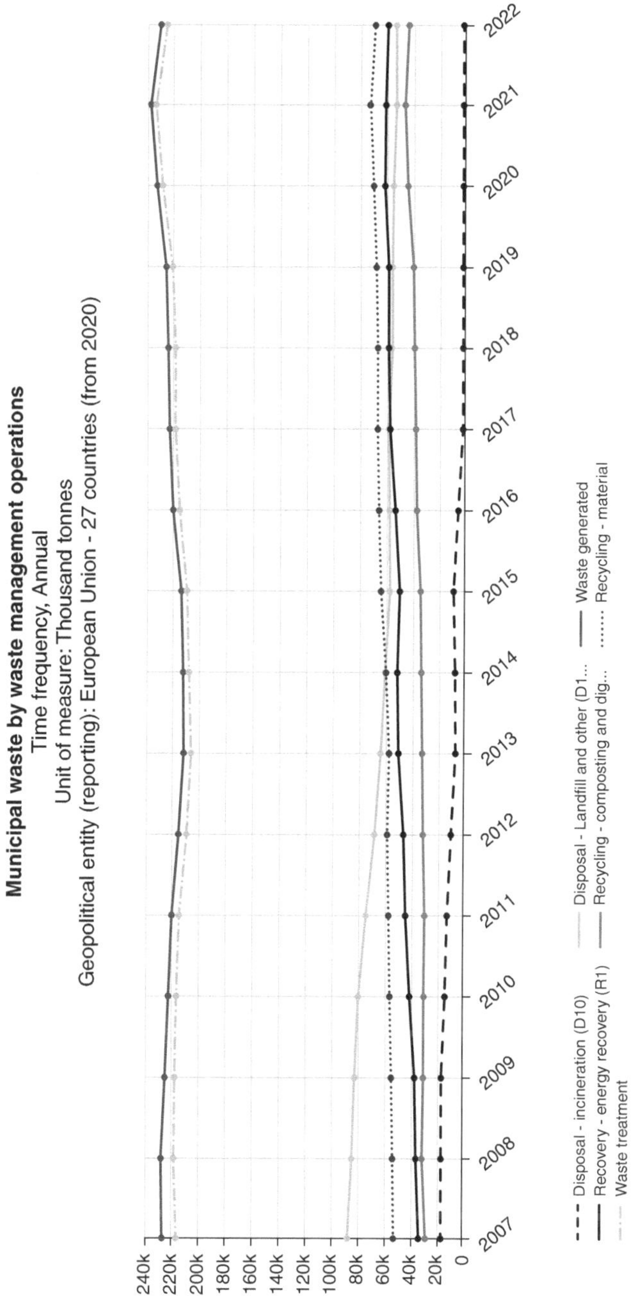

Figure 5.1 Municipal Waste by Waste Management Operations.

energy-from-waste as an alternative to fossil fuels. Indeed, on the proviso that energy was being recovered (as electricity, heat, or combined-heat-and-power), emissions from waste incineration had to be reported in the energy sector. The IPCC guidelines also introduced a distinction between biogenic and fossil CO2 emissions from incinerated waste in order to differentiate the emissions from the combustion of biomass materials (e.g. paper, food, wood waste) from those of fossil origin.

This allowed the energy recovery process, assumed to be a substitute for fossil fuels, to be recognized as a way of decarbonizing. Waste could stand as an alternative source of energy and was promoted as such by incineration companies. Energy from incineration was also championed as a solution for cutting landfill methane emissions. With their call for "energizing waste", Europe-wide incineration organizations (e.g. the Confederation of European Waste-to-Energy Plants-CEWEP), participated in the development of an **energy narrative of waste**. However, estimating GHG emissions from waste is far from being an evidence-based exercise, with struggles intensifying throughout the 1990s and 2000s as a result. Numerous expert analyses and statements released by incineration promoters and challengers reflect these struggles and testify to the precarious convergence of waste and climate-energy agendas. For instance, GHG calculating methods disseminated by the CEWEP (2008) appear to be rather extensive. On the other hand, Friends of the Earth (2006) insist that incineration generates underestimated amounts of fossil-fuel-derived GHGs and that other treatment options (recycling or anaerobic digestion) provide better options in terms of climate change, representing an interesting alternative to energy from waste. The unresolved question –Should energy from waste be considered and supported as a renewable energy? – was being answered by means of energy accounting standards. Faced with difficulty in recognizing waste as a source of renewable energy, on the same level as solar or wind power, the 2009 EU Directive on Energy from Renewable Sources recognized only the biodegradable portion of waste – estimated to represent 50 percent of the total waste – as a renewable energy source. This accountancy standard has important financial consequences: In France, a 50 percent renewable mix means that district heating networks can benefit from reduced VAT and public subsidies.

Placing Energy Recovery on the Waste Hierarchy

Through climate policies, energy recovery has gained unprecedented impetus, although not without being challenged. Energy recovery is generally accompanied by controversy, as incineration has proven to be a highly challenging mode of waste treatment. Waste incineration, while allowing the local use of energy, faces poor social acceptance vis-à-vis plants (Bobbio et al. 2016; Lougheed et al. 2017; Rocher 2009). Pollution scandals involving dioxins and furans, due to a lack of control, arose in France and elsewhere in Europe, leading to opposition movements getting particularly angry about the opening of new plants. Environmental and sanitary issues were not the only motive for a challenge that soon turned into a global approach to waste, linking disposal possibilities with the generation of waste and recycling. The over-supplying of incineration plants (by creating more garbage) was denounced for undermining both material recycling efforts (set from the mid-1990s at the European level) and "wasting less" objectives (which became the main narrative from the early 2000s). Thus, as climate and energy concerns offered incineration new legitimacy, controversies hardened, whereby energy recovery was blamed by NGOs for competing with (material) recycling.

The Waste Hierarchy was introduced in the 2008 EU Waste Framework Directive as a response to the controversial debates about competing modes of waste. According to the Hierarchy, waste prevention should be given priority, followed by product reuse, material recycling, energy recovery, and then landfilling as the last resort (see Chapter 15). While not legally binding, this framework was meant to align the policies of the member states that had developed their own waste hierarchies (Buclet and Godard 2001). In addition to prioritizing a 'wasting less narrative' over a 'less landfilling narrative' in 'the most ecumenical way', the Hierarchy model 'also ranks various ways of retrieving value from waste' (Corvellec and Hultman 2012). Prioritization of material recycling over energy recovery, long claimed by NGOs, was settled as a major principle and accompanied by technical specifications relating to energy performance levels. The "R1 Energy Efficiency formula", based on energy efficiency standards that had been introduced in 2001 in Europe and in 2002 in France, formalized a recovery ratio of 0.6 (for existing plants) and 0.65 (for plants created after 2008) in order to "rendering renewable" energy from these plants (Behrsin 2019). From 2009 and on, energy performance, amongst other environmental criteria, was included in the waste treatment tax in France. Nonetheless, the incineration processes were criticized by NGOs for their low-energy performance, notably when electricity alone is generated without heat recovery.

The 2008 framework directive, though it undoubtedly represents an important step forward in ranking energy recovery amongst treatment options, did not, however, end the debate on the Waste Hierarchy. In January 2017 the European commission released a communication entitled 'The role of waste-to-energy in the circular economy'. This communication is an attempt to make the recovery of energy from waste meet the 2015 EU Circular Economic Action Plan, as well as EU legislation on waste, the Energy Union Strategy, and the Paris Agreement, and to ensure that it is 'firmly guided by the EU waste hierarchy'. It is a testament to the realignment of waste along the CE narrative, by tackling the contradictions inherent in waste-to-energy, while ignoring the contradiction between 'offering a transformative agenda with significant new jobs and growth potential' (European Commission 2017: 2) and, above all, waste minimization (Desvaux 2017). This official release signals the need to adapt the hierarchy framework to a new, albeit unstable, waste-to-energy reality that consists of a variety of processes and a complexity of

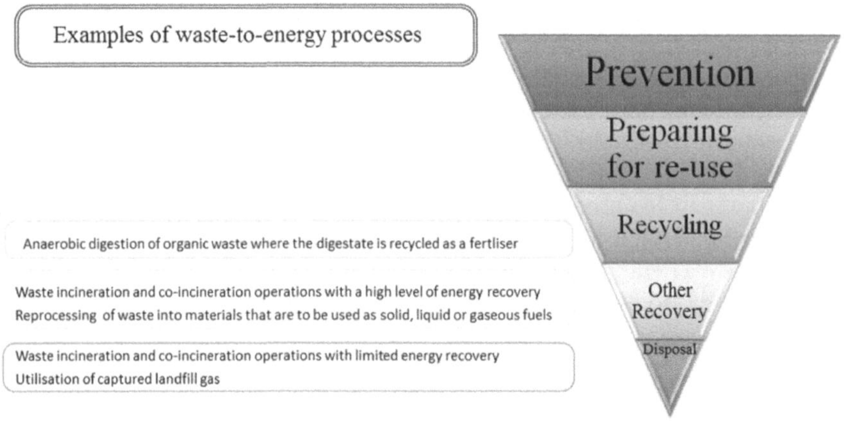

Figure 5.2 The Waste Hierarchy and Waste-to-Energy Processes (European Commission 2017, 4).

issues. Indeed, various waste-treatment processes that generate energy are positioned along the waste hierarchy, with a view to directing the funding and planning of public financial support. Beyond dedicated incineration, a distinction is made between the different energy flows in order to rank them as being equal not only to "recovery", but also to recycling or disposal. Thus, biogas from the anaerobic digestion of organic waste, on the proviso that the digestate is recycled as a fertilizer, is regarded to be a recycling operation. On the other hand, biogas from landfill is classified as disposal. Incineration and co-incineration are ranked as "other recovery" or disposal, depending on their recovery performance.

The Multiple Energy Output of Waste Treatment

Some significant changes indicate that energy output from waste is multiplying (technically and legally), revealing an energy shaping of waste that is intensifying. Waste treatment techniques most commonly allow the valuation of heat, gas, and/or generating power, but these potential solutions are unevenly being encouraged by public policies. Besides local constraints, legal regulations, prices, and financial support prove decisive when making a choice between one way or another of recovering energy. Heat recovery and power generation, or both (i.e. combined heat and power), are the main modes of energy recovery from waste incineration. Choosing one or the other of these solutions depends on local factors (the existence and proximity of a district heating network), but also on the economic rationale used, which is highly dependent on incentives. Power generation (though criticized for its low-energy performance) has until recently been supported by guaranteed feed-in tariffs, whereby electricity companies are obliged to buy electricity-from-waste at a fixed price for 15 years. Heat recovery has also benefited from financial support, by means of subsidies directed at ensuring that district heating uses at least 50 percent of renewable and recovered heat. As a result, combined heat and power, seen as the most efficient and preferred solution due to its seasonal flexibility, increased a lot in the last 15 years. But the end of guaranteed electricity feed-in tariffs might reverse this situation: This could result in a preference for heat use over electricity. Similar changing valuation conditions have occurred on the gas side, in the context of extended valuation possibilities regarding waste-derived biogas. In France, power generation was the only recovery possibility until 2011. However, as a result of the obligation to capture landfill methane emissions, and of the development of anaerobic digestion units, biogas – which increased in production – was allowed to be injected into the gas grid.

For all these treatment modes, what remains at stake is the making of public policies that favor the most efficient forms of recovery (heat and gas injection) without hampering others (electricity) which could appear consistent, particularly when there is no local network. The compensatory device being proposed by the French government; that is, to replace electricity feed-in tariffs, has met opposition from the European Commission, reluctant to supporting the production of electricity from unsorted waste (this applies to incineration and landfill). However, if public financial support were only applicable to the renewable part of waste, then electricity generation would not be economically viable. These examples signal that, parallel to a broadening of the recovery options, the financial tools that accompany these are creating competition between energy outputs. Hesitation regarding the making of these policies mirror the dilemmas surrounding the recognition of waste as a renewable energy. Ultimately, this suggests that the more waste processing choices rely on factors pertaining to energy outputs, the more energy will take the lead in waste management.

Waste as Energy: When Waste Becomes Fuel

Solid Recovery Fuel (SFR) designates a new category of waste intended for use as a fuel for energy plants. The creation of this category in Europe in the early 2010s is another illustration of the fact that energy concerns are taking the lead in waste management and, above all, of the redefinition of what constitutes waste. SFRs are made of refuse material from the sorting and recycling of non-hazardous waste which, depending on its components, may have a high calorific value. These materials can be used at incineration plants, in co-incineration (e.g. cement kilns), and at energy plants, depending on their calorific value and environmental criteria (mercury concentration, chlorine content). The waste industry has lobbied for the development of the SFR sector and named it "the missing link of circular economy", while NGOs were reluctant to endorse the creation of this category (Zéro Déchets 2017). The making of public policies aimed at developing SFR industries rely on national governments. In France, the SFR sector (mainly from industrial and commercial waste) is considered to have a greatly underexploited potential (ADEME 2012). Yet, it is in need of structuring to prevent these materials from being sent abroad. A 2016 ordinance recognized and framed this use of waste by introducing a new SFR-based energy plant classification. These plants can only be operated if they meet the high energy-efficiency standards (based on the calorific value of incoming materials) associated with local energy needs.

However, the French SFR framework is far from becoming stabilized. First, it faces the difficulty of designing public support tools aimed at electricity generation vs heat only (mentioned above). Moreover, there are struggles between waste actors regarding the categorization of SFR – whether this should be based solely on refuse from recycling or include non-sorted domestic waste. As for the waste hierarchy, SFR (designed as 'reprocessing of waste into material that is to be used as solid, liquid or gaseous fuels') is recognized as a form of energy recovery in respect of the 2017 EU communication. Although seeming very specific and technical, these expert struggles indicate the multiple and intricate channels that energy recovery is entangled with, from the very upstream flows of waste being targeted by reduction and recycling objectives, to the competing energy outputs linked to energy regulations and markets. Whereas in classical incineration, energy is a by-product of a disposal technique, the priorities have been reversed at SFR plants: It is energy outputs that determine the quantities and qualities of the waste to be allowed as fuel.

Case Study: Cities Locked-in Waste-to-Energy

Relying on waste as an energy resource carries profound contradictions cities have to face. While waste represent a local energy resource alternative to fossil fuel, their generation is expected to decrease. In some cities where important investment have been made in district heating supply with a great reliance on waste, a decrease in domestic waste generation means turning to importation. That is what happened for instance in Gothenburg, Sweden (Corvellec et al. 2013), or in Magdeburg, Germany (Florentin 2017), where local authorities had to import waste from other regions or countries. In addition to the negative environmental impact of transporting large volumes of waste, such infrastructural *lock-in* prevents alternative solutions from emerging. In spite of the proximity principle, EU legislation allows waste exportation and importation between member states, provided that it is in line with energy recovery standards.

Ingrid Behrsin and Salvatore Paolo de Rosa (2020) have given an edifying demonstration of the spatial, socio-political and symbolic circulations that enable waste to be transformed into energy. They explain how waste from Naples, whose disastrous local management has led to a health and political crisis, is sent to be incinerated in Zwentendorf, a small Austrian town to which it provides additional income. This situation is highlighted as part of the renewal of the town's industrial identity. The heat generated is then transported to St Pölten, 31 km away, to supply the new district heating network. This network, developed as part of a property development programme, is presented as a pillar of the city's policy of ecological excellence (Behrsin and Rosa 2020).

In Lyon's (France) metropolitan area, waste treatment and district heating infrastructures have been closely associated since the 1960s, and dependencies have developed. The two incineration units built in the 1960s fuel district heating networks. The future of waste treatment, and incineration in particular, cannot be considered in isolation from district heating, which has become a pivotal element of local energy policy since the early 2010s. In recent years, local policies have supported the extension of heating networks and the reduction of waste, notably by biowaste sorting practices. Waste quantities have fallen by 9 percent between 2010 and 2020. The target set by the Waste Master Plan adopted in June 2022 is to reduce waste produced by 25 percent and halve the volume of waste incinerated by 2030. It is therefore planned to limit the capacity of each of the two incineration plants, without affecting the supply of heating networks. To achieve this, cooperation is planned with neighboring local authorities not equipped with incinerators.

Conclusions

Converging agendas of climate and waste resulted in an unprecedented boost for energy recovery. This consisted of framing and locating energy as a key issue in waste management using a set of policy instruments, amongst which accountancy tools played a crucial role. Energy has become a predominant driver of waste policies, mandated to account for their GHG emissions and energy consumption and production, and to integrate numerous incentive and regulatory tools focusing on energy recovery (tax, energy performance standards, and favoring "renewable energy"). Energy recovery became the main reason why incineration gained legitimacy, while simultaneously being challenged by intensified claims and lobbying on the part of both NGOs and industry. The waste Hierarchy introduced in the 2008 EU directive consisted of ranking waste-to-energy as a less preferable option than material recycling, but still better than disposal. The 2017 EU communication, consisting of a re-ranking of energy recovery processes along the Hierarchy and adjusting it to that of the CE, signals a realignment of waste principles in respect of energy outputs.

The refinement of rules and tools, allowing diversified practices of energy recovery, suggests that energy outputs not only appear as byproducts worthy of recovery, but also as ends in themselves that tend to dominate waste policy-making on various levels, and are likely to determine local waste management choices. While different forms of energy recovery from waste are potentially in competition, they are regulated by energy-centric rules (e.g. electricity feed-in tariffs), indicating that energy rationales are taking the lead in waste management. The SFR status, which formats waste as a fuel, is symptomatic of the ability energy has to displace the very boundaries of waste, and to redefine what waste is and what it is not. So doing, the waste-to-energy rationale has shifted to energy-from-waste, in other words, to waste *as* energy.

Questions for Consideration

- Is waste-to-energy compatible with reducing waste in the long term?
- Should the proximity principle apply even in the case of energy recovery from waste, to ensure that waste is a local energy resource?
- Are greenhouse gas accounting methods going to improve in order to take better account of emissions from waste treatment operations?

Further Readings

Behrsin I and Rosa SPD (2020) Contaminant, commodity and fuel: a multi-sited study of waste's roles in urban transformations from Italy to Austria. *International Journal of Urban and Regional Research* 44(1): 90–107.

Gille Zsuzsa and Lepawsky Josh (2022) *The Routledge Handbook of Waste Studies*, Routledge

Rocher L (2020) Waste, A Matter of Energy. A Diachronic Analysis (1992-2017) of Waste-to-Energy Rationales. In: Ek Richard and Johansson Nils (eds), *Perspectives on Waste from the Social Sciences and the Humanities. Opening the Bin*. Cambridge Scholars Publishing. pp. 94–112.

References

ADEME (2009) *Les Déchets et L'effet de Serre. Eléments de Réflexion et D'éclairage*. Note de la Direction Déchets et Sols.

ADEME (2012) *Study on the Production and Use of Solid Recovered Fuels*. Executive summary.

Barles S (2005) *L'invention Des Déchets Urbain. France, 1790-1970*. Cham Vallon. Seyssel.

Behrsin I (2019) Rendering renewable: technoscience and the political economy of waste-to-energy regulation in the European Union. *Annals of the American Association of Geographers* 109(5): 1362–1378.

Behrsin I and Rosa SPD (2020) Contaminant, commodity and fuel: a multi-sited study of Waste's roles in urban transformations from Italy to Austria. *International Journal of Urban and Regional Research* 44(1): 90–107.

Bertolini G (1992) Les déchets: rebuts ou ressources? *Economie et statistique* 258(1): 129–134.

Bobbio L, Melé P and Ugalde V (2016) *Entre conflit et concertation: gérer les déchets en France, en Italie et au Mexique*. ENS éditions. Available at: https://halshs.archives-ouvertes.fr/halshs-01706474 (accessed 7 November 2020).

Brunner PH and Rechberger H (2015) Waste to energy – key element for sustainable waste management. *Waste Management* 37. Special Thematic Issue: Waste-to-Energy Processes and Technologies: 3–12.

Buclet N and Godard O (2001) The evolution of municipal waste management in Europe: how different are national regimes? *Journal of Environmental Policy and Planning* 3(4): 303–317.

Bulkeley H, Watson M and Hudson R (2007) Modes of governing municipal waste. *Environment and Planning A* 39(11): 2733–2753.

CEWEP/FFacts (2008) *Waste-to-energy and the Revision of the Waste Framework Directive. Waste-to-energy's Contribution to Climate Protection.*

Corvellec H and Hultman J (2012) From "less landfilling" to "wasting less": societal narratives, socio-materiality, and organizations. *Journal of Organizational Change Management* 25(2): 297–314.

Corvellec H, Zapata Campos MJ and Zapata P (2013) Infrastructures, lock-in, and sustainable urban development: the case of waste incineration in the Göteborg Metropolitan area. *Journal of Cleaner Production* 50. Special Issue: Advancing sustainable urban transformation: 32–39.

Desvaux P (2017) Économie circulaire acritique et condition post-politique: analyse de la valorisation des déchets en France. *Flux* (108): 36–50.

European Commission (2017) *Communication from the Commission to the European Parliament, the Council, the European Economic and Social Committee and the Committee of the Regions. The Role of Waste-to-Energy in the Circular Economy.*

Friends of the Earth (2006) *Dirty Truths: Incineration and Climate Change*. Summary of the Report "A Changing Climate for Energy from Waste?"

Florentin D (2017) Juxtaposer efficacité énergétique et proximité: contradictions des systèmes de chauffage urbain dans l'Est de l'Allemagne. *Flux* (109–110): 48–60.

Grand Lyon la Métropole (2022) *Schéma directeur déchets 2030 de la Métropole de Lyon. Trajectoire métropolitaine pour la réduction des déchets et la valorisation des ressources*, juin 2022, 48 p.

Gregson N, Crang M, Fuller S, and Holmes H (2015) Interrogating the circular economy: the moral economy of resource recovery in the EU. *Economy and Society* 44(2): 218–43.

Hawkins G (2006) *The Ethics of Waste: How We Relate to Rubbish*. Rowman & Littlefield.

International Panel for Climate Change (1996) *Revised 1996 IPCC Guidelines for National Greenhouse Gas Inventories: Reference Manual.*

International Panel for Climate Change (2006) *IPCC Guidelines for National Greenhouse Gas Inventories. Volume 5: Waste.*

Lougheed SC, Metuzals J and Hird MJ (2017) Modes of governing Canadian waste management: a case study of Metro Vancouver's energy-from-waste controversy. *Journal of Environmental Policy & Planning* 0(0): 1–13.

Melosi MV (2005) *Garbage in the Cities: Refuse, Reform, and the Environment*. Rev. History of the urban environment. University of Pittsburgh Press. Available at: Table of contents www.loc.gov/catdir/toc/ecip0420/2004015714.html.

Record (2008) *Application de la méthode "bilan carbone" aux activités de gestion des déchets.* Etude RECORD no 07-1017/1A.
Rocher L (2009) Les contradictions de la gestion intégrée des déchets urbains: l'incinération entre valorisation énergétique et refus social. *Flux* (74): 22–29.
Rocher L (2020) Waste, A Matter of Energy. A Diachronic Analysis (1992-2017) of Waste-to-Energy Rationales. In: Ek Richard and Johansson Nils (eds), *Perspectives on Waste from the Social Sciences and the Humanities. Opening the Bin.* Cambridge Scholars Publishing. pp. 94–112.
Tarr JA (1984) The search for the ultimate sink: urban air, land, and water pollution in historical perspective. *Records of the Columbia Historical Society, Washington, D.C.* 51: 1–29.
ZeroWaste France (2017) *Cinq Propositions pour un Quinquennat Zéro Déchet.*

6 Consuming Food

Elaine Power

Summary

- The industrialized food system in Canada produces millions of tons of food each year that are lost in production, handling, and processing, then wasted at the retail and household levels.
- Much of this food loss and waste goes to landfill, where it produces methane; a short-acting greenhouse gas, as it decays.
- Reducing the level of food loss and waste has taken on new urgency with the intensification of the climate crisis, and with Canada's commitments to the Paris Climate Accord and the UN's Sustainable Development Goals.
- With millions of Canadians experiencing food insecurity, one popular proposal is to donate edible food waste from retail stores to food banks for redistribution to those who are hungry.
- A more effective response is a guaranteed livable basic income, which could support the transition to a more sustainable food system and justice for food insecure Canadians.

Keywords: Food Loss; Food Waste; Food Charity; Food Insecurity; Industrialized Food System; Guaranteed Livable Basic Income

Introduction

When Justin Kulik learned in 2018 that billions of dollars of food are wasted each year in Canada, he was so upset that he decided to do something. Inspired by a 2015 law in France that prohibits grocery stores from throwing away edible food, the 17-year-old started a petition on Change.org (Kulik 2018). Kulik's petition urged the federal government to implement a food waste law that would prohibit "supermarkets from intentionally destroying and wasting unsold, still edible food" (np) and require them to donate edible food to food banks. Citing the (then) 4 million Canadians who were food insecure, the one

DOI: 10.4324/9781003412526-7

million Canadians relying on food banks, and the detrimental climate effects of food waste going to landfill, Kulik found a winning formula. Perhaps it was the combination of his youthful idealism, the "no-brainer" of not wasting food, the simplicity of matching excess food with hungry people, and the media investigation (Mancini and Vellani 2016) that had put food waste on the political agenda. Recognizing that Kulik's campaign resonated with the public, Change.org boosted his petition with the tags #WhyWasteFood and #FoodDeservesBetter (Butterfield 2018). By the time he presented his petition to the Minister of Agriculture on World Food Day in October 2018, it had garnered more than 165,000 signatures (Henning 2018).

Five years later, the petition was still open, with over 420,000 signatures in the fall of 2023. Signatories decry food waste as "criminal," "foolish," "disgusting," and "shameful." Kulik's solution of having supermarkets donate edible food to food banks was seen as "simple," "cost-effective," a "win-win," and clearly the decent, caring thing to do. Reasons for signing also include "helping the planet," but these types of comments are less frequent than moral outrage about edible food going to landfill while people are hungry.

This chapter considers the problematic aspects of this apparently "simple" solution, which hides bigger problems in the food system and the social injustice of poverty. Donating edible food waste from retail stores to food charities helps to lock the status quo in place and stall the transformations required for genuine change. The evidence presented in this chapter shows that this apparently simple solution neither tackles the massive amounts of food lost and wasted in the industrialized food system, nor addresses the growing numbers of food-insecure Canadians, estimated to be almost 7 million people in 2022 (Li, Fafard St-Germain and Tarasuk 2023). Instead, the downstream focus on donating food waste to community-based charities inhibits structural analysis of underlying causes, and lets global food and agriculture corporations, governments, and global governing bodies avoid system transformation.

Old and New Moral Imperatives

Prohibitions against wasting food and exhortations to share it are deeply rooted moral imperatives. In the territories around the Great Lakes in northeastern Turtle Island where I live, the Dish with One Spoon Wampum agreement binds the Haudenosaunee and Anishinaabe peoples to share the resources of the land and ensure there is enough for everyone. In Leanne Betasamosake Simpson's retelling of the Anishinaabeg story, "Our Treaty with the Hoof Nation," humans broke their agreements with their non-human relatives by wasting food and not sharing it, resulting in human hunger (Betasamosake Simpson 2013). For adherents of the Abrahamic faiths, Judaism, Christianity, and Islam, feeding the hungry is seen as a duty of faith, and many do so by distributing unwanted food (Yoreh and Bede Scharper 2020). Indeed, the world's first food bank, in Phoenix, Arizona, was set up in 1967 to rescue edible food from the garbage for redistribution to those who were hungry (Power 2015).

However, with the industrialized food system producing approximately one-third of all greenhouse gas (GHG) emissions (Crippa et al. 2021), recent interest in reducing food waste is driven primarily by the urgent need to reduce GHG emissions in the context of the climate emergency. Food waste means that the resources used to produce the food are squandered, leaving the detrimental impacts of industrial food production without the benefit of people being fed (United Nations Environment Programme 2021). Moreover, when food waste is sent to landfill, it decomposes and produces methane, a greenhouse gas that is much more powerful over the short term than carbon dioxide in trapping heat in the atmosphere (Moseman and Trancik 2023). For this reason, curbing methane emissions is seen as "low-hanging fruit" in tackling the climate crisis (McKenzie 2023).

Reducing methane emissions was the primary motivation for Environment and Climate Change Canada's (ECCC) 2019 discussion paper: 'Taking Stock: Reducing Food Loss and Waste in Canada.' The discussion paper is a "blueprint" for fulfilling Canada's commitment to the UN's Sustainable Development Goal (SDG) 12, Ensure Sustainable Consumption and Production Patterns (Target 12.3), which sets a goal of cutting per capita food waste in half at the retail and consumer levels by 2030. Following a four-rung "Hierarchy of Solutions to Address Food Loss and Waste" ECCC's discussion paper lists "reducing" food waste and loss as its most preferred solution and "recovering" it as number two. Recovering food waste includes the donation of surplus food to feed people and using food waste for the manufacture of animal feed or other food products.

Though the ECCC discussion paper recommends sending food waste to **food banks**, it explicitly states that "recovery of surplus food to feed people is not proposed as a solution to food insecurity, but instead recognizes that the highest value of food is maintained when it is consumed by people" (2019: 2). Despite the ECCC distinction, the goals of reducing food waste and reducing hunger (commonly used to indicate food insecurity) are usually tightly linked, as in the motto of the largest Canadian food rescue organization, "No Waste No Hunger" (Second Harvest, 2023). Though other hierarchies of food waste reduction separate reuse for human consumption from feeding animals, perhaps ECCC didn't consider what message they send by putting human and non-human animals together in its category of "recovering" food waste. Nor did it consider that the most preferred category in the waste hierarchy, "reduce" food loss and waste at source, adversely impacts the donations that food banks are able to redistribute to those who are food insecure.

By endorsing food charities as the main recipient of food waste, waste hierarchies implicitly support the idea that those who are food insecure do not have a right to the same food as everyone else. South African Nobel Prize winner, Archbishop Desmond Tutu, has told of his childhood experience watching a black boy search in the garbage for food that white students had thrown out. " 'It was perfectly edible food. But I knew it was wrong,' he said. For Archbishop Tutu, the idea that some people have to eat the cast-off food that others do not want is a powerful symbol of profound, systemic injustice" (Power 2019: np).

Food Loss and Waste

Though few countries have robust data on food loss and waste (United Nations Environment Programme 2021), the World Food Programme estimates that across the planet, approximately one-third of the food produced for human consumption is lost or wasted, enough to feed two billion people (World Food Programme 2020).

Case Study: Food Loss Versus Food Waste

Scholars differentiate between food loss and food waste: food loss refers food lost in production, storage, and processing, while food waste refers to edible food that could have been eaten but instead is disposed of at the point of food retail and at home. However, in practice, the two are often combined. For example, although the first UN Food Waste Index Report is focused on *waste* (United Nations Environment Programme, 2021), it opens with the statement, "If food *loss and waste* [emphasis added] were a country, it would be the third biggest source of greenhouse gas emissions" (p. 4). Despite no or weak data from many countries, the Report determined that *household* food waste accounts for the majority of food waste (United Nations Environment Programme, 2021). The report concludes that "action on consumer food waste is needed worldwide" (p. 92) and recommends careful shopping, creative cooking, and making food waste socially unacceptable.

The UNEP is focused on reducing household food waste, but Canadian research suggests that this is a small fraction of the total amount of the food that is lost or wasted. In 2019, the Toronto-based food rescue organization, Second Harvest, in collaboration with Value Chain Management International (VCMI), published the results of a year-long research study on food loss and waste (FLW), described as a "world-first" because of its focus on the whole **food chain** (Gooch et al. 2019). Their report differentiates between "unavoidable" FLW, such as animal bones and inedible peels, and an "avoidable" FLW, generally in the post-processing phase, such as bruised apples. The researchers estimated that the total FLW in Canada amounted to 35.5 million metric tons, of which 32 percent was avoidable, and that the value of avoidable FLW was approximately $49.5 billion, approximately 3 percent of Canada's GDP in 2016. They also concluded that only 14 percent of excess edible food was donated or redistributed. The Second Harvest/VCMI report concluded that "FLW is a systemic issue that results from how the food system presently operates" (ibid: 6). Accordingly, it targets government, industry organizations, and industry for FLW prevention, redistribution, and waste management — not just individual consumers.

The Second Harvest/VCMI researchers estimate the value of avoidable FLW in 2016 to be just over half of the amount that Canadians spent on groceries, a staggering amount of loss and waste. They locate the source of the problem in a "cultural acceptance of waste", which "ultimately emanates from the true costs of waste not being internalized by industry" (Gooch et al. 2019: 38). This includes the benefit of FLW to the food industry because it increases sales. Considering the environmental impact of total FLW, measured in terms of carbon dioxide emissions and water usage, Gooch et al. (2019) find that the impact of food consumed is smaller than the environmental impact of total FLW along the food chain. They conclude, "This raises the question of whether the current food industry is environmentally sustainable" (ibid: 36).

Wastefulness of the Capitalist Industrialized Food System

Critics argue that there is no doubt about the unsustainability of the industrialized food system. As geographer Tony Weis (2017) has summarized, agriculture in wealthy countries has shifted from a relatively "closed loop" system to a "through flow" process, with devastating consequences for Earth. Closed loop agriculture is characteristic of small, mixed, organic farms that grow crops and raise animals together. It uses the sun for energy, via the photosynthesis of plants, biological approaches for soil fertility and pest suppression, and organic waste, especially manure, as fertilizer. In contrast, agriculture as a **through flow** process is dependent on external inputs, including irrigation, chemical pesticides, inorganic fertilizers, and pharmaceuticals. The dominant industrialized food system is highly mechanized and standardized, characterized by the separation of animal and crop farming, and increasing trans-national corporate concentration at every level (Clapp 2020; Weis 2017).

In one component of industrialized agriculture, vast fields of **monocrops** (often from genetically modified seed) are sown and harvested by large machinery, fertilized by inorganic fertilizers, sprayed intensively with pesticides, and mechanically irrigated, creating ground, water, and air pollution, and destroying the soil's delicate eco-system. This type of agriculture uses large amounts of carbon-based fossil fuels and, correspondingly, emits significant greenhouse gases. Moreover, dead soil cannot sequester carbon, as healthy soil can (Weis 2017). In another component of industrialized agriculture, genetically similar animals (cattle, pigs, chickens) are crowded together in large numbers in "**factory farms**," in profoundly unhealthy conditions, and fed crops that they would not otherwise eat. The process of feeding crops to animals, instead of letting them graze grass or eat insects and food waste, is a highly inefficient mechanism for food production (Smil 2004), generating numerous ill effects. For example, the genetic similarity of the animals and poor farm conditions provide ideal conditions for the development and transmission of pathogens. And instead of fertilizing the soil for crop production, as in closed loop agriculture, animal manure becomes yet another waste problem to manage (Clapp 2020; Weis 2017).

The **industrialized food system** has produced bountiful amounts of food at a relatively low price but only because so many of the costs have never been counted and are invisible to most consumers (Weis 2017). While Indigenous peoples have carefully tended and managed Earth's abundance for millennia to provide nourishment for people, the capitalist, industrialized food system creates death, destruction, and waste, turning complex ecosystems into monocrop wastelands, destroying biodiversity, and causing grave harm to human and non-human animals and Earth herself. Perhaps it isn't surprising that such a system of agriculture was developed on land that was stolen and violently occupied by settlers who destroyed the native food systems of the original Indigenous occupants of Northern Turtle Island (Ghosh 2021).

Considering the overall destructive nature and unsustainability of the industrialized food system, the narrow focus on greenhouse gas emissions as its most important problem seems disingenuous, at best. And yet the industrialized food system's contributions to GHG emissions have only just — in 2023 — been officially recognized at the United Nations Climate Change Conference (Bauck 2023). While COP-28 ended with an agreement that sustainable agriculture must be part of the response to reduce GHG emissions, the International Panel of Experts on Sustainable Food Systems (IPES-Food) warned that the UN's use of ambiguous, depoliticized, "smoke and mirrors" language provides a cover to allow "agribusiness as usual," instead of the profound social and environmental transformations required to create a sustainable and just food system (IPES-Food Working Group 2022).

Gooch et al. (2019) suggests that the current food system could be tweaked to reduce or eliminate food loss and waste — and thus reduce greenhouse gas emissions — if the true costs of food waste were accounted for and internalized. However, others argue that waste is not an unfortunate side-effect, but inherent in the dominant food system. For example, Cloke (2020) makes the case that food waste is valuable to transnational food corporations because it speeds up sales and the through flow of food products, thus increasing profits. Cloke's analysis of the crucial role of food waste in enhancing corporate profits leads him to conclude that, in fact, there is no "waste" in the industrialized food system. Of course, there is "food waste" but from the perspective of transnational corporations, this is an integral and valuable feature of the industrialized food system. This means that the physical problem of food loss and waste will not be reduced in any significant way until there is food system transformation (ibid.).

Re-Examining a Food Waste Law in Canada

With this background information, let's return to Jason Kulik's proposed new federal law mandating that edible food from retail food stores be donated to food banks. Would such a law make a dent in the massive problem of food waste? Would it help food charities feed hungry people and result in fewer food insecure people? What impact would it have on GHG emissions?

First, as Gooch et al (2019) reports, the retail sector accounts for only about 12 percent of the total edible food waste in Canada, so the effectiveness of a food waste law in reducing food waste, and thus methane emissions, is limited. Moreover, scientists, such as physicist Raymond Pierrehumbert, are cautioning that the framing of methane as much more potent than carbon dioxide in creating global heating is "inaccurate and misleading" (in McKenzie 2023) because methane and carbon dioxide operate differently as greenhouse gases. Methane has a strong warming effect in the short term, but its impact disappears after 20 years. Carbon dioxide has a much smaller warming effect than methane in the short term, but its warming effects continue for thousands of years. This means that the popular focus on reducing methane emissions to "buy time" for decarbonization is "mass delusion and wishful thinking" according to Pierrehumbert (ibid.: np). A focus on methane emissions in isolation from reducing carbon dioxide provides a distraction from the more challenging work of decarbonizing, a transformative move that oil companies continue to resist (ibid.).

Analysis of the impact of France's food waste law shows that the law has resulted in up to 30 percent more donations to food banks (Mourad, 2022; Saltzman, Bittman and Livesay 2019), but has also prompted food retailers to discount and sell products instead of donating them (Mourad 2022). Retailers get a tax credit for donating to food charities, which has led to suspicions that some might try to "game the system;" indeed, some charities report that they are getting inedible, unusable food (Saltzman et al., 2019) and the amount of food that French food banks throw out has increased (Mourad 2022). When food charities receive donations of food that they can't use or distribute, it becomes their responsibility to dispose of it, creating additional burdens on over-stretched charitable organizations that rely on volunteer labor (Dachner and Tarasuk 2017).

Similarly, a UK study of a partnership between a large supermarket chain and food charities found that there was a "mismatch" between the goal of supermarkets to reduce waste and charities' concern for quality, which sometimes hindered charities' ability to function (Kennedy and Snell 2023). For example, food charities found it difficult to muster enough volunteers to cope with a sudden influx of food about to expire, or donations that were a mix of edible and inedible food.

In his study of food waste reduction at Kroger, the largest supermarket chain in the United States, Warshawsky (2016) concludes that although Kroger's efforts had some positive impacts, overall, food waste reduction served the corporation's brand management and competitive advantage without tackling the underlying causes of food waste. Environmentalists concerned with reducing the environmental impact of food waste, especially methane emissions, maintain that "weak" changes, such as retail donations to food charities (Evans 2011), are primarily "window-dressing," leaving untouched the larger "upstream" problems in the food system that produce the food loss and waste in the first place (Giordano, Falasconi, Cicatiello and Pancino, 2020). As Mourad (2015) argues, "a serious fight against food waste is a fight against the dominant paradigms of the entire food system" (p.27). This suggests that the underlying logic of the contemporary enthusiasm for reducing food waste at the retail and household levels is to provide a cover for maintaining the current system and "business-as-usual."

On the other side of the apparent "win" of donating food waste to charities, anti-poverty scholars argue that food charity is a smokescreen that leaves untouched the structural problems that create food insecurity, a symptom of material deprivation (Kennedy and Snell 2023; Lambie-Mumford 2018). Canadian research shows that only 20–30 percent of food insecure households use food banks (Tarasuk, Fafard St-Germain and Loopstra 2020), and even when they do, they are still food insecure (Loopstra and Tarasuk 2012). A significant body of research demonstrates the ineffectiveness of food charity in addressing food insecurity and shows that the only interventions shown to make an impact are those that increase household income (PROOF: Food Insecurity Policy Research 2022). Critics argue that food banks have come to be an integral component of the industrialized food system, serving multiple functions, including opportunities for multi-national corporations to demonstrate that they are "good citizens" (Warshawsky 2023). Lohnes (2021) suggests that the current food system relies on hunger to solve its food waste problem, though it would be more accurate to say that it relies on hunger to give the appearance of solving food waste. Food banks have become integral to the social welfare system under neoliberal governments, who have downloaded responsibilities for the well-being of their citizens to over-stretched charities

Figure 6.1 Sign Posted on the Side of a Small Town Canadian Food Bank.

(Poppendieck 1998). As Riches concludes, food banks justify feeding "wasted food, surplus to the requirements of a dysfunctional food system, to millions of hungry citizens who are surplus to the requirements of the labor market" (2018: 1).

A Better Response: Guaranteed Livable Basic Income

No one wants to imagine their neighbors going hungry, especially when thousands of kilograms of edible food are wasted each day. Food insecurity and food waste rightly prick our conscience and disturb our moral sensibilities. Both require political solutions, but instead, food banks have depoliticized the problems of food waste and food insecurity. Donating edible food waste to food banks provides a comforting illusion that these problems are being managed, but the evidence presented in this chapter shows otherwise.

As a symptom of material deprivation, food insecurity could be effectively reduced by ensuring all households receive an income that covers necessities (PROOF: Food Insecurity Policy Research 2022). This includes the provision of a living wage for those employed, and a guaranteed livable basic income program to ensure no one lives in deep poverty (PROOF: Food Insecurity Policy Research 2022; Tarasuk 2017). The idea of a guaranteed livable basic income has gained momentum in Canada in the past decade, with a pilot launched in Ontario in 2017 (Swift and Power 2021), a fully costed proposal for a Prince Edward Island demonstration project (Boadway et al. 2023), and much more (see, for example, Coalition Canada: basic income/revenu de base 2023). While food system transformation is complex, a basic income could support new farmers, especially women and BIPOC farmers, who want to farm organically and feed their local communities, providing an alternative to the industrialized, corporate food system (Power and McBay 2022). While basic income can't transform the food system on its own, it can allow us to "make better, freer choices about how we live, what we eat, and how our food is produced, processed, distributed," and thus "could be a potent tool in radical, democratic struggles against systems of oppression and towards justice, in the food system and beyond" (ibid.: 32–33).

Conclusions

The idea that donating retail food waste to food banks for redistribution to those who are food insecure is an easy "win-win-win" to reduce food waste, greenhouse gas emissions, and food insecurity, is not just simplistic: It is wrong. The winners are the corporate players that dominate the capitalist, industrialized food system and the governments who support the status quo. Creating a smokescreen that hides the upstream causes of poverty and food waste, and the transformative systemic work that is required for justice, the logic of such initiatives plays on our deep-seated revulsion about food waste and a moral imperative to look after our neighbors. Compared to Indigenous food systems on Turtle Island that nourish and care for "all our relations," the capitalist, industrialized food system is oriented around profit-making at any cost. Any serious effort to reduce food waste, build a sustainable food system, and ensure that everyone has enough to eat could start with a guaranteed livable basic income.

Questions for Consideration

1) In the face of social problems like food waste and food insecurity, is it better to "do something" than nothing? What would you advise people to do about food waste?
2) Are there other options for using the edible food waste produced by the industrialized food system that are more inclusive and less stigmatizing than donating it to food charities?
3) What difference would having (or having had) a guaranteed livable basic income make in your life? Would it change (or have changed) what you eat, where you shop, and, how you cook or obtain food?

Further Reading

Ghosh, A. (2021). *The Nutmeg's Curse: Parables for a Planet in Crisis.* Chicago: The University of Chicago Press.

Swift, J., & Power, E. (2021). *The Case for Basic Income: Freedom, Security, Justice.* Toronto, ON: Between the Lines Press.

Warshawsky, D. N. (2023). *Food Waste, Food Insecurity, and the Globalization of Food Banks.* Iowa City: University of Iowa Press.

References

Bauck, W. (2023). 'Food is finally on the table': Cop28 addressed agriculture in a real way. *The Guardian.* Retrieved from www.theguardian.com/environment/2023/dec/17/cop28-sustainable-agriculture-food-greenhouse-gases

Betasamosake Simpson, L. (2013). *The Gift is in the Making: Anishinaabeg Stories.* Winnipeg, MB: Highwater Press.

Boadway, R., Corak, M., David, K., Emery, H., Forget, E., Halpenny, C., . . . Stevens, H. (2023). *A Proposal for a Guaranteed Basic Income Benefit in Prince Edward Island.* Retrieved from Charlottetown, PEI: https://static1.squarespace.com/static/6414a3fa59a0c71ae167601e/t/655e0165319bf92e4ef6cbd5/1700659869270/final-report

Butterfield, M. (2018, October 11). B.C. Teen Justin Kulik taking food waste petition with more than 100,000 signatures to Ottawa. *Huffpost.* Retrieved from www.huffpost.com/archive/ca/entry/justin-kulik-food-waste-petition_ca_5cd56e29e4b07bc7297808c0

Clapp, J. (2020). *Food* (3rd ed.). Cambridge: Polity.

Cloke, J. (2020). Interrogating waste: Vastogenic regimes in the 21st century. In C. Reynolds, T. Soma, C. Spring, & J. Lazell (Eds.), *Routledge Handbook of Food Waste* (pp. 65–77). London & New York: Routledge.

Coalition Canada: basic income/revenu de base. (2023). Retrieved from https://basicincomecoalition.ca/en/

Crippa, M., Solazzo, E., Guizzardi, D., Monforti-Ferrario, F., Tubiello, F. N., & Leip, A. (2021). Food systems are responsible for a third of global anthropogenic GHG emissions. *Nature Food, 2*(3), 198–209. doi:10.1038/s43016-021-00225-9

Dachner, N., & Tarasuk, V. (2017, October 26). Corporate food waste isn't the way to solve hunger in Canada. *HuffPost.* Retrieved from www.huffpost.com/archive/ca/entry/corporate-food-waste-isnt-the-way-to-solve-hunger-in-canada_ca_5cd511fbe4b07bc729747c70?utm_campaign=canada_dau

Environment and Climate Change Canada. (2019). *Taking Stock: Reducing Food Loss and Waste in Canada.* . Retrieved from Ottawa, ON: www.canada.ca/en/environment-climate-change/services/managing-reducing-waste/food-loss-waste/taking-stock.html

Evans, D. (2011). Blaming the consumer – once again: The social and material contexts of everyday food waste practices in some English households. *Critical Public Health, 21*(4), 429–440. doi:10.1080/09581596.2011.608797

Ghosh, A. (2021). *The Nutmeg's Curse: Parables for a Planet in Crisis.* Chicago: The University of Chicago Press.

Giordano, C., Falasconi, L., Cicatiello, C., & Pancino, B. (2020). The role of food waste hierarchy in addressing policy and research: A comparative analysis. *Journal of Cleaner Production, 252*, 119617. doi: https://doi.org/10.1016/j.jclepro.2019.119617

Gooch, M., Bucknell, D., LaPlain, D., Dent, B., Whitehead, P., Felfel, A., . . . Maguire, M. (2019). *The Avoidable Crisis of Food Waste: Technical Report.* Toronto, ON. www.secondharvest.ca/getmedia/58c2527f-928a-4b6f-843a-c0a6b4d09692/The-Avoidable-Crisis-of-Food-Waste-Technical-Report.pd

Henning, C. (2018, October 21). 3 British Columbians get creative to stop mountains of food from hitting the trash. *CBC News.* Retrieved from www.cbc.ca/news/canada/british-columbia/food-waste-ideas-bc-daybreak-south-1.4870857

IPES-Food Working Group. (2022). *Smoke and mirrors: Examining competing framings of food system sustainability: Agroecology, regenerative agriculture, and nature- based solutions.* Retrieved from https://ipes-food.org/_img/upload/files/SmokeAndMirrors.pdf

Kennedy, K., & Snell, C. (2023). Relationships between supermarkets and food charities in reducing food insecurity: lessons learned. *Voluntary Sector Review*, 1–10. (published online ahead of print 2023). Retrieved Aug 5, 2024, from https://doi.org/10.1332/20408056Y2023D000000002

Kulik, J. (2018). *End Food Waste in Canada!* Retrieved from www.change.org/p/join-me-in-asking-mclaudebibeau-to-end-food-waste-in-canada-whywastefood?source_location=search

Lambie-Mumford, H. (2018). The growth of food banks in Britain and what they mean for social policy. *Critical Social Policy, 39*(1), 3–22. doi:10.1177/0261018318765855

Li, T., Fafard St-Germain, A.-A., & Tarasuk, V. (2023). *Household Food Insecurity in Canada, 2022.* Retrieved from Toronto, ON: https://proof.utoronto.ca/resource/household-food-insecurity-in-canada-2022/

Lohnes, J. D. (2021). Regulating surplus: Charity and the legal geographies of food waste enclosure. *Agriculture and Human Values, 38*(2), 351–363. doi:10.1007/s10460-020-10150-5

Loopstra, R., & Tarasuk, V. (2012). The relationship between food banks and household food insecurity among low-income Toronto families. *Canadian Public Policy / Analyse de Politiques, 38*(4), 497–514. Retrieved from www.jstor.org.proxy.queensu.ca/stable/41756766

Mancini, M., & Vellani, N. (2016, 26 October). A $31B problem: How Canada sucks at reducing food waste. Other countries crack down on discards, so why are we so far behind? *CBC News.* Retrieved from www.cbc.ca/news/business/canada-food-waste-1.3813965

McKenzie, J. (2023, 18 December). 'Mass delusion and wishful thinking': Why everything you think you know about methane is probably wrong. *Bulletin of the Atomic Scientists.* Retrieved from https://thebulletin.org/2023/12/mass-delusion-and-wishful-thinking-why-everything-you-think-you-know-about-methane-is-probably-wrong/

Moseman, A., & Trancik, J. (2023, 6 July). *Why Do We Compare Methane to Carbon Dioxide over a 100-Year Timeframe? Are We Underrating the Importance of Methane Emissions?* Retrieved from https://climate.mit.edu/ask-mit/why-do-we-compare-methane-carbon-dioxide-over-100-year-timeframe-are-we-underrating

Mourad, M. (2015). Thinking outside the bin: Is there a better way to fight 'food waste?'. *Berkeley Journal of Sociology, 59*, 26–33. Retrieved from https://sciencespo.hal.science/hal-01967927

Mourad, M. (2022). Did France really ban food waste? Lessons from a pioneering national regulation. In S. Busetti & N. Pace (Eds.), *Food Loss and Waste Policy: From Theory to Practice* (pp. 109–123). London: Routledge.

Poppendieck, J. (1998). *Sweet Charity?: Emergency Food and the End of Entitlement.* New York: Viking.

Power, E. (2015). Food banks. In K. Albala (Ed.), *The SAGE Encyclopedia of Food Issues* (pp. 533–559). Thousand Oaks, CA: SAGE Publications, Inc.

Power, E. (2019, 23 May). Sending surplus food to charity is not the way to reduce greenhouse gas emissions. *The Conversation.* Retrieved from https://theconversation.com/sending-surplus-food-to-charity-is-not-the-way-to-reduce-greenhouse-gas-emissions-115685

Power, E., and McBay, A. (2022). Basic income is necessary but insufficient for just food futures. *Canadian Food Studies / La Revue Canadienne Des études Sur l'alimentation, 9*(2), 31–37. Retrieved from https://doi.org/10.15353/cfs-rcea.v9i2.533

PROOF: Food Insecurity Policy Research. (2022). *Food Insecurity: A Problem of Inadequate Income, Not Solved by Food.* Retrieved from Toronto, ON: https://proof.utoronto.ca/wp-content/uploads/2022/10/Food-insecurity-A-problem-of-inadequate-income-not-solved-by-food-PROOF-factsheet-Oct-2022.pdf

Riches, G. (2018). *Food Bank Nations: Poverty, Corporate Charity and the Right to Food.* New York: Routledge.

Saltzman, M., Bittman, M., & Livesay, C. (2019). Is France's groundbreaking food-waste law working? *PBS NewsHour.* Retrieved from https://pulitzercenter.org/stories/frances-groundbreaking-food-waste-law-working

Second Harvest. (2023). *Home Page.* Retrieved from https://secondharvest.ca

Smil, V. (2004). Improving efficiency and reducing waste in our food system. *Environmental Sciences, 1*(1), 17–26. doi:10.1076/evms.1.1.17.23766

Swift, J., and Power, E. (2021). *The Case for Basic Income: Freedom, Security, Justice.* Toronto, ON: Between the Lines Press.

Tarasuk, V. (2017). *Implications of a Basic Income Guarantee for Household Food Insecurity.* Retrieved from Thunder Bay: www.northernpolicy.ca/bigandfoodinsecurity

Tarasuk, V., Fafard St-Germain, A.-A., & Loopstra, R. (2020). The relationship between food banks and food insecurity: Insights from Canada. *VOLUNTAS: International Journal of Voluntary and Nonprofit Organizations, 31*(5), 841–852. doi:10.1007/s11266-019-00092-w

United Nations Environment Programme. (2021). *Food Waste Index Report 2021.* Retrieved from Nairobi, Kenya. www.unep.org/resources/report/unep-food-waste-index-report-2021

Warshawsky, D. N. (2016). Food waste, sustainability, and the corporate sector: Case study of a US food company. *The Geographical Journal, 182*(4), 384–394. doi:https://doi.org/10.1111/geoj.12156

Warshawsky, D. N. (2023). *Food Waste, Food Insecurity, and the Globalization of Food Banks.* Iowa City: University of Iowa Press.

Weis, T. (2017). A political ecology approach to industrial food production. In M. Koç, J. Sumner, & A. Winson (Eds.), *Critical Perspectives in Food Studies* (pp. 118–134). Don Mills, ON: Oxford University Press.

World Food Programme. (2020, 2 June). *Five Facts About Food Waste and Hunger.* Retrieved from www.wfp.org/stories/5-facts-about-food-waste-and-hunger

Yoreh, T., & Bede Scharper, S. (2020). Food waste, religion, and spirituality. In C. Reynolds, T. Soma, C. Spring, & J. Lazell (Eds.), *Routledge Handbook of Food Waste* (pp. 55–64). London & New York: Routledge.

7 Consuming Pets

Josh Milburn

Summary

- Dogs and cats have an adverse impact on the environment, primarily because we feed dogs and cats meat. We produce meat via animal agriculture, which is very bad for the environment (and for animals).
- Possible alternatives to 'slaughter-based' pet foods include pet foods based on cultivated meat or insects, or vegan pet foods. Since these do not rely on animal agriculture, they may be significantly less environmentally damaging.
- Vegan pet foods have limited uptake among guardians of dogs and cats, who worry that vegan pet foods may be 'unnatural' or unhealthy. Meanwhile, critics charge guardians of animals fed vegan diets with forcing their ideologies on animals.
- Recent research suggests that vegan pet foods are just as palatable, and at least as healthy, for dogs and cats as slaughter-based pet foods.
- Quantifications of pet food's impact show that switching dogs and cats to vegan diets globally would drastically reduce the number of animals farmed, and thus the greenhouse gas emissions, land use, and freshwater use of animal agriculture.

Keywords: Dogs, Cats, Pet Food, Food, Pets, Meat, Vegan, Plant-Based, Vegetarian

Introduction

On a 2010 episode of the British comedy panel show *QI* (Series H, episode 9), the host Stephen Fry shows a 'modern family', and asks how they can (legally) reduce their 'ecological footprint'.[1] The comedians on the panel offer some suggestions: Bill Bailey says the family should stop breathing; Alan Davies suggests they should stop defecating. Fry clarifies that the answer must be

DOI: 10.4324/9781003412526-8

legal *and biologically possible*. Sensing the direction of the conversation, Danny Baker falls on his sword, suggesting that the family give up their car. An alarm sounds – Baker has triggered a trap set by the question writers.

Davies suggests that the family eat their dog. *Yes*, eating (or otherwise 'getting rid of') the dog is the best strategy. 'Keeping a dog', Fry claims, has 'the equivalent [ecological footprint] to two Toyota Land Cruisers'. He explains to the flabbergasted panellists that this is because of 'the meat [the dog] eats'. But, Baker contends, *he* eats meat. Fry responds that we can't get rid of humans *legally*, but getting rid of a dog is merely *unkind*. (We can kill dogs 'legally but not ethically', Bailey quips.) 'Even a cat', Fry adds, 'is the equivalent of a Volkswagen Golf', including both manufacture and use of the car. Eddie Izzard asks if it would be better if the dogs and cats ate vegetables. Fry is sceptical: 'They are just born to eat meat, I fear'.

There are many ways that keeping companion animals causes environmental strain. Companions need water; they excrete; they're often bought (plastic) toys, bedding, and clothing; and so on. But central to companions' 'ecological pawprint' is the environmental impact of these animals' diets.

Questions about *human* diets are familiar to environmentally minded consumers, activists, and producers. But the diets of companion animals have been a comparative blind spot – even among those *most* committed to raising questions about the food system, like animal advocates. But familiar concerns about animal agriculture's carbon emissions, land use, and water consumption apply whether farmers produce food for humans or for animals. Animals raised for food (for humans or animals) face confinement, suffering, and early death. Industrial animal agriculture relies on extensive antibiotic use, contributing to antibiotic resistance. And intensively farmed animal populations can be breeding grounds for zoonotic diseases.

Is it time, as Fry suggests, to 'get rid of' our companion animals? That's one possibility. Some authors suggest switching to herbivorous companions, like rabbits, or at least *smaller* dogs and cats (e.g., Okin 2017). But perhaps a more fundamental change would be to shift towards making pet food in different ways. That's what I explore here.

Though I focus on dogs and cats, when we think about feeding meat to animals, we realize that this issue stretches beyond dogs and cats – and beyond the reptiles, fish, and other meat-eating 'pets' (Milburn 2022). We should consider the feeding of dogs and cats in shelters (Giroux, Voigt, and Pepper 2023); of animal 'neighbours' in our parks and gardens (Milburn 2022, chap. 4); of wild animals in sanctuaries and rehabilitation centres (Abbate 2016); and of free-living wild animals (Palmer 2021). Put another way, questions about the ethics of animal diets stretch beyond what the psychologist Hank Rothgerber (2013) calls 'the vegetarian's dilemma', which is the tension that some vegetarians feel when they feed meat to companions.

I begin by identifying three alternatives to familiar meat-based pet food. (I'll use the phrase 'slaughter-based' to refer to meat produced via slaughter – 'meat-based' is ambiguous.) My focus will be on plant-based ('vegan') pet food, because this a better developed (and better-researched) industry sector. In the second section, I explore the ethics of switching dogs and cats to vegan diets. In the final section, I summarize recent research quantifying the environmental benefits of shifts from slaughter-based to vegan pet food. A 'case studies' box provides some details about some of the companies that produce alternative pet foods.

Alternatives to Slaughter-based Pet Foods

Pet food is big business. A guardian visiting a pet shop may find products purporting to be balanced especially for young, old, small, large, or active dogs and cats; made with 'ancestral', 'human-grade', 'organic', 'raw', or 'natural' ingredients; or formulated to be hypoallergenic, or combat any number of health concerns relating to animals' coats, digestion, odour, or energy levels. Producers gear marketing claims towards humans rather than companions. And guardians should treat them with a dose of scepticism.

Until recently – excluding the occasional therapeutic food – almost all commercial pet foods had something in common: meat. It might not be *much* meat; producers bulk out pet foods with cheap plant products. It might be meat from any number of animals. And it might not be *appetizing* meat; the origins of the pet food industry lie with slaughterhouse operators seeking to profit from slaughter by-products. Major slaughter by-products – or, perhaps more accurately, *co*-products – used in pet food today include 'hides and skins, bones, blood, hoofs and horns', as well as materials derived from these, such as 'meals', which results from rendering material like that just mentioned into stable products (Knight 2023, 28). In response to concerns about the impact of slaughter-based meat in pet food – environmental and public health strain, health and safety for companions, harms to 'food' animals, and so on – alternatives began to appear on shelves.

Cultivated Meat

One alternative remains hypothetical. Technological innovations in 'cellular agriculture' have allowed the creation of cultivated meat. This is meat grown outside animals' bodies in bioreactors. The idea is that if the animal is all but removed, we can radically reduce the negative impacts of meat production. At the time of writing, there remain significant socio-cultural and technological barriers for cultivated meat to overcome, and it has extremely limited commercial availability.

Researchers and commentators have hypothesized that cultivated meat in pet food may *not* face some of the challenges to uptake that cultivated meat as human food faces. For example, pet food may be subject to different regulatory pathways, and dogs and cats presumably will not feel disgust at the thought of 'laboratory-grown' meat in the way that some humans do. Initial research indicates demographic differences between those open to purchasing pet food based on cultivated meat and those open to purchasing cultivated meat for their own consumption. While vegetarians and vegans are unlikely to purchase cultivated meat for themselves, many express willingness to purchase it for their companions (Oven, Yoxon, and Milburn 2022).

Many companies have begun exploring the production of cultivated meat for pet food. A 2022 research paper listed 'Because Animals, Pristine Pet Food, and Wild Earth in the United States; Appleton Meats in Canada; Good Dog Food in the UK; and Five Letter Foods in Finland' (Oven, Yoxon, and Milburn 2022: 2–3) as companies that had explored cultivated pet food. However, this is a fast-moving area, and this list already looks out of date. You can find some companies producing cultivated meat pet food detailed in the 'case studies' box below.

Invertebrates

Could we reduce the impact of pet food by making it from invertebrates, like insects? Humans consume thousands of insect species worldwide, and producers industrially farm several species (and thus trillions of individuals annually). Nonetheless, efforts to encourage people in the global north to switch from vertebrate meat to insects have had a limited impact. This comes down to an aesthetic aversion on the part of consumers. Of course, dogs and cats don't have this aversion.

There's already a market for insects as animal food in the global north. This includes a small market for pet foods (lots of pet shops stock live crickets, for example, as feed for reptiles), but, more significantly, it includes farmers raising insects to feed to farmed animals – especially farmed fish.

Given this background, it perhaps is no surprise that companies producing insect-based pet foods have emerged. Shahida Siddiqui and colleagues (2023) recently identified 43 brands worldwide – mostly Europe-based – actively selling insect-based food for dogs and cats. Though 'regional companies and startups' dominated the market through the 2010s, both Mars and Nestle launched insect-based foods in the early 2020s (Siddiqui et al 2023: 1). You can find out more in the 'case studies' box below.

Most of the 43 brands actively selling insect-based pet food products used black soldier flies, with fewer than ten bands using yellow mealworms, and fewer still using other insects. Most brands used insects to produce complete dry dog foods (Siddiqui et al 2023). Nutritionally complete and balanced foods contain all the nutrients that an animal needs in the right amounts – the animals could thrive if fed solely that product.

We can't explore all potential challenges and benefits of insect-based pet foods. But it's worth noting that insect-based pet foods remain ethically fraught. This isn't only because support for insect farming may bolster industries farming vertebrate animals, since the livestock industry is such an important customer of the insect industry. It's also because insects themselves may be morally considerable, meaning that raising and killing them may be morally wrong itself (Sebo and Schukraft 2021). And if they are morally considerable, that's terrible: industrial insect production involves huge numbers of animals. The question of whether insects are morally considerable comes down to whether these animals are sentient – roughly, whether they are thinking, feeling beings. This question is the subject of scientific controversy and ongoing research. We should thus be careful about labelling insect farming morally innocuous.

Vegan Pet Food

Dogs evolved alongside humans, typically eating whatever humans threw away. (For better or worse, this has fallen out of favour in the industrialized north.) No doubt, historically, many dogs have eaten entirely or primarily plant-based diets. (For example, the now extinct Hawaiian Poi Dogs were fed poi, a staple food made from taro roots.) Cats are different – though cats have lived among humans for millennia, they have traditionally been less directly reliant on humans for food.

There are dozens of brands worldwide producing nutritionally complete and balanced vegan dog and cat foods. Manufacturers typically use familiar non-animal protein sources, like beans (including soy) and grains (including rice), but they may also draw upon more exotic ingredients. Manufacturers will almost always fortify these foods with various amino acids, vitamins, and minerals, replacing nutrients that wild animals would acquire from animal-based foods with synthetic alternatives. And they will include various flavour enhancers, and other additives, like preservatives. (This high level of processing is typical of pet food manufacturing.) I explore three brands more closely in the 'case studies' box below.

No doubt the coverage of suppliers is patchy, and more foods are available for some companions than others. But, for many of the guardians reading this chapter, there will be an array of options available. And interest in this area is rising quickly; there's every chance that, by the time you read this, vegan pet food will be far more accessible than it is when I am writing.

A small number of guardians – perhaps in response to problems of availability – feed companions a wholly home-cooked vegan diet. While it's possible to do this well, neither vets nor advocates of vegan pet foods typically recommend it. This is because home cooking – vegan or otherwise – comes with the challenge of ensuring that the diet offered to the companion is nutritionally complete and balanced.

Case Study: Some Companies Producing Alternative Pet Foods

Because Animals received international attention when they debuted 'Harmless Hunt' cat treats in 2021. These biscuits contained cultured mouse meat, but Because Animals explicitly framed them as supplementary, and not a nutritionally complete and balanced food. Though the company did accept preorders for the product, it no longer features on their website. In 2023, Because Animals rebranded as **BioCraft Pet Nutrition**. It now focuses on working with pet food manufacturers to incorporate cultivated meat. If cultivated meat is going to provide a viable alternative to slaughter-based meat for pet food – we might think – it is the work of BioCraft Pet Nutrition that will be vital, rather than the development of products like Harmless Hunt treats.

BioCraft Pet Nutrition's cultivated meat may not be the first to market. The Czech firm **Bene Meat** announced in November 2023 that they had received certification of a new raw material on the European Union's Feed Materials Register. On their website, they claim that this makes them the first company anywhere in the world allowed to sell cultivated meat for pet food. Meanwhile, **Good Dog Food**, which rebranded to **Meatly** in 2023, claims on their website that they will be the first company to sell cultivated meat pet food. They are targeting the UK market, and explain that they are working closely with the British Food Standards Agency and Department for Environment, Food & Rural Affairs, seeking approval for their cultivated chicken.

Purina, owned by Nestle, launched a **Nature's Protein** range through its **Beyond** brand in 2020, initially in Switzerland. One of the products contained black soldier fly, plus chicken and fava beans – this product, though significant as a foray into insect protein for a major manufacturer of pet food, is not a genuine 'alternative' to slaughter-based pet food. Consequently, Mars's product is more interesting. **Lovebug** is a cat food brand owned by Direct2Pet Europe B.V, a Dutch Mars Petcare subsidiary. Its product, launched in the UK in 2021, is 30% dried insect meal, made from black soldier fly larvae. Unlike the Nature's Protein pet food, it does not contain vertebrate animal protein.

V-dog – a British company founded in 1980 – prominently claims on their website that they have 'the Worlds [sic] oldest commercial plant-based vegan dog food'. Their nutritionally complete and balanced Traditional Flakes dry dog food (which looks a bit like muesli) contains (in order by weight): Corn, wheat, corn protein meal, oats, peas, beans, 'minerals', sunflower oil, a 'botanical blend', vegetable stock, alfalfa (a fodder or cover crop occasionally eaten by humans), sweet potato, vegetable fibres, and nutritional yeast. V-dog also produces a Crunchy Nuggets dry food. This – which looks more like a 'typical' dry dog food – is also nutritionally complete and balanced. It contains wheat, maize gluten, peas, sunflower oil, maize, sweet potato, linseed, rice, beet pulp, brewers' yeast, 'minerals', alfalfa, vegetable stock, and a 'botanical blend'. As should be clear, neither of V-dog's foods contain anything particularly unusual or mysterious. They are highly processed, but this is typical of pet food (and basically inevitable when it comes to dry food).

Benevo is another British company producing vegan pet food. Benevo has produced a nutritionally complete and balanced vegan cat food since 2005, which, they explain on their website, nutritionists have independently confirmed meets the nutrition guidelines of the Association of American Feed Control Officials and the European Pet Food Industry Federation. Benevo claim that this product was the first nutritionally complete and balanced meat-free cat food in the UK. Their Adult Original cat food contains (in order): soya, wheat, maize gluten, corn, rice, sunflower oil, sugar beet, brewers' yeast, vegetable stock, 'minerals', linseed, seaweed, fructooligosaccharide (a naturally occurring plant sugar included as a prebiotic), spirulina (a dietary supplement made from algae), and extracts from the Mojave yucca plant. These ingredients are perhaps a little more exotic than those used in V-dog's dog foods. Benevo also produces vegan dog food (including a puppy food) and other pet products.

Amì Planet is an Italian company that claims on their website to be the 'first entirely plant-based pet food company in the world'. They were founded in 2002. They produce dry food for cats and dogs, as well as wet food for dogs. Their dry cat food contains corn gluten, corn, corn oil, yeast, potato protein, 'minerals', peas, vegetable proteins, cellulose, rice protein, linseed, and Mojave yucca. Their wet dog food comes in several flavours, but, for example, their Amì Red contains red beans, tomatoes, beetroot, courgette, parsnip, rice, sunflower oil, pea protein, plus various mineral and vitamin additives.

Challenges to Moving Away from Meat

In an international 2019 study, over half of dog and/or cat guardians expressed at least one worry about slaughter-based pet food. Nonetheless, 97% of dogs and 99% of cats in the study ate slaughter-based meat. Even among guardians who were themselves vegan, only 27% fed their companion animal(s) a plant-based diet (Dodd et al 2019). Guardians offer several reasons to explain or justify their reluctance. In this section, I offer brief responses to some of the most common.

First, consumers worry that there is something 'unnatural' about feeding plants to companion animals. This isn't a compelling argument. It's unclear what it means to talk about 'naturalness' in relation to companion animals, given that they are, themselves, 'unnatural'. (Even if they weren't, it's unclear why we should consider slaughter-based pet food a 'natural' product.) And, more fundamentally, it's unclear why a claim of something's 'naturalness' should be an argument in its favour. Lots of natural things are awful, and lots of *unnatural* things are good. Disease is presumably natural, and life-saving medicine unnatural. But that's a terrible argument against medication. Maybe something similar applies to pet food.

Second, guardians might – understandably – worry about the health impact of vegan pet food. After all, dogs and cats have evolved to eat meat. Indeed, cats are obligate carnivores. In 'nature' – so much as the idea makes sense – they'd acquire certain important nutrients only from other animals. But dogs and cats don't need key *ingredients* to be healthy; they need key *nutrients* (Knight and Leitsberger 2016: n.p.). There's no reason we couldn't provide these nutrients in ways different to how these animals would acquire them 'in nature'. (Indeed, pet food depends upon this. No dogs can 'naturally' open cans. No cats – descended from desert-dwellers – would 'naturally' encounter tuna.) There are many nutritionally complete and balanced vegan pet foods on the market. These typically contain additives providing nutrients that, 'in nature', dogs and cats would find in meat. For example, food technologists can synthesize taurine, an amino acid 'only' found in meat, without the need for animal input. This is frequently added to both vegan and slaughter-based pet foods.

Population-level studies of dogs and cats indicate that the health outcomes for companions fed vegan pet food are at least as good as for those fed slaughter-based pet food. A recent systematic review 'found that there is no convincing evidence of major impacts of vegan diets on dog or cat health', but that there is 'evidence of benefits for animals arising as a result of feeding them vegan diets'. Researchers identified these benefits partly through surveys of guardians – which 'can be subject to selection biases' – but 'these beneficial findings were relatively consistent across several studies and should, therefore, not be disregarded' (Domínguez-Oliva et al 2023: n.p.).

Third, critics might object to vegan guardians imposing their choices on companions. But this isn't a very good argument, either. If we're really worried about imposing choices on animals, we should be more worried about the choices we impose on those animals killed to make pet food. In any case, we make choices on behalf of our companions all the time – where they can go, how they can express themselves, who they can socialize with, and so on. There are undoubtedly important questions to ask about the way we impose on our companions (see, e.g., Healey and Pepper 2021). But this goes far deeper than questions about which brand of pet food we buy.

Presumably, the worry is that the choice of vegan foods is not a choice that the companion *themselves* would make. There are at least two things that we can say about this. First, let's grant that unpalatable vegan food could have health/welfare implications for companions (Brown 2009: 141). But the largest published study on the subject indicates that there are few differences in palatability between vegan and slaughter-based pet food in either dogs or cats (Knight and Satchell 2021) – indicating that, on average, dogs and cats don't prefer slaughter-based pet foods. Of course, dogs and cats are individuals, and population-level studies cannot determine what any *particular* dog or cat will prefer (Milburn, forthcoming). But there's every reason for us to think that our companions *will* be happy with vegan pet food – especially if we introduce them to it in the right way, and perhaps try out a few different brands.

But this leads to my second response, which is that companion choice cannot be sovereign. When companions would choose to do something that negatively impacts others – as a companion's 'choice' to eat meat would – we have good reason not to respect that choice. And that's true even if we should give companions a lot more freedom than we do at present.

Quantifying the Costs of Meat-based Pet Food

Andrew Knight (2023) recently calculated the potential environmental benefits of shifts to vegan pet food. Knight's calculations were deliberately conservative. That is, the impact of current companion animal diets (and the potential benefits of widespread shifts to vegan diets for companions) are likely greater than these numbers suggest.

Assuming constant population levels (based on worldwide companion animal populations from 2018), switching all humans to vegan diets would result in the slaughter of 71.3 billion fewer terrestrial vertebrates annually. Switching dogs to vegan diets would result in the slaughter of 6 billion fewer terrestrial vertebrates annually. Switching cats to vegan diets would result in the slaughter of 900 million fewer terrestrial vertebrates annually. (Switching dogs and cats to vegan diets would also mean we'd kill billions fewer aquatic animals.)

These numbers might surprise readers familiar to thinking of pet food as produced from 'by-products' of slaughter (Bosch and Swanson 2021: 795). But one of the insights of Knight's research is that we should be wary of this assumption. 'For dog food, [human-consumable] ingredients comprised 47.4% of all animal-sourced ingredients, and meat comprised 66.2% of this [human-consumable] group. For cat food, [human-consumable] ingredients comprised 49.2% of all animal-sourced ingredients, and meat comprised 50.0% of this [human-consumable] group' (Knight 2023: 11–12). But it was actually the non-human-consumable sources of animal protein – mostly animal meal, which is highly processed parts of animal bodies not eaten by humans – that 'were less efficient than [human-consumable] sources, requiring more livestock animals to produce – 1.352 times as many, for dog food, and 1.879 times as many, for cat food' (ibid: 26).

We must move away from the idea that non-human-consumable ingredients would 'go to waste' if we didn't include them in pet food. That may have been the case in the early days of the pet food industry, but no longer. Today, producers will use 'excess' products of slaughter in many products. Using these co-products of slaughter 'within pet food increases overall demand for [animal by-products] – and hence, the number of livestock animals [killed] to provide them' (ibid: 28). In short, if we make pet food out of animal bodies, even the parts of animals that humans don't eat, we need to kill *many* more animals

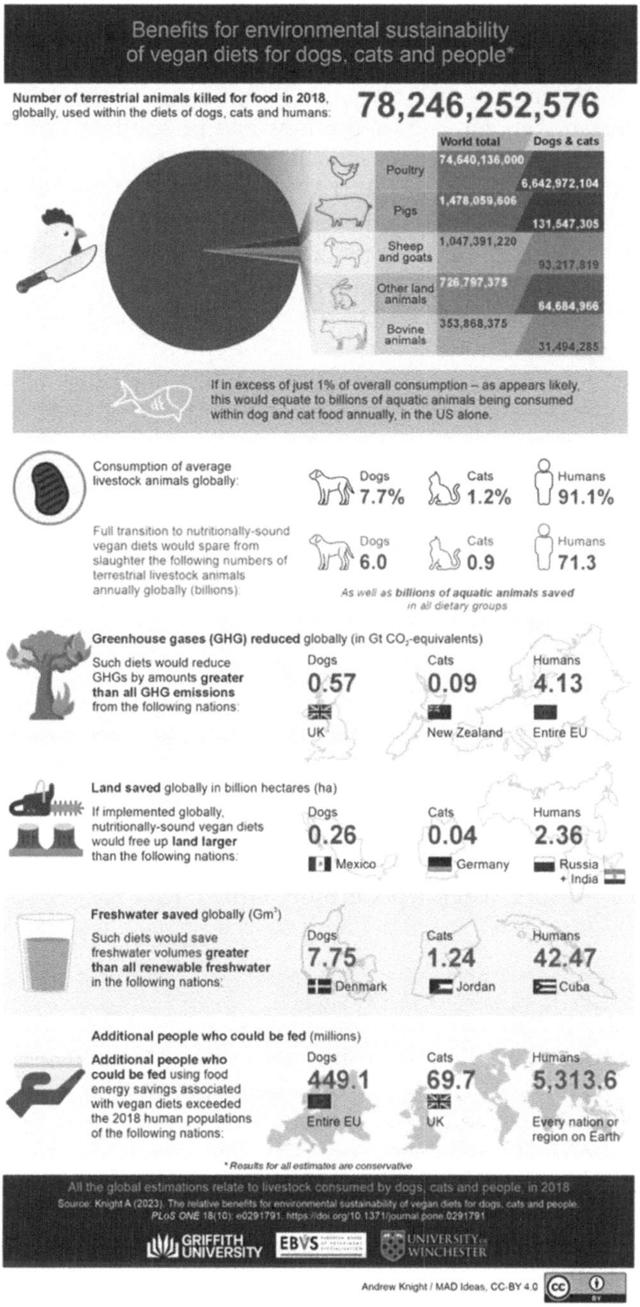

Figure 7.1 Image from www.andrewknight.info/articles/pet-food/, based on Knight 2023; copyright Andrew Knight/MAD Ideas, released under Creative Commons Attribution 4.0.

than we would otherwise. And if we need to kill many more animals, we need to farm many more animals. And that's very bad for the environment. (Not to mention the animals.)

The environmental benefits of the reduction in animal agriculture resulting from a move to vegan diets for dogs and cats would be substantial. Knight (ibid: 22) calculates that switching dogs globally to vegan diets would reduce worldwide greenhouse gas emissions by 0.57 gigatonnes CO_2-eq annually. 0.57 gigatonnes CO_2-eq means the equivalent impact of 0.57 gigatonnes of carbon dioxide – that's more than the annual emissions of greenhouse gases from the United Kingdom. Switching cats to vegan diets would reduce emissions by 0.09 gigatonnes CO_2-eq annually. That's more than the annual emissions of New Zealand.

Meanwhile, Knight (ibid.: 20–21) calculates that switching dogs globally to vegan diets would result in 0.26 billion hectares of land becoming available – that's a larger area than Mexico or Saudi Arabia. Switching cats globally to vegan diets would result in 0.04 billion hectares of land becoming available. That's an area larger than Japan or Germany. There would also be significant freshwater savings, Knight (ibid.: 21) calculates; switching dogs to vegan diets would save 7.75 cubed gigametres of water annually. That's more than all renewable fresh water in Denmark. Switching cats to vegan diets would save 1.24 cubed gigametres of water annually, which is more than all renewable fresh water in Jordan.

Knight (ibid.: 22–25) also calculated the number of additional people that the global food system could feed with the dietary energy savings resulting from switching dogs and cats to vegan diets. Switching the world's dogs to vegan diets would free up food energy sufficient to feed 449.1 million people – greater than the population of the entire European Union. Switching cats to vegan diets, meanwhile, could free up dietary energy sufficient to feed 69.7 million people – more than the population of the UK.

Conclusions

The environmental impact of our companion animals is substantial. Individually and collectively, we can reduce these animals' impact – impact on animals killed for food and on the wider environment – by switching them away from diets rich in slaughter-based meat, and towards vegan diets. (Insect-based diets or, in time, diets based on cultivated meat represent other options.) The existing research indicates that vegan diets are both as palatable and (at least) as healthy for dogs and cats as diets rich in slaughter-based meat.

Making this switch is not a silver bullet. But perhaps now is the time for us to recognize that it's not just *our* consumption habits that matter. The consumption habits of our dogs and cats, too, can change. And if we're serious about limiting the impact of our lives on the planet and other animals, they *should* change.

Questions for Consideration

- Should we have companion animals?
- What values should influence our choices over what to feed our companion animals?
- What challenges might pet foods based on cultivated meat or insects raise?
- What is the relationship between the systems used to produce food for humans and the systems used to produce food for companion animals?
- How central should questions about companion animals be when we reflect on how we can live sustainable lives?

Note

1 My thanks to Andrew Knight, Susana Pickett, and Alice Oven for comments.

Further Reading

Milburn, Josh. 2022. *Just Fodder: The Ethics of Feeding Animals.* Montreal and Kingston: McGill-Queen's University Press.

Nestle, Marion. 2008. *Pet Food Politics: The Chihuahua in the Coal Mine.* Oakland: University of California Press.

Ward, Ernie, Alice Oven, and Ryan Bethencourt. 2019. *The Clean Pet Food Revolution: How Better Pet Food Will Change the World.* Brooklyn: Lantern Media.

References

Abbate, Cheryl. 2016. How to help when it hurts: The problem of assisting victims of injustice. *Journal of Social Philosophy* 47 (2): 142–70.

Bosch, G., and K. S. Swanson. 2021. Effect of using insects as feed on animals: Pet dogs and cats. *Journal of Insects as Food and Feed* 7 (5): 795–805.

Brown W. Y. 2009. Nutritional and ethical issues regarding vegetarianism in the domestic dog. *Recent Advances in Animal Nutrition – Australia* 17: 137–143.

Dodd, Sarah A. S., Nick J. Cave, Jennifer L. Adolphe, Anna K. Shoveller, and Adronie Verbrugghe. 2019. Plant-based (vegan) diets for pets: A survey of pet owner attitudes and feeding practices. *PLOS One* 14 (1): e0210806.

Domínguez-Oliva, Adriana, Daniel Mota-Rojas, Ines Semendric, and Alexandra L. Whittaker. 2023. The impact of vegan diets on indicators of health in dogs and cats: A systematic review. *Veterinary Sciences* 10 (1): 52.

Giroux, Valery, Kristin Voigt, and Angie Pepper (Eds.). 2023. *The Ethics of Animal Shelters.* Oxford: Oxford University Press.

Healey, Richard, and Angie Pepper. 2021. Interspecies justice: Agency, self-determination, and assent. *Philosophical Studies* 178: 1223–43.

Knight, Andrew. 2023. The relative benefits for environmental sustainability of vegan diets for dogs, cats and people. *PLOS ONE* 18 (10): e0291791.

Knight, Andrew, and Madelaine Leitsberger. 2016. Vegetarian versus meat-based diets for companion animals. *Animals* 6 (9): 57.

Knight, Andrew, and Liam Satchell. 2021. Vegan versus meat-based pet foods: Owner-reported palatability behaviours and implications for canine and feline welfare. *PLOS ONE* 16 (6): e0253292.

Milburn, Josh. 2022. *Just Fodder: The Ethics of Feeding Animals.* Montreal and Kingston: McGill-Queen's University Press.

Milburn, Josh. Forthcoming. The ethics of plant-based pet food. In: *The Plant-Based and Vegan Handbook: Psychological and Multidisciplinary Perspectives*, edited by Yanoula Athanassakis, Renan Larue, and William O'Donohue. Cham: Springer.

Okin, Gregory S. 2017. Environmental impacts of food consumption by dogs and cats. *PLOS ONE* 12 (8): e0181301.

Oven, Alice, Barbara Yoxon, and Josh Milburn. 2022. Investigating the market for cultivated meat as pet food: A survey analysis. *PLOS ONE* 17 (12): e0275009.

Palmer, Clare. 2021. Should we provide the bear necessities? Climate change, polar bears and the ethics of supplemental feeding. In: *Animals in Our Midst: The Challenges of Co-Existing with Animals in the Anthropocene*, edited by Bernice Bovenkerk and Josef Keulartz, pp. 377–98. Cham: Springer.

Rothgerber, Hank. 2013. A meaty matter. Pet diet and the vegetarian's dilemma. *Appetite* 68: 76–82.

Sebo, Jeff, and Jason Schukraft. 2021. Don't farm bugs. Aeon. https://aeon.co/essays/on-the-torment-of-insect-minds-and-our-moral-duty-not-to-farm-them

Siddiqui, Shahida A., Thomas A. Brunner, Iwan Tamm, Paul van der Raad, Gautam Patekar, Nur Alim Bahmid, Kees Aarts, and Aman Paul. 2023. Insect-based dog and cat food: A short investigative review on market, claims and consumer perception. *Journal of Asia-Pacific Entomology* 26: 102020.

8 Consuming Plastics

Tony R. Walker

Summary

- Unsustainable plastics production, over consumption and plastics mismanagement threatens environmental, social and economic sustainability.
- More than 9.2 billion metric tons of plastics have ever been produced, but waste mismanagement has resulted in 76% of this plastic now exists as waste in landfills, dumps, or the natural environment.
- Societal dependence on plastics, especially single-use plastics and leakage into the environment has resulted in widespread marine, freshwater, terrestrial and atmospheric impacts globally.
- Most plastics are derived from fossil fuels and account for 6% of global oil consumption.
- Plastic production and incineration produce greenhouse gas emissions during every step of the plastic life cycle, contributing to climate change.
- Widespread consumer demand for plastics have placed enormous pressure on the planet's limited resources and has resulted in widespread plastic pollution in every environmental compartment on Earth.
- The international community and national governments are implementing solutions and establishing ambitious targets to reduce plastic pollution and improve sustainability, yet plastic production, over consumption and waste generation is still outpacing these new policies and regulations.

Keywords: Plastic Production, Single-Use Plastics (SUPS), Plastic Consumption, Plastic Waste Mismanagement, Plastic Pollution, Sustainable Alternatives, Zero-Plastic Waste

DOI: 10.4324/9781003412526-9

Introduction

Plastic is ubiquitous in modern society, yet current consumption is unsustainable (Borrelle et al. 2020; Walker and McGuinty, 2020; McGuinty and Walker 2021; Walker 2021). Society relies on plastic for many common consumer products (Walker et al. 2021; Kitz et al. 2022). Since the development of the first commercial **plastic polymers** in the 1950s, approximately 9200 million metric tons of plastic has been produced and consumed, but roughly 6900 million metric tons is now waste and has already ended up in landfills around the world, or into the environment (Geyer et al. 2017; Brooks et al. 2018). In 2022, global plastic production reached 390 million metric tons per year (Statista, 2023), but may double within 20 years (Lebreton and Andrady 2019; Walker and McGuinty 2020). As most consumer plastics are intended for **single-use** with limited recyclability, it has driven increased global production, consumer demand and over consumption leading to unprecedented plastic waste generation and widespread plastic pollution (Schnurr et al. 2018; Lau et al. 2020; Walker and McGuinty 2020).

Pervasive plastic pollution affects all marine, freshwater, and terrestrial ecosystems globally and plastics are even transported in the atmosphere (Walker and McGuinty 2020; Ryan et al. 2023). Once plastics enter the environment, they continuously break down into increasingly smaller particles called microplastics (<5 mm) (Hartmann et al. 2019; Allen et al. 2022). Due to low degradation coupled with unsustainable production, consumption and disposal, plastic pollution has become a severe transboundary threat to natural ecosystems and human health (Ambrose et al. 2019; Prata et al. 2019; Walker 2023a). There is a growing body of evidence reporting that the presence of plastics in agricultural soils (Hofmann et al. 2023) and in aquatic biota poses potential risks to human health through ingestion in food consumed by humans (Karbalaei et al. 2018, 2019; Conti et al. 2020; Danopoulos et al. 2020; Sequeira et al. 2020; Walker et al. 2022).

Global plastic waste generation worsened during the COVID-19 pandemic resulting in increased use and disposal of **personal protective equipment** (PPE) and single-use plastics (SUPs) due to food safety concerns (Prata et al. 2020; Kitz et al. 2022; Silva et al. 2020, 2021; Molloy et al. 2022b; see Case Study). Mismanagement of PPE during the peak of the COVID-19 pandemic resulted in an estimated 129 billion face masks and 65 billion gloves being used each month globally (Prata et al. 2020). Even before the COVID-19 pandemic, Borrelle et al. (2020) estimated that between 19–23 million metric tons of plastic waste generated globally in 2016 entered aquatic and marine ecosystems and is predicted to reach 53 million metric tons annually by 2030. In response to the global plastic pollution problem, multilevel mitigation strategies have been proposed, along with innovative approaches to reduce and transform the global plastics economy (Ellen MacArthur Foundation 2020; Walker and McGuinty 2020).

Case Study: Tracking Canadian Government Responses to Plastic Pollution Before and During the COVID-19 Pandemic

Single-use plastics (SUPs) are major contributors to local and global plastic pollution. There have been numerous studies examining policy and legislative tools to reduce plastic pollution, particularly SUPs (e.g., plastic bags, microbeads, straws, plastic cutlery) (da Costa et al. 2020). Although early government policy responses targeted plastic bags, there has also been an increase in policies targeting other SUPs (e.g., microbeads, straws, plastic cutlery). Although there has been an increase in the number of national legislative strategies to address plastic pollution, these have also been accompanied by recent increasing non-legislative interventions to mitigate SUPs by individuals and industry that complement government policies. Recently, the COVID-19 pandemic severely disrupted plastic reduction policies at local and national levels and resulted in increased plastic waste generation, negative impacts on the environment and increased plastic pollution. Before the COVID-19 pandemic, governments in Canada and globally had implemented, or were planning to implement, policies to curb SUP use, combined with strong consumer support (Xanthos and Walker 2017; Schnurr et al. 2018). This strong consumer support to reduce plastic pollution and pro-environmental behaviour prior to COVID-19 was consistent with other consumer survey studies from high-income countries (Walker et al. 2023). However, the COVID-19 pandemic disrupted many of these initiatives and changed consumer attitudes (Silva et al. 2020). Two national survey studies measured changes in Canadian consumer attitudes toward SUPs, in 2019 (pre-pandemic) by Walker et al. (2021) and 2020 (during the pandemic) by Kitz et al. (2022). Before the COVID-19 pandemic, most participants were motivated to reduce SUP consumption. Although Canadians were highly motivated to reduce SUPs, they were less willing to pay for sustainable alternatives (Walker et al. 2021). This was mirrored in a regional Atlantic Canadian and a municipal study in Halifax in Nova Scotia pre-pandemic (Varkey et al. 2021; Molloy et al. 2022a; Molloy et al. 2022b). Results from four Atlantic Canadian provinces showed strong consumer support for SUP bag bans, and for further plastic pollution reduction legislation, likely because three of these provinces were the first in Canada to implement provincial-wide policies for plastic bag reduction (Molloy et al. 2022a). Results from Halifax indicated strong support in SUP reduction, as well as concerns among business owners about sourcing sustainable alternatives (Varkey et al. 2021). However, during the pandemic, roughly half of participants were concerned about food safety due to COVID-19 transmission, but there was only a slight decline in motivation to reduce

SUPs. Unfortunately, results showed a decline in support for tighter regulations or bans on SUPs, along with an increase in consumers' willingness to pay for alternatives (Kitz et al. 2022). Molloy et al. (2022b) investigated opportunities to reduce SUPs in the food service sector in Nova Scotia because the COVID-19 pandemic resulted in an increase in SUP consumption due to public health and safety concerns. Molloy et al. (2022b) conducted semi-structured interviews and focus groups with stakeholders from the food service sector. Although many participants had already implemented SUP reduction strategies prior to the COVID-19 pandemic, many businesses were forced to pause their SUP reduction strategies. However, Molloy et al. (2022b) found that reusable items could be used safely when using basic hygiene measures, allowing SUP reduction strategies to be implemented despite the COVID-19 pandemic (Walker et al. 2023)

As global plastic production and waste continues to increase, so does the number of national and international actions to reduce plastic pollution (Xanthos and Walker 2017; UNEP 2018; Walker and McGuinty 2020). National governments are implementing bans, levies or taxes on certain single-use plastic consumer products (Schnurr et al. 2018; Adam et al. 2020; Clayton et al. 2020; Bezerra et al. 2021). However, most of these downstream strategies to curb plastic pollution are consumer focused and are ineffective in the face of increased upstream plastic production (Walker 2023a). Thus, at the international level, the international community has now recognized that a more holistic approach is required to reduce plastic pollution. In March 2022, the United Nations Environment Assembly adopted a resolution to curb plastic pollution with the development of a legally binding Global Plastics Treaty (Walker 2022). To be successful, the Global Plastics Treaty must include caps on plastic production, eliminate harmful chemicals and be legally binding and adopted by all United Nations member states (Walker 2022; Bergmann et al. 2022; Dey et al. 2022).

To curb plastic over consumption and to achieve a zero-plastic waste future, unprecedented solutions, approaches, and mitigation strategies must be widely adopted and implemented (Borrelle et al. 2020; Lau et al. 2020). However, despite these national and international commitments, plastic over consumption and widespread plastic mismanagement continues to threaten the ability of the global community to meet any of the United Nations (UN) Sustainable Development Goals (SDGs) (Walker 2021; Figure 1). This presents immense challenges for governments and organizations to implement reliable reporting and monitoring of SDGs due to the pervasive nature of plastic pollution impacting the environment, society and the economy (Walker 2021).

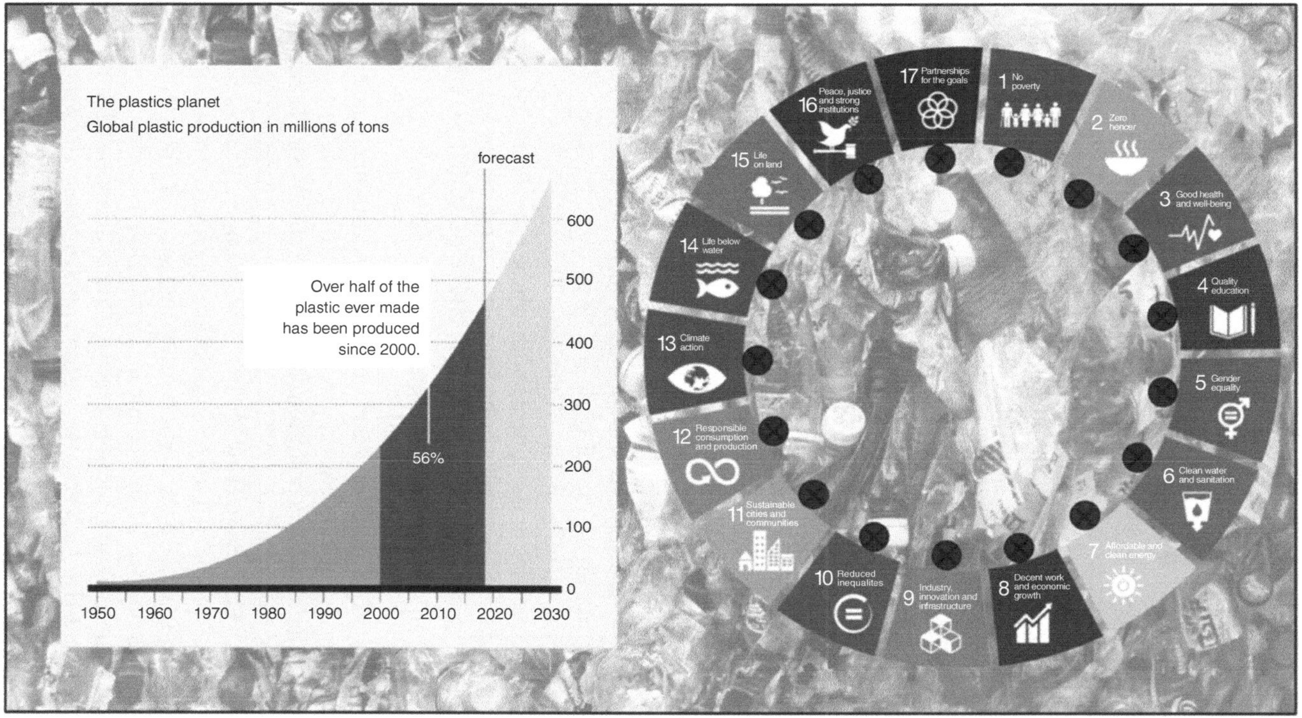

Figure 8.1 Global Plastic Production from 1950 in Million Tons (left). Over Half of this Plastic has been Produced Between 2000 and 2020. This Global Plastic Production Combined With Consumer Over Consumption of Plastics also does not Align With the UN SDGs (right) (adapted from PLASTIKATLAS, CC BY-SA 4.0, https://commons.wikimedia.org/wiki/File:Der_Kunststoff-Planet.svg).

Plastic Waste and Plastic Pollution

Most (98–99%) consumer plastics are derived from fossil fuels and consist of hundreds of polymers with wide-ranging properties (Zhu 2021). Consumer plastic products are often numbered and labeled with resin identification codes to help consumers determine **recyclability** (Walker and McGuinty 2020). Plastic production, use and disposal, particularly single-use plastic packaging, has grown 20-fold since the 1950s (Geyer et al. 2017). Plastics consumed for single-use has increased with a global shift from reusable to single-use consumer products (Jambeck et al. 2015; Walker and McGuinty 2020). Although single-use plastics (SUPs) are lightweight, strong and durable providing many consumer benefits, they create end-of-life disposal issues due to persistence in the environment and limited recyclability (Singh and Walker 2024). Thus, many SUPs are difficult to recycle or can only be recycled a few times before they become waste (Singh and Walker 2024).

According to Brooks et al. (2018) half of the world's mismanaged plastic waste is generated by just five countries: China, Indonesia, the Philippines, Vietnam, and Sri Lanka. However, these countries have also imported poor quality plastic waste from high-income countries for recycling (Walker 2023a). Imports of poor-quality plastic (e.g. contaminated plastics, co-mingling with low values after-market plastics) results in disproportionately higher plastic waste generation per capita. Much of this unregulated imported plastic waste is landfilled, incinerated or leaks into the environment (Law et al. 2020; Liu et al. 2021; Walker 2023b). However, recent amendments to the Basel Convention are designed to restrict international trade in plastic waste to reduce leakage into the environment (Gündoğdu and Walker 2021).

In low-income countries in the global south where potable drinking water is unavailable, the use of SUP sachets or bottled water for drinking has resulted in increased plastic waste (Adam et al. 2020). These discarded SUP sachets have been linked with destructive flooding causing stagnation and creating breeding grounds for mosquitoes and cholera (Adam et al. 2020; Walker 2023a). Indiscriminate disposal of plastics in countries with inadequate waste management systems is choking critical urban infrastructure, resulting in widespread and unsustainable plastic pollution (Jambeck et al. 2018). Plastic waste and pollution costs society up to US$2.5 trillion per year based on reduced ecosystem services (Beaumont et al. 2019). For example, Beaumont et al. (2019) reported that plastic pollution causes severe negative economic impacts on communities and negative impacts on ecosystem services, most notably in coastal communities in low-income countries in the global south.

Until 2018, high-income countries exported their domestic plastic waste to China (Liu et al. 2018; Walker 2018). China imported recyclable materials to supplement its domestic manufacturing industries (Ellen MacArthur Foundation et al. 2018). However, much of this plastic waste was contaminated with food, mixed with other plastic materials (i.e., co-mingled) or comprised of difficult to recycle plastics, so could not be recycled and ended up as waste or leaking into the environment (Walker 2023a). Thus, many high-income countries have failed to incorporate the true environmental costs of managing plastic waste and so the circular economy has not yet become mainstream enough to adapt to global plastic waste diversion changes (Walker 2018; Law et al. 2020; Walker 2023a).

Plastic waste, especially from SUP packaging has increased public awareness about the negative impacts of plastic pollution (Walker et al. 2021). Few consumer plastics are fully biodegradable and thus accumulate in the natural environment and landfills (Walker and Xanthos 2018; Walker 2023c). Plastic polymers are derived from fossil fuels and plastics account for 6% of global oil consumption (Zhu 2021). Furthermore, public understanding of the correlation between fossil fuel extraction, use of petroleum for plastic production, greenhouse gas emissions and climate change has increased given they are inextricably linked with every step of the plastic life cycle from production to waste disposal (Walker and McKay 2021). Impacts of fossil fuel-based plastic production and waste are indisputable and are currently unsustainable (Walker 2021; Walker and Fequet 2023). Increased consumer awareness of waste from plastic and the direct linkage between plastic consumption and climate change helps drives industrial innovation to design plastic products for end-of-life for improved recyclability for a circular economy (Zink and Geyer 2017; Ellen MacArthur Foundation 2020). This can be achieved via improved waste management, improved product designs, financial instruments (taxes and incentives) and better collection strategies at regional levels financed by collection of taxes or levies (Brooks et al. 2018).

Globally, only 9% of all plastic waste is recycled, 12% incinerated, and the remaining 79% accumulates in natural ecosystems (Geyer et al. 2017). To ensure sustainable consumption, production and to reduce plastic waste, extraordinary efforts are required by the international community. For example, dramatically decreasing production and consumption of plastics, develop circular economies where end-of-life plastics are valued rather than becoming waste and dramatically increasing domestic recycling rates without relying on the global plastic waste trade (Walker 2018; Gündoğdu and Walker 2021). To lessen consumption and to adopt zero plastic waste strategies all stakeholders (individuals, governments and industry) need to reduce, reuse and recycle SUPs (Walker and Xanthos 2018; Diggle and Walker 2020).

Solutions for a Transition to a Zero-Plastic Waste Future

Addressing the complex issue of plastic over consumption, plastic waste generation and plastic pollution on the global scale, requires international agreements (such as the Global Plastics Treaty), national and regional policies, and industry action (Walker 2022; Bergmann et al. 2022; Dey et al. 2022). These government actions coupled with strong consumer, government and industry-level support can lead to a large paradigm shift in plastic use and over consumption (Walker et al. 2021; MacDonald et al. 2023). Solutions required from all stakeholders to reduce plastic waste are diverse. Some solutions, approaches, and mitigation strategies to reduce plastic over consumption, improve management of plastic waste and to reduce plastic pollution include:

- Extended producer responsibility programs that make the producer of an item accountable for the end-of-life management of that item, thus improving recycling efforts and supporting waste reduction goals (Diggle and Walker 2020; Diggle et al. 2023);
- Prevention initiatives to reduce difficult to recycle SUPs and other non-essential plastics including consumer behavioural changes using economics incentives (Xanthos and Walker 2017; Schnurr et al. 2018; Adam et al. 2020; Clayton et al. 2020; Bezerra et al. 2021; MacDonald et al. 2023);
- Circular economy systems development, corporate social responsibility including more robust financial and environmental reporting standards, increased consumer awareness and improved performance measures (Diggle et al. 2023);
- The Global Plastic Treaty must introduce legally binding and time-bound caps on plastic production, especially non-essential and SUPs (Bergmann et al. 2022).

Conclusions

Plastic pollution threatens global social, environmental, and economic sustainability. Plastic production use and disposal, particularly single-use plastic packaging, has grown 20-fold in the past 50 years. Many single-use plastic items are difficult to recycle or can only be recycled a few times before they become waste. Ambitious responses to plastic waste reduction from governments, industry, and consumers have not keep pace with current unsustainable plastic production and use. Thus, caps on global plastics production are required. Addressing the multi-faceted global issue plastic waste and pollution requires extraordinary efforts to transform the global plastics economy to achieve zero-plastic waste. To achieve this, specific time-bound actions are required beyond national level legislation and policy-driven changes. The Global Plastics Treaty must be legally binding and adopted by all countries to reduce plastic consumption and resulting plastic pollution. The world needs to stimulate consumer behaviour change. Extraordinary efforts from all stakeholders including extended producer responsibility, partnerships with cutting-edge packaging producers, reduction initiatives, circular economy systems, education increased awareness at the consumer level, and performance measures are essential to mitigate further harm from the global problem of plastic over consumption, plastic waste, and plastic pollution.

Questions for Consideration

- What is plastic over consumption?
- How can individuals find solutions to reduce plastic over consumption?
- What are governments doing to reduce plastic over consumption?

Further Reading

Molloy, S., Varkey, P., & Walker, T.R. (2022b). Opportunities for single-use plastic reduction in the food service sector during COVID-19. *Sustainable Production and Consumption*, *30*, 1082–1094. https://doi.org/10.1016/j.spc.2022.01.023

Schnurr, R.E., Alboiu, V., Chaudhary, M., Corbett, R.A., Quanz, M.E., Sankar, K., ... & Walker, T.R. (2018). Reducing marine pollution from single-use plastics (SUPs): A review. *Marine Pollution Bulletin*, *137*, 157–171. https://doi.org/10.1016/j.marpolbul.2018.10.001

Varkey, P.S., Walker, T.R., & Saunders, S.J. (2021). Identifying barriers to reducing single-use plastic use in a coastal metropolitan city in Canada. *Ocean & Coastal Management*, *210*, 105663. https://doi.org/10.1016/j.ocecoaman.2021.105663

Walker, T.R., McGuinty, E., Charlebois, S., & Music, J. (2021). Single-use plastic packaging in the Canadian food industry: Consumer behavior and perceptions. *Humanities and Social Sciences Communications*, *8*, 80. https://doi.org/10.1057/s41599-021-00747-4

References

Adam, I., Walker, T.R., Bezerra, J.C., & Clayton, A. (2020). Policies to reduce single-use plastic marine pollution in West Africa. *Marine Policy*, *116*, 103928.

Allen, S., Allen, D., Karbalaei, S., Maselli, V., & Walker, T.R. (2022). Micro (nano) plasticssources, fate, and effects: What we know after ten years of research. *Journal of Hazardous Materials Advances*, *6*, 100057. https://doi.org/10.1016/j.hazadv.2022.100057

Ambrose, K.K., Box, C., Boxall, J., Brooks, A., Eriksen, M., Fabres, J., ... & Walker, T.R. (2019). Spatial trends and drivers of marine debris accumulation on shorelines in South Eleuthera, The Bahamas using citizen science. *Marine Pollution Bulletin*, *142*, 145–154.

Beaumont, N.J., Aanesen, M., Austen, M.C., Börger, T., Clark, J.R., Cole, M., ... & Wyles, K.J. (2019). Global ecological, social and economic impacts of marine plastic. *Marine Pollution Bulletin*, *142*, 189–195.

Bergmann, M., Almroth, B.C., Brander, S.M., Dey, T., Green, D.S., Gundogdu, S., ... & Walker, T.R. (2022). A global plastic treaty must cap production. *Science*, *376*(6592), 469–470.

Bezerra, J.C., Walker, T.R., Clayton, C.A., & Adam, I. (2021). Single-use plastic bag policies in the Southern African development community. *Environmental Challenges*, *3*, 100029.

Borrelle, S.B., Ringma, J., Law, K.L., Monnahan, C.C., & Lebreton, L. (2020). Predicted growth in plastic waste exceeds efforts to mitigate plastic pollution. *Science*, *369*(6510), 1515–1518.

Brooks, A.L., Wang, S., & Jambeck, J.R. (2018). The Chinese import ban and its impact on global plastic waste trade. *Science Advances*, *4*(6), eaat0131.

Clayton, C.A., Walker, T.R., Bezerra, J.C., & Adam, I. (2020). Policy responses to reduce single-use plastic marine pollution in the Caribbean. *Marine Pollution Bulletin*, *162*, 111833.

Conti, G.O., Ferrante, M., Banni, M., Favara, C., Nicolosi, I., Cristaldi, A., ... & Zuccarello, P. (2020). Micro-and nano-plastics in edible fruit and vegetables. The first diet risks assessment for the general population. *Environmental Research, 187*, 109677.

da Costa, J.P., Mouneyrac, C., Costa, M., Duarte, A.C., & Rocha-Santos, T. (2020). The role of legislation, regulatory initiatives and guidelines on the control of plastic pollution. *Frontiers in Environmental Science, 8,* 104. https://doi.org/10.3389/fenvs.2020.00104

Danopoulos, E., Jenner, L.C., Twiddy, M., & Rotchell, J.M. (2020). Microplastic contamination of seafood intended for human consumption: A systematic review and meta-analysis. *Environmental Health Perspectives, 128*(12), 126002.

Dey, T., Trasande, L., Altman, R., Wang, Z., Krieger, A., Bergmann, M., ... & Almroth, B.C. (2022). Global plastic treaty should address chemicals. *Science, 378*(6622), 841–842.

Diggle, A., & Walker, T.R. (2020). Implementation of harmonized Extended Producer Responsibility strategies to incentivize recovery of single-use plastic packaging waste in Canada. *Waste Management, 110*, 20–23.

Diggle, A., Walker, T.R., & Adams, M. (2023). Examining potential business impacts from the implementation of an extended producer responsibility program for printed paper and packaging waste in Nova Scotia, Canada. *Circular Economy, 2*(2), 100039.

Ellen MacArthur Foundation, ARUP, McKinsey & Company, & UNCTAD. (2018). The Circular Economy Opportunity for Urban & Industrial Innovation in China. www.ellenmacarthurfoundation.org/urban-and-industrial-innovation-in-china

Ellen MacArthur Foundation. (2020). Global Commitment. New Plastics Economy. www.newplasticseconomy.org/projects/global-commitment

Geyer, R., Jambeck, J.R., & Law, K.L. (2017). Production, use, and fate of all plastics ever made. *Science Advances, 3*(7), e1700782.

Gündoğdu, S., & Walker, T.R. (2021). Why Turkey should not import plastic waste pollution from developed countries?. *Marine Pollution Bulletin, 171*, 112772.

Hartmann, N.B., Hüffer, T., Thompson, R.C., Hassellöv, M., Verschoor, A., Daugaard, A.E., ... & Wagner, M. (2019). Are we speaking the same language? Recommendations for a definition and categorization framework for plastic debris. *Environmental Science & Technology, 53*(3), 1039–1047.

Hofmann, T., Ghoshal, S., Tufenkji, N., Adamowski, J.F., Bayen, S., Chen, Q., ... & Wilkinson, K.J. (2023). Plastics can be used more sustainably in agriculture. *Communications Earth & Environment, 4*(1), 332. https://doi.org/10.1038/s43247-023-00982-4

Jambeck, J.R., Geyer, R., Wilcox, C., Siegler, T.R., Perryman, M., Andrady, A., Narayan, R., & Law, K.L. (2015). Plastic waste inputs from land into the ocean. *Science, 347*(6223), 768–771.

Jambeck, J., Hardesty, B.D., Brooks, A.L., Friend, T., Teleki, K., Fabres, J., ... & Wilcox, C. (2018). Challenges and emerging solutions to the land-based plastic waste issue in Africa. *Marine Policy, 96*, 256–263.

Karbalaei, S., Hanachi, P., Walker, T.R., & Cole, M. (2018). Occurrence, sources, human health impacts and mitigation of microplastic pollution. *Environmental Science and Pollution Research, 25*(36), 36046–36063.

Karbalaei, S., Golieskardi, A., Hamzah, H.B., Abdulwahid, S., Hanachi, P., Walker, T.R., & Karami, A. (2019). Abundance and characteristics of microplastics in commercial marine fish from Malaysia. *Marine Pollution Bulletin, 148*, 5–15.

Kitz, R., Walker, T.R., Charlebois, S., & Music, J. (2022). Food packaging during the COVID-19 pandemic: Consumer perceptions. *International Journal of Consumer Studies, 46*(2), 434–448. https://doi.org/10.1111/ijcs.12691.

Lau, W.W., Shiran, Y., Bailey, R.M., Cook, E., Stuchtey, M.R., Koskella, J., ... & Palardy, J.E. (2020). Evaluating scenarios toward zero plastic pollution. *Science, 369*(6510), 1455–1461.

Law, K.L., Starr, N., Siegler, T.R., Jambeck, J.R., Mallos, N.J., & Leonard, G.H. (2020). The United States' contribution of plastic waste to land and ocean. *Science Advances, 6*(44), eabd0288.

Lebreton. L., & Andrady, A. (2019). Future scenarios of global plastic waste generation and disposal. *Palgrave Communications, 5*(1), 1–11.

Liu, Z., Adams, M., & Walker, T.R. (2018). Are exports of recyclables from developed to developing countries waste pollution transfer or part of the global circular economy? *Resources, Conservation & Recycling, 136*, 22–23.

Liu, Z., Liu, W., Walker, T.R., Adams, M., & Zhao, J. (2021). How does the global plastic waste trade contribute to environmental benefits: Implication for reductions of greenhouse gas emissions?. *Journal of Environmental Management, 287*, 112283.

MacDonald, A., Allen, D., Williams, L., Flowers, P., & Walker, T.R. (2023). People, plastic, and behaviour change–a comment on drivers of plastic pollution, barriers to change and targeted behaviour change interventions. *Environmental Science: Advances, 2*(4), 551–557.

McGuinty, E., & Walker, T.R. (2021). Solutions, Approaches and Mitigation Strategies for Plastic Waste Management. In: Horton, A. (Ed.). *Plastic Pollution in the World's Oceans.* World Scientific Press.

Molloy, S., Medeiros, A.S., Walker, T.R., & Saunders, S.J. (2022a). Public perceptions of legislative action to reduce plastic pollution: A case study of Atlantic Canada. *Sustainability, 14*(3), 1852. https://doi.org/10.3390/su14031852

Molloy, S., Varkey, P., & Walker, T.R. (2022b). Opportunities for single-use plastic reduction in the food service sector during COVID-19. *Sustainable Production and Consumption, 30*, 1082–1094. https://doi.org/10.1016/j.spc.2022.01.023

Prata, J.C., Silva, A.L., Walker, T.R., Duarte, A.C., & Rocha-Santos, T. (2020). COVID-19 pandemic repercussions on the use and management of plastics. *Environmental Science & Technology, 54*(13), 7760–7765.

Prata, J.C., Silva, A.L.P., da Costa, J.P., Mouneyrac, C., Walker, T.R., Duarte, A.C., & Rocha-Santos, T. (2019). Solutions and integrated strategies for the control and mitigation of plastic and microplastic pollution. *International Journal of Environmental Research and Public Health, 16*(13), 2411.

Ryan, A., Allen, D., Allen, S., Maselli, V., LeBlanc, A., Kelleher, L., Krause, S., Walker, T.R., Cohen, M. (2023). Transport and deposition of ocean-sourced microplastic particles by a North Atlantic hurricane. *Communications Earth & Environment, 4*, 442. https://doi.org/10.1038/s43247-023-01115-7

Schnurr, R.E., Alboiu, V., Chaudhary, M., Corbett, R.A., Quanz, M.E., Sankar, K., Srain, H.S., Thavarajah, V., Xanthos, D., & Walker, T.R. (2018). Reducing marine pollution from single-use plastics (SUPs): A review. *Marine Pollution Bulletin, 137*, 157–171.

Sequeira, I.F., Prata, J.C., da Costa, J.P., Duarte, A.C., & Rocha-Santos, T. (2020). Worldwide contamination of fish with microplastics: A brief global overview. *Marine Pollution Bulletin, 160*, 111681.

Silva, A.L.P., Prata, J.C., Walker, T.R., Campos, D., Duarte, A.C., Soares, A.M., ... & Rocha-Santos, T. (2020). Rethinking and optimising plastic waste management under COVID-19 pandemic: Policy solutions based on redesign and reduction of single-use plastics and personal protective equipment. *Science of the Total Environment, 742*, 140565.

Silva, A.L.P., Prata, J.C., Walker, T.R., Duarte, A.C., Ouyang, W., Barcelò, D., & Rocha-Santos, T. (2021). Increased plastic pollution due to COVID-19 pandemic: Challenges and recommendations. *Chemical Engineering Journal, 405*, 126683.

Singh, N., & Walker, T.R. (2024). Plastic recycling: A panacea or environmental pollution problem. *npj Materials Sustainability, 2*, 17. https://doi.org/10.1038/s44296-024-00024-w

Statista. (2023). Global plastics industry – statistics & facts. www.statista.com/topics/5266/plastics-industry/

UNEP. (2018). Single-use plastics: A roadmap for sustainability. Retrieved from: www.unenvironment.org/resources/report/single-use-plastics-roadmap-sustainability

Walker, T.R. (2018). China's ban on imported plastic waste could be a game changer. *Nature, 553*(7689), 405.

Walker, T.R. (2021). (Micro)plastics and the UN sustainable development goals. *Current Opinion in Green and Sustainable Chemistry, 30*(8), 100497. https://doi.org/10.1016/j.cogsc.2021.100497

Walker, T.R. (2022). Calling for a decision to launch negotiations on a new global agreement on plastic pollution at UNEA5.2. *Marine Pollution Bulletin, 176*, 113447. https://doi.org/10.1016/j.marpolbul.2022.113447

Walker, T.R. (2023a). The tropics should not become the world's plastic pollution problem. *Journal of Tropical Futures, 1*(1), 12–24. https://doi.org/10.1177/27538931231165273

Walker, T.R. (2023b). The Maldives should not become the world's garbage dump by importing plastic waste. *Marine Pollution Bulletin, 189*, 114749.

Walker, T.R. (2023c). What not to do with dog poop. *Science of The Total Environment, 896*, 165332.

Walker, T.R., & Xanthos, D. (2018). A call for Canada to move toward zero plastic waste by reducing and recycling single-use plastics. *Resources, Conservation & Recycling, 133*, 99–100.

Walker, T.R., & McGuinty, E. (2020). Plastics. In: C. Constance (ed.), *The Palgrave Handbook of Global Sustainability*, (pp. 1–12). Springer International Publishing. https://doi.org/10.1007/978-3-030-38948-2_55-1

Walker, T.R., & McKay, D.C. (2021). Comment on "five misperceptions surrounding the environmental impacts of single-use plastic". *Environmental Science & Technology, 55*(2), 1339–1340.

Walker, T.R., & Fequet, L. (2023). Current trends of unsustainable plastic production and micro (nano) plastic pollution. *TrAC Trends in Analytical Chemistry, 160*, 116984.

Walker, T.R., McGuinty, E., Charlebois, S., & Music, J. (2021). Single-use plastic packaging in the Canadian food industry: Consumer behavior and perceptions. *Humanities and Social Sciences Communications, 8*, 80. https://doi.org/10.1057/s41599-021-00747-4.

Walker, T.R., Wang, L., Horton, A., & Xu, E.G. (2022). Micro (nano) plastic toxicity and health effects: Special issue guest editorial. *Environment International, 170*(11), 107626. https://doi.org/10.1016/j.envint.2022.107626
Walker, T.R., Baechler, B., Markley, L., Grünzner, M., Akuoko, I., Bowyer, C., ... & Cowan, E. (2023). Plastic pulse of the public: A review of survey-based research on how people use plastic. *Cambridge Prisms: Plastics, 1*, E8. https://doi.org/10.1017/plc.2023.8
Xanthos, D., & Walker, T.R. (2017). International policies to reduce plastic marine pollution from single-use plastics (plastic bags and microbeads): A review. *Marine Pollution Bulletin, 118*(1-2), 17–26.
Zhu, X. (2021). The plastic cycle–An unknown branch of the carbon cycle. *Frontiers in Marine Science, 7*, 609243. https://doi.org/10.3389/fmars.2020.609243
Zink, T., & Geyer, R. (2017). Circular economy rebound. *Journal of Industrial Ecology, 21*(3), 593–602. https://doi.org/10.1111/jiec.12545

9 Consuming Electronics

Patrick Brodie

Summary

- Scholars of "environmental media" have conceived of various ways that media technologies, specifically the expansion of digital media systems and infrastructures, are creating new challenges for environmental justice and ecological relations.
- Through a genealogy of contemporary studies of media and materiality, we can see how a shift from the "consumption" of media technologies to a more holistic view of technological and infrastructural systems is required to conceive of the impact of digital economies on the environment.
- United by a heuristic of "extractivism," three different approaches to environmental media materialities help push forward more justice-orientated approaches to technology: resources, energy, and waste.
- A dynamic analysis and political mobilisation of these anti-extractive understandings are required for a coalitional approach to cease the destructive consumption of planetary resources within legacies of colonial capitalism.

Keywords: Extractivism, Environmental Media, Digital Infrastructure, Media Technologies

Introduction

While naturalised descriptions of "the cloud" and "streaming," as well as proclamations of data itself as the "new oil" or "new gold" of various emerging resource regimes, recall a more atmospheric and innocuous form of capitalism through Industry 4.0, data-intensive industries remain extremely resource-intensive. As data infrastructures in particular become more important to "green" transitions away from fossil fuels, whether in making "smart" energy consumption and grid tech or drawing from renewable energy sources, the

DOI: 10.4324/9781003412526-10

transformations in these material economies require more precise critical engagement. Digital data, like the networks and infrastructures of the capital it is built on top of, is a world-eating device for extraction and exploitation along its supply chains, and its energetic and resource-making politics are crucial to understanding how the "twinned transitions" of digitalisation and decarbonisation are rolling out under the powerful influence of multinational tech companies.

In this chapter, I outline three ways that scholars of "environmental media" have conceived of this resource-intensivity within digital capitalism: the energy and emissions impacts of digital technologies and infrastructures; the extraction of minerals and pollution required for manufacture of devices and technologies; and the economies of waste and obsolescence driving accumulation of "e-waste." I attune each of these areas of study to their role in maintaining unsustainable and uneven geographical development at the world scale, demonstrating the ways in which they map onto networks of imperial capitalism and its enduring infrastructures. I conclude by demonstrating that shifting the lens from "consumption" to more holistic (but targeted) views of technological supply chains will be required for climate action more closely attuned to planetary environmental justice.

Environmental Media and Political Ecology

Scholars have long thought about how media systems, technologies, and content overlap with environments. Sean Cubitt and his collaborators, in their pioneering work in "**ecomedia**," found that approaches to engaging environmental problems through media could be thought about beyond, for example, how works of media represented or communicated environmental information and culture (Rust et al. 2015). Building on a longer history of studying science and specifically environmental communication (Cox and Depoe 2022), which still deals with translating and expressing complex planetary processes and concepts in and through the social lenses and affordances of various media (see Lakoff 2010), Cubitt, among many other scholars (see Iheka 2021; Shriver-Rice and Vaughan 2020), have recognised that engaging these metabolisms between media and the environment beyond purely scientific information and culture demonstrated deeper entanglements between the materials, resources, energetic processes, and infrastructures of media. Contemporaneous studies, united within the developing subfield of "environmental media studies" (Chang et al. 2019; Shriver-Rice and Vaughan 2020), have variously understood how we can thus "green" the media (Maxwell and Miller 2012), think about "sustainability" through media systems (Starosielski and Walker 2016), understand media's "hidden" environmental costs (Vaughan 2019), or, most crucially for this chapter, foreground media's material substrates (Mattern 2017; Parks et al. 2023; Parks and Starosielski 2015; Starosielski 2015), elements (Parikka 2015; Peters 2015; Starosielski 2019), and wastes (Gabrys 2011; Lepawsky 2018).

The centrality of electronic media technologies within the emerging social systems and networks of **digital economies** – think the explosion of personal computers, smart phones, and IoT devices alongside the supporting infrastructures required to facilitate them for extraction, distribution, and operation – has been well-documented by scholars in critical media studies since the 1990s and 2000s (Barney 2004; Castells 2010; Curtin et al. 2014), especially in research looking at the intersections of media, industries, infrastructures, and environments (Cubitt 2005; Maxwell and Miller 2012; Starosielski and Walker 2016; Taffel 2023). Below, I outline some ways in which scholars have conceived of the sometimes incomprehensibly complex planetary ecological implications of digital technologies.

In considering the dynamics of extraction and consumption at the base of digital media economies, it is worth considering a concept developed by political ecologists Alexander Dunlap and Jostein Jakobsen (2020). In describing the "violent technologies of extraction" developing during the transition to "renewable" energy (a term that Dunlap dismantles in other work (Dunlap 2021)), they warn us about "the **capitalist world-eater**," a concept which sharply and polemically raises the stakes surrounding the ongoing expansion of capitalist enterprise in the face of climate and overall ecological crisis (2020). The heuristic of "extractivism" as a framework for understanding these material dimensions of emerging "green" economies is thus especially useful for our purposes (see Chagnon et al. 2022; Gago and Mezzadra 2018; Voskoboynik and Andreucci 2022), especially in terms of the imperatives for "critical" and/or "tech" minerals at multiple policy levels. As Transnational Institute researcher Maximilian Jung argues, "digital media is a mine, not a cloud" (2023), emphasising the extractive dimensions that are at the very *base* of digital media economies. In spite of policy discourses pairing "digitalisation and decarbonisation," we cannot "dig our way to a just transition," as a team of geologists recently proposed (McGrath 2023), without fundamentally addressing the *absence of justice* within existing extractive and energy regimes (see Gómez-Barris 2017). In each approach below, I reflect on how the heuristic of extractivism helps us to escape the frequent double-binds presented by climate and environmental action amidst overwhelming planetary systems, representing alternatives to business-as-usual solutions to the businesses consuming the planet.

Three Approaches to Environmental Media Materialities

Resources

Digital media studies needs to reckon with resource-making as a process (Bridge 2011) – one that is both increasingly enabled by digital technologies through forms of mediation and datafication, as well as required for the energetic and thermal processes that make electronic computing happen (Pasek et al. 2023). There has been a significant body of work on "data extractivism" as a heuristic for understanding how digital data industries demonstrate familiar dynamics of extractive economies – for example, the classification of data (withdrawn from human life itself) as a "resource" for increasingly naturalised digital processes (Couldry and Mejias 2019; Srnicek 2016). As Nick Couldry and Ulises A. Mejias argue, "Extractive rationalities need to be naturalized or normalized, and, even more fundamentally, the flow of everyday life must be reconfigured and re-presented in a form that enables its capture as data" (2019). They reference political ecologist Jason Moore's concept of the production of "cheap nature" for capital as a way to comprehend the interlocking processes that make data a resource for capital – situating this within much longer histories of colonial exploitation of "natural" resources, they develop the concept of "**data colonialism**" to describe the material and discursive stakes of the planetary expansion of data economies (2019). These processes are made possible by the immense consumption – and required storage – of media content on and through digital devices.

However, as Jung argues polemically, buying into these durable narratives about data-as-resource:

> belittles the violence involved in extracting the materials used to create the digital transformation and the exploitation that makes it work, whether it be mining for metals, manufacturing parts, brutalising communities and depriving them of vital resources, dumping toxic waste in landfills or offloading the worst horrors of content moderation onto traumatised 'click workers'. And ultimately it depoliticises those decisions that brought about the digital economy and seeks to rob us of the means to envisage different futures.
>
> (2023: np)

While data is certainly a "resource" by particular resource-making regimes emerging through digital technologies, it is also not possible to emerge as such without the material and energetic processes of digital computing, which, in the electronic processing of information, are inescapably energetic in content (see Pasek 2023) and traverse immense and imbalanced geographical scales (see Brodie 2023). The elemental make-up of digital media technologies – from minerals to manufactured synthetic components down to the water, air, and electrons flowing through them – is core to their communicative and information storage capabilities, as the "marvelous cloud," to quote the title of John Durham Peters' famous book, is an ecological as much as technological paradigm (Peters 2015). The geologies and atmospherics of media technologies, in Jussi Parikka's *A Geology of Media* conceived in their origins as mineral resources and their durable aftermaths as toxic residues permeating the earth (2015), are of as much explanatory importance as the extractive processes of data. The scars on the Earth, whether cobalt mines or abandoned chip manufacturing facilities, are the legacies of this world-eating desire.

Since Harold Innis and Marshall McLuhan were tracing the material components of "staple" economies in early settler colonial Canada (see Young 2017, 2020), media scholars have grappled with the fundamental material elements that constitute media systems and technologies. However, what contemporary studies of data and extractivism have brought to the fore are these processes of coloniality embedded within digital materialities, especially in the enduring forms of classification which designate landscapes as wastes and material as resources (see Bresnihan and Brodie 2021, 2023; Liboiron 2021; Taylor 2019). Paola Ricaurte's framework for the "coloniality of data" is useful in mapping the multi-layered processes and dimensions that sustain data-driven global economies (2019) – it acts as a heuristic and a reminder that what undergirds the operationality of digital devices, from their sourcing to their energetic processes to their wasting, is extractivism and exploitation in the global south (Gago and Mezzadra 2018; Mezzadra and Neilson 2019).

Energy

Much like Innis and McLuhan were interested in the metabolic processes that constituted networks of trade and communication in the Canadian settler colony (see also Ruiz 2021), the energetic functions and impulses of human society have similarly integrated "natural" landscapes and ecologies into the progressive processes of colonial and capitalist modernity, growth, and accumulation. Cara New Daggett presents us with an alternative history of "energy" which situates its ideology at the heart of the modern, cis-hetero-patriarchal capitalist project – the transformation of "energy" from nature to labour to society was a process of lumpy and violent integration of energetic processes through technology (see 2019). However, these vital dimensions of energy, which scholars have developed to understand the atmospheric and thermal processes by which sun and heat sustain life and industry alike (e.g. After Oil Collective 2022; Starosielski 2021), must also be accounted for at the material level within the electronic conductive processes that are required for digital communications across points (Pasek 2023).

Media's energetic properties have similarly been occluded within the naturalisation of media as a process whose "**backends**," as Lisa Parks, Julia Velkova, and Sander de Ridder term the behind-the-scenes and substrata of media systems, are primarily out of sight. Infrastructure, after all, while frequently conceived as "invisible" or "ambient" until it breaks down, is actually much more frequently at the foreground of global experience *in its very operation* as intrusive, unfinished, or underdeveloped (see Carse and Kneas 2019; Larkin 2013). The same goes for digital technology, which, while increasingly naturalised, is also, in its everyday consumptive use, a constant interaction with energetic processes. Think about how frequently phones die and need charging, or Bluetooth or Wi-Fi signal is activated between devices, or overloaded computer tabs kick your laptop fan into overdrive to cool its overheated components. Each of these situations also interfaces with wider energetic and ecological systems, each with potentially toxic or otherwise environmental implications, whether the electric grid (carbon-fuelled in most parts of the world), atmospheric and radiative signals (which many argue have potentially misunderstood health effects), or lithium battery storage (requiring extensive mining which damages and displaces Indigenous communities from the Atacama to Australia). Thus, at the larger scale, we must also think about the energy required to power the cloud, the "**externalities**" that produces, and the wider but ambivalent political ecologies of data at a global scale in its multiple uses (see Hogan 2018; Goldstein and Nost 2022). As Maxwell and Miller emphasise, physical media – from paper to film stock – has always been a material, and frequently toxic, prospect (2012). The energetic requirements of digital infrastructures thus sit within a lineage of extractive, polluting activities (and backing epistemologies) that are at the heart of modern communication.

Case Study: Data Centres, Energy, and Extraction

One of the major offshoots of the energetic requirements of digital media is the outsourcing of digital operations to large-scale data centres since the late-2000s, the infrastructural backbone of the "cloud computing" (Hogan 2021; Holt and Vonderau 2015; Mosco 2014). These usually multinational infrastructures, while globally distributed, require large-scale nodes like the big tech "hyperscale" cloud facilities of Amazon Web Services, Google, and Microsoft. These facilities utilise an immense amount of electricity and introduce significant ecological and energy transition policy issues in the places where they are most heavily concentrated (for example, Ireland, where they used 18% of the country's energy daily in 2022), and are required to operate not only daily consumer internet traffic but also most "smart" systems and, increasingly, the storage and training of data for AI. These energetic systems metabolise with the resources available in the place they are built – to extend the Ireland example, an energy mix of wind and natural gas on the national grid as well as backup diesel fuels, natural gas-fired generation on-site, and lithium batteries in the case of short-term generation failure. These wind farms are frequently built in energy poor rural places, dependent on solid fuels and heating oil to warm poorly insulated houses, while industrial-scale, multinational renewable energy installations contracted to data centre companies are built nearby, sometimes damaging bog ecologies and disrupting local economies like eco-tourism. In this and other ways, data centres operate within an "unjust transition" by facilitating and reproducing the unequal relations of ruralisation that have sustained Irish postcolonial modernity and now the burgeoning "eco-modernity" of green techno-solutions (Bresnihan and Brodie 2021). As scholars have increasingly begun to emphasise, especially in the consolidating sphere of "critical data centre studies" (Edwards et al. 2024), the infrastructural ecologies managed through these facilities represent productive critical apertures into a multitude of extractive processes (Hogan 2018; Brodie 2023). Jordan Kinder, for example, demonstrates that even when looking at individual platforms, the interlocking of energy and digital infrastructure in Canada, "lubricated by ongoing settler colonialism, have brought the data frontier into contact with a historical one. Hydroelectricity providers like Hydro-Québec mobilize green discourses, for instance, to describe Québec as 'home to clean clouds' " (2023, 107). As Kinder continues, such discourses greenwash not only the "data centre industrial complex" (Hogan 2021), but the history of colonial place-making – and the violent displacement and subjugation of Indigenous peoples – which produced those hydroelectric dams and the modern Québec energy grid in the first place.

One of the primary and frequently misapprehended element of these processes (see case study) is in the circulation, emission, waste, and sometimes re-use of heat within the climatic systems and politics of large-scale digital infrastructures. Due to data centres' extreme energy use, which is primarily drawn to cool (as well as run) the servers, the immense amounts of waste heat have been proposed as a circular solution to the excessive energy use of digital media. Velkova, for example, has written extensively about the politics and recycling of waste heat from data centres and other computing infrastructures (2016, 2021) from domestic to industrial levels. However, related to the final approach to digital media materialities that I will outline, the assumption of ongoing digital growth in spite of the environmental impacts by applying "sustainable" solutions like waste heat usage (among other processes, as I will begin with below), reproduces the unsustainable – and unequal – processes of digital capitalism at a global scale. This idea of re-using heat energy also demonstrates a kind of entropy of colonial thinking. STS scholar Max Liboiron, in their book *Pollution Is Colonialism*, demonstrates that the base *epistemology* that waste is a necessary outcome of human activity rests on a colonial ideology of excess classification, use, and consumption of land and resources embedded within colonial capitalism and its modes of valuing (and discarding) forms of life and knowledge not deemed valuable for capital (2021). In the final section, then, I will show that the offshoot of digital media's extractive economies is the elemental detritus they produce and necessitate.

Waste

As the conclusion above illustrates, a primary offshoot of the over-consumption of electronic energy is the production – and then necessary distribution – of waste heat, whether from servers or in the combustion and use of energy

Figure 9.1 The Front Gate of an Amazon Web Services (AWS) Data Centre in Drogheda, Co. Louth in 2023 (photo by author).

required to power the servers in the first place (of which the waste heat is obviously in itself a product). Utilising this waste heat represents a "circular," "sustainable" solution for digital growth, within which waste becomes an essential element of emerging green infrastructures, for example in the form of district heating infrastructures. But this is not the only "circular" economy being experimented with in and through data centres and their operating companies, and remains open to argument whether such re-use actually constitutes circularity in any meaningful measure (see Chapters 5 and 16). The valuation of waste as an infrastructural component of digital economies extends beyond data processing facilities specifically. In Ireland, Microsoft is involved in projects that are meant to sequester carbon pollution in peatlands as a way to manage the ongoing effects of fossil fuel pollution and atmospheric emissions through Ireland's ecologies (Bresnihan and Brodie 2023). They are also experimenting with their facilities absorbing excess energy produced by intermittent renewable energy that cannot be fully consumed by the grid (see Brodie forthcoming). This energetic and ecological management of emerging forms of extractivism – also being designed to potentially manage Ireland's "untapped" offshore wind reserves – demonstrates that the dynamic of waste and excess is at the heart of data economies and their infrastructures.

None of this is to mention the obsolescence of digital technologies themselves, including data centres, whose internal life-cycles are measured in short years (think Theseus' ship, but with servers), and who are subject to becoming "cloud ruins" if market decisions mean that they cease to be useful within a particular location (Brodie and Velkova 2021). These life-cycles produce immense amounts of electronic waste in the form of computers, if we are looking just at data centres, but also the endless array of smart devices and consumer technologies that provide access to these increasingly naturalised systems and infrastructures (see Taffel 2023). These wasteful economies expel and accumulate both their trash and the toxic elements in the landscapes and bodies of peripheralised communities in the global south (see Gabrys 2011; Maxwell and Miller 2012), but also represent an emerging resource economy in and of themselves due to the potentially useful elements contained within (see Kama 2015). Within these durable legacies of colonial capitalism reproduced within digital economies, especially the ongoing voracious appetite for land and resources, everything becomes a source of extraction, and thus these materialities are at the centre of all digital processes of consumption – not externalities, but constituent processes. The consequences of "consuming the planet" are the detritus of consumption, the abandonment of the bodies and materials deemed "surplus," "abandoned," or "discarded" by political economies of capitalist growth (see Tadiar 2009).

Conclusions: Against the World-Eater

I want to conclude this brief chapter with two points. First, as Maxwell and Miller acknowledge in their early treatise on "greening the media" (more accurately a calling for greening media *studies*), recourses to consumer activism are not only the answer, but fall into the worst traps of media studies' focus on audiences as consumers, reproducing the "individualist fantasy of reader/audience/consumer/player autonomy – the libertarian intellectual's wet dream of music, movies, television, and everything else converging under the sign of empowered fans" (2012, 13). I agree that this is no way to do climate action, at least not the kind those facing the most extreme effects of capitalism's environmental impacts urgently need. Laurie Parsons, speaking in the very different context of fast fashion, is similarly strong in his polemic about consumer activism – in spite of the horrific forms of exploitation and pollution that occur in the production of fast fashion, the most important tactic is to organise and ensure that the productive forces dictating these economies are disputed and disrupted *across the board*, starting with the levers of power (2021). It is not about conscious consumers, it is about organising to affect direct political change and to disrupt supply chains and the processes of accumulation that, on the one hand, generate obscene wealth for some, while on the other, accumulate toxic residues among the many. While there has been much talk about e-waste and our excessive use of smart technologies, there has been less discussion about growth and accumulation as historically durable political economic circumstances of the capitalist world system (see Chapter 16).

Second, we need to perhaps re-conceive our understanding of the environmental politics of digital technologies not as necessarily the technical affordances of industrial production and consumption practices that require them, but rather as the basis of the imbalanced metabolism across so-called "nature" and capitalism as it is being re-shaped by "industry 4.0". As Liboiron argues, it is the basic process of designating environmental systems and "resources" as useful for capital that reproduces the colonial relationalities at the heart of what gets called the "climate crisis" in the first place (2021) – a crisis classified as such via an often flattened planetary responsibility that negates the culpability of European colonial capitalism and its enduring consequences. In my conception, we can understand these endurances through the heuristic of extractivism, which applies these technoscientific rationalities of planetary mastery to different ways of withdrawing resources, on the one hand, while treating landscapes, people, and materials as the necessary "waste" of these activities that sustain capital on the other. This is true whether dealing with the more familiar extractive/polluting activities of Rio Tinto or the more developed models of extraction pioneered by ostensibly green and/or digital corporations.

As Maxwell and Miller offer an olive branch to audience scholars, media scholars must also avoid buying

> into the corporate fantasy of control – the political economists arid nightmare of music, movies, television, and everything else converging under the sign of empowered firms. Those antinomies shadow the fetish of innovation that informs much discussion about media technology, while ignoring the environmental destruction and centralized power that underpin it.
> (2012: 13)

But while systems transcend the actions of individual firms and analysis must be scaled up to reflect this, there is thus still significant work to be done in connecting the power of big tech multinationals within these environmental media assemblages, and in de-emphasising the role of consumers in the expansion of these economies. Recent examples of tech workers mobilising across borders against their multinational employers for their environmental policies and complicity in genocidal regimes and activities represents hopeful futures for these types of organisation. I am referencing, for example, the 2019 lawsuit against major tech companies including Apple, Dell, Google, Microsoft, and Tesla for their use of cobalt mined by children in the Democratic Republic of the Congo, as well as the No Tech for Apartheid campaign amongst tech workers demanding Amazon and Google divest from technologies supporting the Israeli occupation of Palestinian territory, specifically Project Nimbus (Gebru n.d.) (lest we forget the devastating climate impacts of warfare and the environmental destruction of settler colonial ecocide in poisoning and cutting off lifeways of food and water). The business models of endless growth accelerated by digital technologies, along with the states and international systems that are in place to facilitate this expansion, are party to an exceedingly profane global apparatus of material violence, and we need to make more concrete analytical connection with the environmental and infrastructural substrates that support life itself at base. After all, these analytical connections can only partially describe the ecological lifeways that connect water theft at a lithium mine in the Atacama with the energy use and water pollution at a Tesla Gigafactory in Germany. These systems, woven together by imperialist supply lines, are planetary in scope and thus hard to wrap one's head around. But that is why projects and analytics that attempt to do so – whether starting with the digital systems themselves (e.g. Brevini 2022) or the sites of extraction (e.g. Arboleda 2020) – deserve the sustained critical attention of sustainability researchers.

Questions for Consideration

- How does extraction specifically offer a lens through which to understand the dynamics of over-consumption and under-development which map durable imperial relations across the global south and global north?
- What other frameworks might offer complementary paradigms to "environmental media studies" for thinking about the environmental impacts of media technologies and infrastructures?
- How can scholars work with activist campaigns to promote environmental and global justice in and beyond the classroom?

Further Reading

Goldstein, Jenny and Eric Nost, editors. 2022. *The Nature of Data: Infrastructures, Environments, Politics.* University of Nebraska Press.

Maxwell, Richard and Toby Miller. 2012. *Greening the Media.* Oxford University Press.

Parikka, Jussi. 2015. *A Geology of Media.* University of Minnesota Press.

Pasek, Anne, Cindy Lin, Zane Griffin Talley Cooper, and Cindy Lin. 2023. *Digital Energetics.* University of Minnesota Press.

References

After Oil Collective. 2022. *Solarities: Seeking Energy Justice.* University of Minnesota Press.

Arboleda, Martín. 2020. *Planetary Mine: Territories of Extraction under Late Capitalism.* Verso.

Barney, Darin. 2004. *Prometheus Wired: The Hope for Democracy in the Age of Network Technology.* University of Chicago Press.

Bresnihan, Patrick and Patrick Brodie. 2021. "New Extractive Frontiers in Ireland and Moebius Strip of Wind/Data." *Environment and Planning E: Nature and Space,* vol. 4, no. 4: 1645–1664.

———. 2023. "Data Sinks, Carbon Services: Waste, Storage, and Energy Cultures on Ireland's Peat Bogs." *New Media and Society*, vol. 25, no. 2: 361–383.
Brevini, Benedetta. 2022. *Is AI Good for the Planet?* Polity.
Bridge, Gavin. 2011. "Resource Geographies 1: Making Carbon Economies, Old and New." *Progress in Human Geography*, vol. 35, no. 6: 820–834.
Brodie, Patrick. 2023. "Data Infrastructure Studies on an Unequal Planet." *Big Data and Society*, vol. 10, no. 1: 1–14. https://doi.org/10.1177/20539517231182402.
———. 2024. "Smarter, Greener Extractivism: Digital Infrastructures and the Harnessing of New Resources." *Information, Communication and Society*, online first: 1-20. https://doi.org/10.1080/1369118X.2024.2341013.
Brodie, Patrick and Julia Velkova. 2021. "Cloud Ruins: Ericsson's Vaudreuil-Dorion Data Centre and Infrastructural Abandonment." *Information, Communication and Society*, vol. 24, no. 6: 869–885.
Carse, Ashley and David Kneas. 2019. "Unbuilt and Unfinished: The Temporalities of Infrastructure." *Environment and Society*, vol. 10, no. 1: 9–28.
Castells, Manuel. 2010. *The Rise of the Network Society*. Second edition. Wiley Blackwell.
Chagnon, Christopher W., Francesco Durante, Barry K. Gills, Sophia E. Hagolani-Albov, Saana Hokkanen, Sohvi M. J. Kangasluoma, Heidi Konttinen, Markus Kröger, William LaFleur, Ossi Ollinaho, and Marketta P. S. Vuola. 2022. "From Extractivism to Global Extractivism: The Evolution of an Organizing Concept." *The Journal of Peasant Studies*, vol. 49, no. 4: 760–792.
Chang, Alenda, Adrian Ivakhiv, and Janet Walker. 2019. "States of Media + Environment." *Media + Environment*, vol. 1, no. 1: n.p. https://doi.org/10.1525/001c.10795.
Couldry, Nick and Ulises A. Mejias. 2019. "Data Colonialism: Rethinking Big Data's Relation to the Contemporary Subject." *Television & New Media*, vol. 20, no. 4: 336–349.
Cox, Robert and Stephen Depoe. 2022. "Emergence and Growth of the Field of Environmental Communication." In *The Routledge Handbook of Environment and Communication*, edited by Anders Hansen and Robert Cox. Routledge.
Cubitt, Sean. 2005. "Distribution and Media Flows." *Cultural Politics*, vol. 1, no. 2: 193–213.
Curtin, Michael, Jennifer Holt, and Kevin Sanson, editors. 2014. *The Distribution Revolution: Conversations about the Digital Future of Film and Television*. University of California Press.
Daggett, Cara New. 2019. *The Birth of Energy: Fossil Fuels, Thermodynamics, and the Politics of Work*. Duke University Press.
Dunlap, Alex. 2021. "Renewable Energy and the War of Progress." *The Peace Chronicle: The Magazine of the Peace and Justice Studies Association*, Spring. www.peacejusticestudies.org/chronicle/9-renewable-energy-and-the-war-of-progress/.
Dunlap, Alex and Jostein Jakobsen. 2020. *The Violent Technologies of Extraction: Political ecology, critical agrarian studies and the capitalist worldeater*. Palgrave Macmillan.
Edwards, Dustin, Zane Griffin Talley Cooper, and Mél Hogan. 2024. "The Making of Critical Data Centre Studies." *Convergence* (online first): 1–18. https://doi.org/10.1177/13548565231224157.
Gabrys, Jennifer. 2011. *Digital Rubbish: A Natural History of Electronics*. University of Michigan Press.

Gago, Verónica and Sandro Mezzadra. 2018. "A Critique of the Extractive Operations of Capital: Toward an Expanded Concept of Extractivism." *Rethinking Marxism*, vol. 29, no. 4: 574–591.
Gebru, Timnit. n.d. "#Notechforapartheid." *DAIR*. Last accessed 17 January 2024. www.dair-institute.org/blog/NoTechForApartheid/.
Goldstein, Jenny and Eric Nost, editors. 2022. *The Nature of Data: Infrastructures, Environments, Politics*. University of Nebraska Press.
Gómez-Barris, Macarena. 2017. *The Extractive Zone: Social Ecologies and Decolonial Perspectives*. Duke University Press.
Hogan, Mél. 2018. "Big Data Ecologies." *Ephemera: Theory and Politics in Organisation*, vol. 18, no. 3: 631–657.
———. 2021. "The Data Center Industrial Complex." In *Saturation: An Elemental Politics*, edited by Melody Jue and Rafico Ruiz. Duke University Press.
Holt, Jennifer and Patrick Vonderau. 2015. " 'Where the Internet Lives': Data Centers as Cloud Infrastructure." In *Signal Traffic: Critical Studies of Media Infrastructures*, edited by Lisa Parks and Nicole Starosielski. University of Illinois Press.
Iheka, Cajetan. 2021. *African Ecomedia: Network Forms, Planetary Politics*. Duke University Press.
Jung, Maximilian. 2023. "Digital capitalism is a mine not a cloud: Exploring the extractivism at the root of the data economy." *Transnational Institute*, 10 February. www.tni.org/en/article/digital-capitalism-is-a-mine-not-a-cloud.
Kama, Karg. 2015. "Circling the Economy: Resource-Making and Marketization in EU Electronic Waste Policy." *Area*, vol. 47: 16–23.
Kinder, Jordan. 2023. "Ambivalence and Intensity: On the Platform Energetics of NationBuilder." In *Digital Energetics*, edited by Anne Pasek, Cindy Lin, Zane Griffin Talley Cooper, and Jordan Kinder, 96–120. University of Minnesota Press.
Lakoff, George. 2010. "Why it Matters How We Frame the Environment." *Environmental Communication*, vol. 4, no. 1: 70–81.
Larkin, Brian. 2013. "The Politics and Poetics of Infrastructure." *Annual Review of Anthropology*, vol. 42, no. 1: 327–343.
Lepawsky, Josh. 2018. *Reassembling Rubbish: Worlding Electronic Waste*. MIT Press.
Liboiron, Max. 2021. *Pollution Is Colonialism*. Duke University Press.
Mattern, Shannon. 2017. *Code and Clay, Data and Dirt: Five Thousand Years of Urban Media*. University of Minnesota Press.
Maxwell, Richard and Toby Miller. 2012. *Greening the Media*. Oxford University Press.
McGrath, Eoin, Eoin O'Donnell, and Koen Torremans. 2023. "Digging Our Way to a Just Transition." *Geological Society, London, Special Publications*, vol. 526: 175–182.
Mezzadra, Sandro and Brett Neilson. 2019. *The Politics of Operations: Excavating Contemporary Capitalism*. Duke University Press.
Mosco, Vincent. 2014. *To the Cloud: Big Data in a Turbulent World*. Routledge.
Parikka, Jussi. 2015. *A Geology of Media*. University of Minnesota Press.
Parks, Lisa, Julia Velkova, and Sander de Ridder, editors. 2023. *Media Backends: Digital Infrastructures and Sociotechnical Relations*. University of Illinois Press.
Parks, Lisa and Nicole Starosielski, editors. 2015. *Signal Traffic: Critical Studies of Media Infrastructures*. University of Illinois Press.
Parsons, Laurie. 2021. *Carbon Colonialism: How Rich Countries Export Climate Breakdown*. Manchester University Press.

Pasek, Anne. 2023. “From Atoms to Electrons: An Energy History and the Future of Computing.” In *Digital Energetics*, edited by Anne Pasek, Cindy Lin, Zane Griffin Talley Cooper, and Cindy Lin, 15–42. University of Minnesota Press.

Pasek, Anne, Cindy Lin, Zane Griffin Talley Cooper, and Cindy Lin. 2023. *Digital Energetics*. University of Minnesota Press.

Peters, John Durham. 2015. *The Marvelous Clouds: Towards a Philosophy of Elemental Media*. University of Chicago Press.

Ricaurte, Paola. 2019. “Data Epistemologies, The Coloniality of Power, and Resistance.” *Television and New Media*, vol. 20, no. 4: 350–365.

Ruiz, Rafico. 2021. *Slow Disturbance: Infrastructural Mediation on the Settler Colonial Resource Frontier*. Duke University Press.

Rust, Stephen, Salma Monani, and Sean Cubitt, editors. 2015. *Ecomedia: Key Issues*. Routledge.

Tadiar, Neferti. 2009. “Life-Times of Disposability within Global Neoliberalism.” *Social Text*, vol. 31, no. 2: 19–48.

Taffel, Sy. 2023. “AirPods and the Earth: Digital Technologies, Planned Obsolescence and the Capitalocene.” *Environment and Planning E: Nature and Space*, vol. 6, no. 1: 433–454.

Taylor, A.R.E. 2019. “Data Centres as Technological Wilderness.” *Culture Machine*, vol. 19 : 1-30. https://culturemachine.net/wp-content/uploads/2020/10/Taylor-proofs-f-ed_compressed.pdf.

Shriver-Rice, Meryl and Hunter Vaughan. 2020. “What Is Environmental Media Studies?” *Journal of Environmental Media*, vol. 1, no. 1: 3–13.

Srnicek, Nick. 2016. *Platform Capitalism*. Polity.

Starosielski, Nicole. 2015. *The Undersea Network*. Duke University Press.

———. 2019. “The Elements of Media Studies.” *Media + Environment*, vol. 1, no. 1: n.p. https://doi.org/10.1525/001c.10780.

———. 2021 “Beyond the Sun: Embedded Solarities and Agricultural Practice.” *South Atlantic Quarterly*, vol. 120, no. 1: 13–24.

Starosielski, Nicole and Janet Walker, editors. 2016. *Sustainable Media: Critical Approaches to Media and Environment*. Routledge.

Vaughan, Hunter. 2019. *Hollywood’s Dirtiest Secret: The Hidden Environmental Costs of the Movies*. Columbia University Press.

Velkova, Julia. 2016. “Data that Warms: Waste Heat, Infrastructural Convergence and the Computation Traffic Commodity.” *Big Data and Society*, vol. 3, no. 2. https://doi.org/10.1177/2053951716684144.

———. 2021. “Thermopolitics of Data: Cloud Infrastructures and Energy Futures.” *Cultural Studies*, vol. 35, no. 4-5: 663–683.

Voskoboynik, Daniel Macmillan and Diego Andreucci. 2022. “Greening Extractivism: Environmental Discourses and Resource Governance in the ‘Lithium Triangle.’” *Environment and Planning E: Nature and Space*, vol. 5, no. 2: 787–809.

Young, Liam Cole. 2017. “Innis’s Infrastructure: Dirt, Beavers, and Documents in Material Media Theory.” *Cultural Politics*, vol. 13, no. 2: 227–249.

———. 2020. “Salt: Fragments from the History of a Medium.” *Theory, Culture & Society*, vol. 37, no. 6: 135–158.

10 Consuming Knowledge

Lara Houston

Summary

- The number of digital devices is growing, yet their useful lifetimes are shortening, which accelerates negative environmental impacts.
- Arjun Appadurai and Igor Kopytoff follow the 'social life' of things, from their production through to their eventual discarding. We can use this approach to think through the barriers that prevent digital products from living longer.
- Appadurai makes a broad distinction between the 'production knowledge' that gathers around a thing during manufacturing and 'consumption knowledge' about its appropriate consumption in specific settings. Some barriers to repair result from asymmetries between these.
- Community repair organisations aim to impact consumption knowledge by giving members of the public the experience of fixing their stuff alongside a skilled volunteer.
- 'Right to Repair' campaigners in the USA and EU lobby for legal changes to compel manufacturers to share production knowledge needed for repair, including schematics, manuals, tools, and software.

Keywords: Repair; Consumption; Electronics; Right to Repair; Social Life of Things; Product Lifetimes

Introduction

Over the last few decades, consumer electronics have proliferated. As 'consumers' or 'users', we know most about these devices at the point of purchase, when we begin to weave them into our everyday lives. However, as these notoriously short-lived devices start to break down or obsolesce, we don't necessarily know how to maintain or repair them. Short product lifetimes go

DOI: 10.4324/9781003412526-11

on to contribute to an out-of-control electronic waste (e-waste) mountain, and drive greenhouse gas emissions higher.

This chapter describes key barriers that prevent us from repairing our digital stuff. We may be sophisticated users – but not necessarily skilled fixers – of our things, which have become more complex than ever before. A focus on innovation and novelty may render repair invisible in contemporary material cultures in some parts of the world, leading to difficulties even imagining repair as a pathway to extend the lives of digital things. Companies who manufacture digital devices contribute to this situation by controlling the availability of **production knowledge** that is necessary for repair, such as schematics, manuals, tools, and software. Manufacturers use a range of strategies to nudge us towards purchasing a new device, rather than making it easy to repair an older one.

However, recent years have also seen a surge in repair activism, and in this chapter, we explore two cases. Firstly, we describe the repair events that community repair organisations have developed both to serve members of the public in need of a fix, and to widen the appeal of repair. Secondly, we examine the coalitions that have formed to lobby for new 'Right to Repair' legislation in the United States of America (USA) and the European Union (EU) that seek to use legal tools to drive manufacturers to share production knowledge with users.

The Environmental Consequences of Digital Production

This chapter begins with the idea that the digital products that we use have their own social lives. This is the central insight of anthropologists Arjun Appadurai and Igor Kopytoff, who were reflecting in the late 1980s on the increasingly globalised nature of commodities, and their increasing circulation across wide geographical and cultural distances (Appadurai 1986; Kopytoff 1986). When we look at the social lives of things, we open up a temporal viewpoint into the conditions under which things are made, then consumed in people's everyday lives, and how they obsolesce, break down, and are wasted (or sometimes recycled).

Since then, huge numbers of consumer electronic 'things' have been invented and placed on the global market. We have never before lived with more digital devices. This expansion is most visible in wealthy homes in the global North, where new connected technologies such as smartphones and smart watches accompany people's bodies, providing new forms of intimate data. These homes may be newly fitted with connected devices – including smart doorbells, speakers, and thermostats and contain leisure electronics – from TVs to gaming consoles and connected toys. However, just as the number of digital products is increasing, their useful lifetimes are also getting shorter (Bakker et al. 2014).

The social life of things framing helps us to make the environmental consequences of this digital proliferation more visible. In her book *Digital*

Rubbish, Jennifer Gabrys takes us on a tour through the most polluted sites of Silicon Valley, the famed centre for computing and technological innovation in the USA. The production of microchips for digital products has left an accumulation of toxic chemicals in the area's soils, such as the known carcinogen trichloroethylene (Gabrys 2011 p. 2). Although the microchips made there have long since fallen out of use, they have left toxic legacies that continue to be felt today. In addition to issues with toxic contamination, the global manufacturing of Information and Communications Technologies (ICTs) alone were estimated to cause 580 million metric tons of greenhouse gases emissions (Singh and Ogunseitan 2022), fuelling climate breakdown. Estimates of the global emissions from all of the life stages of ICTs are as high as 2.1–3.9% (Freitag et al. 2021) and set to increase.

We encounter a similar story when turning from the manufacture of digital devices to their endings. The global e-waste mountain is estimated at 53.6 million metric tons (an all-time high) and is growing at almost two million metric tons per year (Forti et al. 2020 p. 14). A fraction of this—17.4%—has been documented as recycled (ibid.) or more accurately 'downcycled,' since shredding devices inevitably generates lower quality materials. The geography of waste is incredibly uneven, and marginalised bodies (often in the global South) tend to bear the greatest burden. Chemicals contamination can cause severe health consequences for workers involved in dismantling e-waste, while local soils and waterways are contaminated through the burning and burying of discards (Forti et al. 2020).

The social lives of things framing illuminates the stark contrasts between the short lives of digital products and the toxic legacies of production and e-waste discarding that persist even across intergenerational timelines. It invites us to consider what needs to change, in order to move from short-term consumption of devices to longer-lived connections with our digital things.

Under What Conditions Do Digital Things Fail?

Although products are mass manufactured under (relatively) standardised conditions, digital things end their useful lives idiosyncratically, as they are woven into people's everyday routines. They are 'continually evolving, positioned within and affected by an ongoing flow of consumer practice, as well as enabling of practices' (Gregson et al. 2009: 250). What follows from this observation, is that whether things 'work' or not is also a question of everyday (social and material) happenings in a particular situation. As Law and Singleton observe, 'for something to work takes work: a performance' (Law and Singleton 2000: 771). The idea of a social life of things helps us to see these performances as contingent: as inevitably subject to change across time, as they come 'unstuck' for a variety of reasons (ibid).

This perspective helps us to go further than the materialist binary of working versus broken, and to explore the quality of relationships between people and things. Although the lives of devices do sometimes end abruptly—as anyone who has dropped their mobile phone down the toilet will surely know—survey research with a group of global Northerners showed that 'most products were replaced while they were still performing their main function, but showing a loss in performance' (Magnier and Mugge 2022: 1). Although these things were technically working, they were no longer working for people in a particular situation.

On the one hand, people play an active role in deciding how to live with their digital things, and when the useful lives of these will end. People value their devices through an active process that intertwines functional, emotional, and social dimensions. However, this sense of value tends to wane over time (Guiltinan 2010). Research on 'satiety' suggests that we get bored with our digital stuff with repeated exposure, and that at the same time we look forward to the benefits of an updated product (Hou et al. 2020).

On the other hand, manufacturers also shape the conditions under which devices fail. Manufacturers provide short windows of software support: Apple designate their products 'vintage' after they have been off the market for five years, and 'obsolete' after seven years (MacRumors 2024). When this support is withdrawn a device's functionality is significantly impacted, since the newest applications can no longer be installed. Digital devices are also increasingly 'tethered' (Zittrain 2008) to their manufacturers, meaning that they can be remotely accessed after purchase. Examples of how this power has been misused are easy to find. In 2016, Revolv smart home hubs were remotely killed following the company's takeover by the rival firm Nest, rendering them useless (Hern 2016). The idea that manufacturers design products with an artificially shortened life span is known as premature obsolescence. Though manufacturers deny engaging in this practice, they have been fined for deliberately slowing down devices – as in 2018 when Apple and Samsung were fined by the Italian national competition authority for issuing software updates that slowed older smartphones (Gibbs 2018). Significant asymmetries come into view when considering the control that users have over their devices, in contrast to the control that manufacturers retain.

Distributions of Knowledge

These asymmetries are the central focus of this chapter. Appadurai observes that 'if we regard commodities as having "life histories" or "careers" in a meaningful sense, then it becomes useful to look at the distribution of knowledge at various points in their careers' (Appadurai 2013: 45). He makes a broad distinction between 'the knowledge (technical, social, aesthetic, and so forth) that goes into the production of the commodity; and the knowledge that goes into appropriately consuming the commodity' (Appadurai 2013: 45) in a particular setting. For digital things, production knowledge generated at the beginning of a product's life, is required in order to undertake repairs as the product ages. Therefore, the dislocation between production knowledge and consumption knowledge is a key barrier to repairing products in order to extend their lifetimes. As such, working to enable expanded access to knowledge has been a key part of repair activism.

Turning first to consumption-related knowledge and activism, our collective focus on innovation and invention places an unsustainable emphasis on the creation of digital things over their everyday use, meaning that the majority of their social lives slide out of view (Houston et al. 2016). Particularly within the global North, acts of maintenance, repair and care are 'rendered invisible under our normal modes of picturing technology' (Jackson 2014: 225). This invisibility has consequences. Survey research in Europe indicates that most people replace their electronic things while they are either working well, or have suffered a partial loss of performance (Magnier and Mugge 2022: 10). Only around a third of respondents considered repairing their smartphones, vacuum cleaners and televisions, revealing that 'a big group of individuals do not consider repairing their products at all' (ibid.) when they begin to fail, or completely break down.

However, in other parts of the world, consumption knowledge concerning the social lives of things is more expansive. The work of inventively assembling temporary connections across the seams of digital infrastructures is captured in terms such as 'gambiarra', a Portuguese word that in Brazil means 'any quick-fix solution made with whatever happens to be at hand' (Rosas 2008: 344), similar to the practice of 'jugaad' in India (Rai 2019). Gambiarra—like jugaad— is also 'a mode, modus operandi, a stratagem, a guerrilla tactic' (Rosas 2008: 351) that stands for an alternative orientation towards digital things that more readily recognises and works with the different temporal conditions of digital things and infrastructures.

Community repair events are an important form of repair activism that has directly focused on expanding the nature of consumption knowledge about digital devices. Their story begins in 2009, when Martine Postma organised the first Repair Café in Amsterdam, in the Netherlands. This was a temporary, 'pop-up' community repair event, where people were invited to bring along their broken things, to be matched with a skilled volunteer. Since 2011, the Repair Café Foundation has been helping others to organise their own Repair Café events locally. They usually take place in public or semi-public spaces such as community centres or libraries for a few hours at a time. Over 2500 Repair Cafés are now running globally, although the majority are organised in the global North. In 2012, The Restart Project began to organise pop-up repair events specifically dedicated to electronics, which has since grown to more than 600 groups in 20 countries.

At a community repair event, there's no guarantee of a fix. Instead, the owner and the volunteer work collectively through a process of enquiry. The aim is to move from an unstructured problem, towards a narrower range of possibilities that can form the basis for action. Narrative is an important way in which information is shared (Orr 1996). Owners tell stories about how both humans and machines behave in the malfunctioning situation and volunteers listen for clues.

In the case of a suspected hardware fault, the outer casing of a device is removed in order to see what's going on inside. Repair is a profoundly embodied activity, where the look, smell (and sometimes even taste) of a device interior can yield clues. Internet sources such as the open access website iFixit. com, are often used to check if the internal components look as they should. Here, owners encounter the 'micropolitical level of design' (Hertz and Parikka 2012: 425) of glued components, and heat-welded plastics, where ease of manufacture has been prioritised over ease of repair. Dealing with a more general complaint of a slow-running laptop (or other software problem) is more difficult. Volunteers can run basic checks and undertake maintenance. More often, they work around the lack of operating system support by installing the open-source operating system Linux. Of course, 'people problems' are also important sources of breakdown, and volunteers help owners to learn how to use their devices effectively (Orr 1996: 83).

Community repair events are profoundly social. They are 'not only about mending or fixing an item but also about sharing the experience with others' (Bradley and Persson 2022: 1328). Broken things cannot be dropped off as they would be in a commercial setting. Owners must participate in attempts to fix, even if that means simply watching and listening. This entails a 'balancing act between the material and social function of the Repair Cafés, which can't be disentangled, but which at the same time need to be constantly negotiated' (van der Velden 2021: 8).

The rationale for community repair is that attendees come to see repair as a viable response to a breakdown, rather than turning first to product replacement. Community repair organisations articulate their work in terms of reawakening a disappearing repair imaginary, where 'lots of people have forgotten that they can repair things themselves' (Repair Café n.d.). Through the shared experience, participants are thought to gain the confidence and skills to begin a process of repair enquiry – even if they don't necessarily gain the skills to complete the repair. Engaging in community repair 'is argued to cultivate post-consumerist values through stronger associations with the repaired objects' (Hielscher and Jaeger-Erben 2021: 1) including moral or ethical relations, potentially 'reconfiguring everyday material relations from one of use and disposal to one of care and stewardship' (Hobson 2020: 110). These are prefigurative sites where other pathways for repair are made possible, yet they need to be combined with other transformations to the consumption system.

Production Knowledge and the 'Right' to Repair

Whatever the material culture of repair in a particular place, the repair of some digital systems unavoidably relies on what Appadurai terms production knowledge. He explains that 'factories, fields, forges, mines, workshops, and most other production loci are repositories… of technical production knowledge of a highly standardized sort' (Appadurai 2013: 45). The issue today, is that the standardised knowledge of artefacts needed for repair, such as design

Figure 10.1 iFixit's Self Repair Manifesto. Licensed via Creative Commons.

schematics, product manuals, diagnostic software and software updates are often rigorously controlled by manufacturers. These artefacts are understood to be proprietary knowledge necessary for maintaining competitive advantage. They are often confined to manufacturer-authorised workshops, with independent technicians and users relying on peer-produced 'unofficial' web sources such as iFixit.com or other online forums (Houston 2019).

Repair coalitions seeking to liberate production knowledge have coalesced under the Right to Repair banner. In the USA, electronics repair service industries began organising in the early 2010s – concerned that intellectual property regimes such as copyright and patents were locking independent technicians out, providing significant advantages to manufacturer-authorised repair centres. The industry was grappling with the consequences of new laws such as the 1998 Digital Millennium Copyright Act, which had significantly strengthened the ability of manufacturers to use technological locks to protect their digital code.

During the same period, these issues were also being negotiated in the automotive industry, where independent mechanics were fighting for access to the computer systems on-board cars and other motorised vehicles. It was the independent auto industry who first introduced the 'Right to Repair' (R2R) catchphrase and pursued the strategy of bringing R2R laws to state-level legislatures. In 2012, a successful vote at a R2R referendum in Massachusetts led to a nationwide agreement with auto manufacturers, that allowed independent mechanics and drivers to buy diagnostic tools for their in-car computer systems. When the consumer electronics repair industry founded their own association in 2013, they drew on the same language, and indeed some of the same strategies.

The Repair Association includes a heterogeneous mix of repair and recycling industry representatives, consumer rights groups, community repairers, journalists, and researchers. Along the way, unexpected connections have been made with the farming community (whose equipment is increasingly sensor-enabled and data-paywalled) and medical device users, struggling to maintain life-enhancing machines. At the time of writing the campaign is enjoying surging success, as R2R laws have been passed in four states of the USA, with active campaigns in a dozen more.

In the USA, the right (i.e. the moral entitlement) to repair is anchored in product ownership. The campaign argues that 'ownership should be absolute' (The Repair Association 2024), and that 'if you can't fix it, you don't own it' (Wiens 2010). The right of fair market competition is also a central concern – the Federal Trade Commission has investigated anti-competitive and monopolistic practices in the consumer electronics industry. Taken together it is the twin rights of ownership and of fair competition that are argued to be more important than the rights of manufacturers to protect their intellectual property. R2R legislation seeks the levelling of the asymmetries between production and consumption knowledge by requiring manufacturers to share digital diagnostic tools, replacement parts, product documentation (including manuals and schematics), and in some circumstances the ability to bypass technological locks for the purposes of repair.

The Right to Repair in a Global Frame

The idea of a Right to Repair has also travelled far beyond the US, with policymakers in Canada, New Zealand/Aotearoa, and India working on proposals at the time of writing. Outside of the USA, R2R is most advanced in the EU, a group of 27 Member States that cooperate political and economically. Here—although the terminology of the 'right' to repair is the same—the moral entitlement to repair is grounded differently. In addition to a concern with consumer rights, the R2R is seen as an important way to accelerate the EU's transition to a Circular Economy. In this context, repair is understood as a strategy to make the use of materials more efficient through a hierarchy of preferred action – reuse, repair, remanufacturing, and finally, recycling.

In EU legislation, the Ecodesign Directive partially addresses R2R campaign aims, by requiring manufacturers to provide product manuals, tools and spare parts for selected product groups such as washing machines, smartphones, and tablets – but only to qualified repairers. The EU is currently also implementing a wider R2R Directive that obliges manufacturers to provide repair services for users beyond the legal guarantee period for the first time. This also closes some loopholes around the provision of spare parts, which should be priced fairly and not be subject to technological locks. However, the Right to Repair Europe coalition—of over 100 civil society and repair industry groups—were disappointed that this is not yet a 'universal' R2R law that provides repair information and spare parts to everyone.

Unlike the USA, the right to act physically on one's own purchased property is somewhat de-emphasised within EU R2R actions, as can be seen in the exclusion of users from repair information and the expansion of manufacturers' responsibilities to conduct repairs. Instead, in the EU the moral force of the 'right' to repair comes partly from the need to work collectively to mitigate the environmental damage caused by device production and use, through the central idea and metaphor of the Circular Economy. What form the 'right' to repair may take in emerging campaigns in Canada, New Zealand/Aotearoa, and India remains to be seen. However, these two examples from the USA and the EU point to the role of existing campaigns in forming new coalitions (for example the precursor of the R2R vehicles campaign) and the pragmatic fitting of repair rights to existing policy discourses and policy frameworks (around ownership and the Circular Economy transition – see Chapters 5 and 16).

Conclusions

The social life of things framing pioneered by Appadurai and Kopytoff (1986) helps us to comprehend that different bodies of knowledge gather around digital devices across their lifetimes. Appadurai makes a broad distinction between the knowledge that goes into appropriately consuming commodities (in a particular place and time) and the knowledge that goes into producing them (Appadurai 2013, p. 45). The core argument of this chapter has been to highlight the fraught power dynamics that unfold across these, and in particular to show how different forms of repair activism and advocacy have focused on tackling the asymmetries between them.

Community repair aims to extend consumption knowledge in global sites—but particularly within the global North—by opening up a shared social process of enquiry that cracks open a device's case and explores the possibility of diagnosing a fault and taking remedial action. The object biographies shared during diagnostic work, surface the rich, mutually shaping relations that we hold through co-living with things, including the emotional landscape of affection, attachment, and frustration. In some cases, community repairers seek to make the possibility of repair thinkable again for those people who would otherwise replace their product directly (without ever considering a fix). Although the number of community repair events is dwarfed by the scale and intensity of the consumption of our electronic stuff, they act prefiguratively to show us other ways of being, doing, and feeling.

At the same time, broad coalitions in the USA and the EU have won partial victories in the campaign to free production knowledge under the R2R campaign. Since production knowledge is broadly protected by the legislative frameworks of intellectual property law, R2R campaigns have also focused on legislative action, by arguing that repair is an exceptional act. However, the different moral basis for repair's exceptionality depends on how campaigners have built on existing alliances and salient social narratives, favouring ownership in the USA and sustainability in the EU. One concern is that doubling down on ownership in the USA campaign embeds individualistic approaches, while the EU's Circular Economy narrative—although limited in multiple ways—at least brings collective action on climate into view.

Appadurai's classic work on the social lives of things remains particularly salient today. Thinking about technological things in terms of their social lives helps us to avoid the myopia that ties the value of technological devices to newness at the point of production or the point of sale, and crucially it brings into view the huge environmental costs that accrue in production and disposal (even via recycling). It allows for the layering of timelines and the juxtaposition of questions of value, as the handful of years that a smartphone is used is spliced against the intergenerational timelines of toxicity that can be caused through their production and discarding.

Questions for Consideration

- What repair skills do you have? Have you ever diagnosed a problem, and attempted to fix it?
- Can you map the social life of one of your own electronic devices, from purchasing through to discarding? What needs to change at each stage, to create products with longer lifetimes?

- What do you think about the 'right to repair'? How should the rights of consumers and manufacturers be balanced?

Further Reading

Appadurai, A. (1986) 'Introduction: Commodities and the Politics of Value', in A. Appadurai (ed.) *The social life of things: commodities in cultural perspective.* 1st. ed. Cambridge: Cambridge University Press, pp. 3–63.

Houston, L. *et al.* (2016) 'Values in Repair', in *Proceedings of the 2016 CHI Conference on Human Factors in Computing Systems.* New York, NY, USA: Association for Computing Machinery (CHI '16), pp. 1403–1414.

Jackson, S.J. (2014) 'Rethinking Repair', in T. Gillespie, P.J. Boczkowski, and K.A. Foot (eds) *Media technologies: essays on communication, materiality, and society.* Cambridge, [Massachusetts] London: The MIT Press (Inside technology), pp. 221–239.

References

Appadurai, A. (1986). 'Introduction: Commodities and the Politics of Value', in Appadurai A. (ed.) *The social life of things: commodities in cultural perspective*, 1st. ed. Cambridge: Cambridge University Press, pp. 3–63.

———. (2013). *The future as cultural fact: essays on the global condition.* Politics/anthropology. London New York: Verso.

Bakker, C., Wang, F., Huisman, J., & den Hollander, M. (2014). 'Products that go round: exploring product life extension through design', *Journal of Cleaner Production*, 69: 10–6. DOI: 10.1016/j.jclepro.2014.01.028

Bradley, K., & Persson, O. (2022). 'Community repair in the circular economy – fixing more than stuff', *Local Environment*, 27/10–11: 1321–37. Routledge. DOI: 10.1080/13549839.2022.2041580

Forti, V., Baldé, C.P., Kuehr, R., & Bel, G. (2020). *The Global E-waste Monitor 2020: Qualities, flows and the circular economy potential.* Bonn, Germany; Geneva, Switzerland; Rotterdam, Netherlands: United Nations University (UNU); United Nations Institute for Training and Research (UNITAR); co-hosted SCYCLE Programme; International Telecommunication Union (ITU) and International Solid Waste Association (ISWA). Retrieved February 7, 2024, from https://ewastemonitor.info/wp-content/uploads/2020/11/GEM_2020_def_july1_low.pdf

Freitag, C., Berners-Lee, M., Widdicks, K., Knowles, B., Blair, G.S., & Friday, A. (2021). 'The real climate and transformative impact of ICT: a critique of estimates, trends, and regulations', *Patterns*, 2/9: 100340. DOI: 10.1016/j.patter.2021.100340

Gabrys, J. (2011). *Digital rubbish: a natural history of electronics.* Ann Arbor, MI: University of Michigan Press. DOI: 10.2307/j.ctv65swcp

Gibbs, S. (2018). 'Apple and Samsung fined for deliberately slowing down phones'. *The Guardian.*

Gregson, N., Metcalfe, A., & Crewe, L. (2009). 'Practices of object maintenance and repair: how consumers attend to consumer objects within the home', *Journal of Consumer Culture*, 9/2: 248–72. SAGE Publications. DOI: 10.1177/1469540509104376

Guiltinan, J. (2010). 'Consumer durables replacement decision-making: an overview and research agenda', *Marketing Letters*, 21/2: 163–74. DOI: 10.1007/s11002-009-9085-2Hern, A. (2016). 'Revolv devices bricked as Google's Nest shuts down smart home company'. *The Guardian*.

Hertz, G., & Parikka, J. (2012). 'Zombie Media: Circuit Bending Media Archaeologyinto an Art Method'. *Leonardo*, 45/5: 424–30. DOI:10.1162/LEON_a_00438.

Hielscher, S., & Jaeger-Erben, M. (2021). 'From quick fixes to repair projects: insights from a citizen science project', *Journal of Cleaner Production*, 278: 123875. DOI: 10.1016/j.jclepro.2020.123875

Hobson, K. (2020). '"Small stories of closing loops": social circularity and the everyday circular economy', *Climatic Change*, 163/1: 99–116. DOI: 10.1007/s10584-019-02480-z

Hou, C., Jo, M.-S., & Sarigöllü, E. (2020). 'Feelings of satiation as a mediator between a product's perceived value and replacement intentions', *Journal of Cleaner Production*, 258: 120637. DOI: 10.1016/j.jclepro.2020.120637

Houston, L. (2019). 'Mobile Phone Repair Knowledge in Downtown Kampala: Local and Trans-Local Circulations', in Strebel I., Bovet A., & Sormani P. (eds) *Repair work ethnographies: revisiting breakdown, relocating materiality*. Singapore: Palgrave Macmillan, pp. 129–60.

Jackson, S.J. (2014). 'Rethinking Repair', in Gillespie T., Boczkowski P.J., & Foot K.A. (eds) *Media technologies: essays on communication, materiality, and society*, Inside technology. Cambridge, [Massachusetts] London: The MIT Press, pp. 221–39.

Kopytoff, I. (1986). 'The Cultural Biography of Things: Commoditization as Process', in Appadurai A. (ed.) *The social life of things: commodities in cultural perspective*, 1st ed. Cambridge: Cambridge University Press, pp. 64–91.

Law, J., & Singleton, V. (2000). 'Performing technology's stories: on social constructivism, performance, and performativity', *Technology and Culture*, 41/4: 765–75. [The Johns Hopkins University Press, Society for the History of Technology].

MacRumors, S. (2024). 'Vintage and Obsolete Apple Products'. *MacRumors*. Retrieved February 7, 2024, from www.macrumors.com/guide/vintage-and-obsolete/

Magnier, L., & Mugge, R. (2022). 'Replaced too soon? An exploration of Western European consumers' replacement of electronic products', *Resources, Conservation and Recycling*, 185: 106448. DOI: 10.1016/j.resconrec.2022.106448

Orr, J.E. (1996). *Talking about machines: an ethnography of a modern job*. Collection on technology and work. Ithaca, NY: ILR Press.

Rai, A.S. (2019). *Jugaad time: ecologies of everyday hacking in India*. ANIMA: Critical Race Studies Otherwise. Durham, NC: Duke University Press.

Repair Café. (n.d.). 'Why a Repair Café?'. *Repair Café?* Retrieved February 7, 2024, from www.repaircafe.org/en/about/

Rosas, R. (2008). 'The Gambiarra: Considerations on a Recombinatory Technology', in Boler M., Schmidt A., Boler M., Magnan N., Renzi A., & Boler M. (eds) *Digital media and democracy*. Cambridge, MA: The MIT Press, pp. 343–54. DOI: 10.7551/mitpress/7687.003.0019

Singh, N., & Ogunseitan, O.A. (2022). 'Disentangling the worldwide web of e-waste and climate change co-benefits', *Circular Economy*, Urban Mining, 1/2: 100011. DOI: 10.1016/j.cec.2022.100011

The Repair Association. (2024). 'Our Mission and History'. *Repair.org*. Retrieved February 8, 2024, from www.repair.org/history

van der Velden, M. (2021). '"Fixing the World one thing at a time": community repair and a sustainable circular economy', *Journal of Cleaner Production*, 304: 127151. DOI: 10.1016/j.jclepro.2021.127151

Wiens, K. (2010). 'Self-Repair Manifesto'. *iFixit.* Retrieved February 7, 2024, from www.ifixit.com/News/14266/self-repair-manifesto

Zittrain, J. (2008). *The future of the Internet and how to stop it.* New Haven [Conn.]: Yale University Press.

11 Consuming Fashion

Sofi Thanhauser

Summary

- Export Processing Zones are legal entities within countries that allow foreign companies to take advantage of low labor costs.
- The garment industry relies on EPZs around the world, and the clothing trade is a full globalized one.
- The globalization of the garment trade came about in large part because of US Cold War policy.
- From 1974–2005, some of the most extreme consequences of this globalized trade were held in check by tariff agreements, but now the garment industry is unrestrained in its use of cheap labor around the world.
- This has led to serious environmental consequences, and undone the work of labor unions in the US to make garment production a decent livelihood.

Keywords: Export Processing Zone; Globalization; Tariffs; Microfiber

Introduction

In Ho Chi Minh City, in January 2019, I went shopping for some "career wear" at Zara. By "career wear" I mean something like "professional," or "business casual," but I also mean a class of garments invented for the American market by East Asian countries when tariff walls went up in the 1970s—a value-added product, geared towards the American women just then entering the workforce, that could earn more per unit than t-shirts and help exporters to recoup the losses that would come from working under a quota system. The reason for my shopping trip was as follows: I had just found out that my ruse to get into the Linh Trung Export Processing Zone by pretending to be Chris, the assistant to an invented Brazilian investor, had worked. I didn't think Chris would arrive at a business meeting in my loose faded linen skirt

DOI: 10.4324/9781003412526-12

and Birkenstocks, so I went to the Zara in the Vincom Center, a mall in the ritzy part of District I. A costume designer I had once chatted with at a party had told me that when he wanted to make a character look rich, he shopped at Zara. (This is in partly because Zara so effectively steals intellectual property, lifting graphic design elements to print on clothing items from illustrators without paying them, for instance). Not that I wanted to look rich, really. I wanted to look like somebody who wanted to look rich. I also wanted to spend 400,000 Vietnamese dong or less, about 20 US dollars.

My fiction was mostly a fiction born of necessity. I had written several emails to the management of Linh Trung that had gone un-replied to for weeks. When Tom Robinson the investor wrote, on the other hand, he received a reply on the following business day. I found a black knit dress with white panels down the sides for 399k. It was tighter than what I normally wear, maybe the kind of thing that would have appealed to me in high school. I thought it made me look commanding, or at least as commanding as a sales girl at Sephora. There was a long line at the checkout, all Vietnamese middle class, and waiting in it, I felt exuberant. I almost never buy new clothes, and it's fun. The tag on the dress said, "Join Life." Was I finally, in becoming Chris, joining life? Entering intelligibility? Was this how American women had felt in the 1970s in their brand new "career wear"? As Chris, I was going to project professional competence, power, or at least that type of power that comes from being an appendage to power. I was finally speaking a language people understood. "Investment Feasibility Study was the subject line I had settled on for the email from Tom.

The next morning, I took a cab to the Linh Trung Export Processing Zone as Chris. "We are a Brazilian clothing brand", I coached myself on the drive. "We would like to begin manufacturing in Vietnam because of opportunities created by the TPP." The Trans-Pacific Partnership (TPP) was the centerpiece of US President Barack Obama's strategic pivot to Asia, and before President Donald Trump withdrew the United States in 2017, the TPP was set to become the world's largest free trade deal, covering 40 percent of the global economy. Even without the US, it was huge. And it meant a Brazilian garment company could more easily do business in Vietnam.

"You have a meeting with Mr. Banh?" said the young woman at the front desk. In the lobby there was a fake orchid and a watercolor of a boy on a water buffalo. I nodded and smiled. She walked me up a flight of stairs and ushered me into a slightly shabby conference room with four bottled waters and a MacBook on the table. On the wall behind the table's head was a large map of Vietnam, and on the wall behind where I sat, maps showed Linh Trung 1, 2, and 3, with a detailed map of Lin Trungh 1, its companies. Each of these Lin Trunghs was what is known as an "Export Processing Zone."

Export Processing Zones trace their lineage as legal entities to the 19th century free trade zones at ports in Singapore and Hong Kong but became widely popular in the 1970s. EPZs are little duchies carved out of larger states that operate under different legal structures than the country in which they are located. These legal differences have as their goal the facilitating trade of a particular kind. They permit the duty-free import of raw materials and serve as a way to entice firms and their capital equipment into the host country. Inside the zones, these capital goods are combined with domestic labor to produce finished goods that are then sold abroad. By the mid-1980s, more than 40 EPZs existed in Asia alone, employing nearly half a million people. (Warr 1989).

Mr. Bahn arrived and took a seat across from me. He told me that some of the companies' 20-year leases were coming to an end, and he was planning to tear those buildings down and put up multi-story factories that we—we meaning Tom's fictive Brazilian clothing company—could rent by the floor. His answers to my first question, about water, electricity, and security, were straightforward: He gestured to the brochure on the table, that listed all of the zones' appurtenances. On taxes there was more to say. It used to be that EPZs in Vietnam provided a ten-year tax holiday for businesses, he said. Now, in the developed areas that was no longer true. However, in areas like where Lin Trungh 3 is located, where the government still wanted to create incentives to develop, there was a ten-year tax holiday. No matter which I selected, however, I would pay no income taxes for five years, and enjoy complete absence of export taxes. Mr. Banh assured me that yes, our company could be 100 percent foreign owned. The EPZ itself was under 50 percent Chinese ownership, he pointed out. The whole thing about export processing zones is, he explained, that you are producing a product that will not enter the Vietnamese market.

This, critics point out, is one of the problems with EPZs. Their total insulation from the host country means that they are effectively detached entities, that don't purchase local goods, or help local businesses grow. Even the economic benefit to the host country most frequently cited in favor of Export Processing Zones by their boosters—the wages paid to workers—can be largely illusory, as these wages are rarely enough to lift anyone out of poverty.

I asked Mr. Banh about labor costs. He said they were going up, but that it wasn't the Export Processing Zones fault: It was because the government kept raising the minimum wage. Minimum wage currently stood around 4 million dong a month, or 180 US dollars. The pay in a garment factory would typically only need to be a little bit above that, for an unskilled worker, for me to be competitive, he thought: Maybe 4.5 million. Although, he pointed out, the Japanese-owned electronics company in Linh Trung paid a lot more as a strategy to keep workers happy: This was another way to approach it. I asked if we would need to build worker housing. He showed me, on a map, where another company had built dormitories. There was no land available at Linh Trung 1 to build more dormitories at the moment, he said, but I could work with leasing companies offsite to help offset housing costs by, say, 20 percent. "The workers are very poor" he said. "Actually, it's funny, they can work their whole lives and not be able to buy a house, even in this area, so far away from the city center." When Mr. Banh said, "funny" his eyes looked sad.

I asked if I would need to give them medical benefits to be competitive. As if to assuage my worry about costs he said, again, "they are *very* poor. It's up to the employer. Say you pay X and they pay X + 50." Here, he used the phone on the desk to represent the competitor, and then walked his pointer and index fingers over to the higher paying job, "They will go over there. So, *you* offer to contribute towards housing costs. They come back to you." His fingers marched back over to my company. I asked to be shown the Zone and a driver pulled around with a van. We drove past the customs gate. He pointed out the Japanese precision mechanics company, Free Trend, a Hong Kong company that manufactures sports shoes for Nike and Adidas, and Upgain, another Hong Kong company that manufactures garments.

Mr. Banh revealed no sinister, sociopathic cruelty in the course of our meeting. Rather, he was doing a job that was obviously regrettable to him in its structural preconditions, acting in accordance with his training and expertise, and the law of the land. The joke was on me. I got to see how my avarice was ignited, how easy it was to fall into the role of Chris, to congratulate myself for even considering paying health care costs, to marvel at how easy it was to syphon off the labor of an entire generation of workers.

Textiles and the Creation of Export Processing Zones

In the early 1950s, the French scholar Paul Mus, who had been raised in the then-French-colony of Viet Nam, wrote the following description of the French colonial highway system:

> [The highways] slice into the rest of the country, cross the rivers, cut through the hills and expropriate the paddy fields. They lead us as if from island to island in our own world. …One instinctively understood that European motorcars could only speed non-stop through the country, between these fragments of another planet, superimposed on the traditional countryside. For that countryside had nothing to do with these other beings, nothing whatsoever.
>
> (Guillebaud and Depardon 1994: 104)

In the early 1990s, the French journalist and former Vietnam War correspondent Jean-Claude Guillebaud invoked Mus' description to describe the way the American military infrastructure had been laid down in Vietnam in the decade between 1965 and 1975. Just like the old French highway system, he wrote, it had nothing at all to do with the life of the country's people. The Export Processing Zone, like the imperial highway system and the infrastructure laid down by the American military infrastructure in Vietnam, is in but not of, the country. It acts in service to an international system in which national borders can be superseded easily.

The current state of play in the garment manufacturing industry, wherein a complex web of contracting spans continents, makes it difficult and sometimes impossible to trace the chain of custody for goods, and is a far cry from the industry standard just half a century ago. And, although it is often configured in the American imagination as an assault from abroad, the incursion of cheaply made goods from Asia into the American market was, in the case of garments, a fact explicitly engineered by the US State Department, as part of its Cold War strategy. If the US fought communism with napalm and Agent Orange in the jungles of Vietnam, it fought it with garment and textile factories elsewhere in the far East.

Case Study: Textiles and the US Cold War Policy

Following WWII, Japan was occupied by US troops under Douglass Macarthur. An immediate postwar priority was to rebuild Japanese industry, particularly its textile industry, to prevent the country from "falling" to communism. More than 80 percent of Japanese textile machinery had been wiped out by the war: Either destroyed, shipped to overseas territories, or repurposed. Japan had been a major producer of silk before the war, and at first the plan was to rebuild silk capacity. However, a new DuPont product, Nylon, had largely displaced silk as the fabric choice for silk stockings. Rayon was considered, but that would depend on costly imports of wood and coal. Ultimately the War Department settled on cotton, and US agricultural interests succeeded in persuading Congress to approve the US army's plans to finance the sale of American raw cotton to Japan. Japan would soon become the largest importer of US Cotton. In the 1953–54 season Japan took 25.7 percent of the US' total cotton exports. With a source of raw cotton secured for Japanese mills, the next challenge was to find a market for Japanese cotton textiles. In 1947 SCAP and the War Department began urging Congress to open America's own markets to Japanese textiles. For 150 years, the US had pursued a policy of trade protections that had, by the end of the war, helped create the stunning successes of American business. In the 1930s the US, like European countries with textile industries, had raised tariffs to protect their textile manufacturers. Now, for the first time in US history, tariffs on textiles and apparel were significantly reduced. In the context of containing communism, the US textile and apparel industries were to be told to simply adjust to, and find ways to compete with, these imports (Rosen 2002: 15).

Between 1954 and 1956, textile imports from Japan rose quickly, and by1956, Japanese textile shipments to the United States were at seven times their 1952 level. US cloth producers were hard hit. They faced a state-of-the-art textile industry in East Asia that had been fueled by US subsidies and foreign aid. While US foreign aid had enabled Asian mills to purchase the newest technology, 65 percent of the machinery in use by US textile producers was obsolete. Between 1947 and 1957, textile worker's wages dropped. "We are face to face with a life or death question of whether our own government will stand idly by and permit low wage competition from Japan to seriously cripple our industry" said the outgoing president of the American Cotton Manufacturers' Institute (ibid. 41, 49, 82, 84).

Japan was not the only source of competition for American cloth and clothing makers produced by US Cold War policy. The US did not occupy South Korea or Taiwan, like it did Japan, but it did engage in direct military interventions to prevent both countries from becoming communist, and then provided massive military defense funds for both countries. Between 1945 and 1958, the US provided 2.6 billion worth of economic aid to South Korea, according to a UN estimate. The US provided extensive support to authoritarian governments in South Korea and Taiwan, while economic aid also went to providing infrastructure: Paved roads, modern harbors, and electrical capacity. The authoritarian regimes supported by the US were able to bring about rapid industrialization in part by repressing labor leaders and thereby ensuring a safe investment environment. The US also channeled largescale funding into industrial revitalization in Taiwan, South Korea, Hong Kong, Malaysia, Thailand, the Philippines, Indonesia, and Singapore. This was intended to link these countries with Japan and therewith, to Western dominated trade and investment networks. Meanwhile, it was preparing for the globalization of the US apparel industry (Rosen 2002: 43–45).

At first, the Japanese imports that most concerned American manufacturers were textiles. Clothing was next. The deluge of cotton blouses from Japan began in 1947. By 1954, with the end of the Korean War, 171,000 cotton blouses were exported to the US from Japan. A year later, it was four million. By the 1960s, Hong Kong and Taiwan had also begun to produce inexpensive women's and children's clothing for export to the US Unions, and were now competing with offshore producers who could work at a fraction of US costs. The earliest cotton blouses to arrive were sold in shops for one dollar, while similar ones made in the US cost three or four dollars. Before the war, Japan had not exported clothing. Leo Ullman, the president of the Clothing Manufacturers Association, wrote in 1959:

> The Japanese consumer does not ordinarily purchase ready-made tailored clothing. The new industry has been organized by so-called American entrepreneurs who have been setting up factories in foreign countries where sweatshop conditions prevail [,] for the sole purpose of exporting such garments to the Unites States.
>
> (ibid.: 103–105)

The people most responsible for the Japanese-made clothing pouring into the US market, in other words, were not Japanese businesses, but American ones.

Japan could undersell US-made garments not only because of the US subsidies in the form of foreign aid, cheap cotton, modern technology, and annual tariff reductions. Their low price tags also came thanks to the extreme gender wage gaps in the countries where they were produced. Modern textile equipment can increase efficiency and lower costs for cloth manufacturers. In garment production, however, there is still no technology more efficient than human hands. Japan relied on a heavy gender wage gap to lower garment costs, just as US manufacturers had done from the time that the first sweatshops emerged in New York and Chicago. In Hong Kong, Taiwan, Japan, and South Korea—the countries from which a deluge of garments would begin to arrive in the U.S—low wages paid to young women was particularly important to keep prices low (ibid.: 83, 87, 117). In other words, as the US State Department created industries in East Asia and opened the US market to their products, it allowed the high **gender wage gap** overseas to erode the progress made against the wage gap by American women unionists. The International Ladies Garment Workers Union had, through hard work and in the face of often violent repression, succeeded in raising garment work

Figure 11.1 A garment factory in Vietnam.

in the US from the misery of the sweatshop into a comfortable middle-class occupation in the years after the disastrous 1911 Triangle Shirtwaist Factory fire. Now, that work was undone.

Textiles and Trade Agreements

When JFK took office, he, like those before him, thought that developing countries must be offered access to the markets of industrialized nations to promote their economic development, and for reasons of military security. In the face of rapidly increasing imports of low wage textiles and garments it became clear, however, that the US could not absorb all of these exports. Kennedy negotiated the short-term Arrangement with the General Agreement on Tariffs and Trade (GATT) nations in 1961, and the long-term arrangement the following year, creating a special trade regime to last until 1971, when negotiations for the longer-lasting **Multifiber Arrangement** began. Kennedy treated garments and textiles as a special case under GATT, not wanting to set a protectionist precedent. The import growth rate for cotton textiles and apparel was set at a maximum of 6 percent each year: Intended to allow the American textile and garment industries time to adjust to low wage competitors. Kennedy also provided tax breaks to southern textile producers to help them upgrade equipment, and established funds to provide for job training and assistance for displaced workers. The bulk of these funds went to industries with mostly male workforces like auto and steel, however, and Reagan cut these job training programs entirely in the 1980s. It was in the context of Kennedy's "compromise" moreover, that Congress was finally made to accept trade liberalization as the new policy paradigm (ibid.: 58, 73–74, 115).

Kennedy's quota regime had been set at the behest of the American Cotton Manufacturers Institute, and thus it only regulated cotton fabric and clothing made from cotton fabric. However, in the 1960s Japan's reconstituted chemical cartels had begun to increase production of human-made fibers, and by 1970 Japan was the world's second largest producer of synthetic fiber. Meanwhile, Japan became a textile supplier to apparel industries in Hong Kong, Taiwan, and South Korea, who in turn began to assemble and export clothing to US contractors, importers, and retailers. As the tariffs went forward, imports of apparel made from human-made fibers increased dramatically. This led, in turn, to manufacturers in the United States increasing their output of synthetics, often at the expense of a natural fiber producer, who tended to be less consolidated. This goes far towards explaining US fashion of the sixties and seventies. Only in 1974, with the Multifiber Arrangement negotiated by Nixon, were quotas imposed on textiles and clothes made of human-made fibers, as well as cotton (ibid.: 43, 92–93, 111–112).

The new Multifiber Arrangement had its own unintended effects. There was, as already mentioned, the invention of a new garment class called "career wear," as East Asian manufacturers began to produce products that targeted the large numbers of American women entering the labor force in the 1970s.

There was, too, the way the new quotas tended to bring even more competitors into the garment trade. Countries who had met their quota cap started outsourcing production to other countries who were new to exporting garments and so weren't yet bound by quota restrictions. For instance, the Association of Southeast Asian Nations (which includes countries like Singapore, Vietnam, and The Philippines) had no quotas and cheaper labor costs than Hong Kong, Taiwan and South Korea. Thus, producers in the latter countries began to subcontract production to the ASEAN (Association of Southeast Asian Nations) countries for export to the US. While Hong Kong, Taiwan, and South Korea remained the biggest source of US imports until the mid 1980s, ASEAN countries began to expand their own exports. By the early 1980s, more than 100 countries were exporting garments to the US market. Between 1974 and 1981, the US trade deficit in apparel reached 7 billion. Meanwhile, between 1973 and 1992, the textile and apparel industries lost 750,000 jobs: Almost half the number of jobs that had existed at the peak level of employment. Organizing became more difficult, and working conditions deteriorated (ibid.: 112–113, 117–118). Sweatshops, having disappeared for over 50 years, re-emerged.

Textiles and Economic Development

The communist 'bogeyman' that had globalized the garment trade would continue to be invoked. In the 1980s Regan declared the presence of a new communist menace emerging in the Caribbean and Central America. In addition to supporting military intervention against the left-wing insurgents, the Caribbean Basin Initiative (CBI), or as it was officially called, the **Caribbean Basin Recovery Act**, was a new trade and investment program designed to promote economic development and political stability. Just as they had in Japan and the far east, textiles and apparel were once more wielded in the name of Cold War strategy. According to the logic of the Caribbean Basin Initiative's trade agenda, the region's quasi colonial trade and investment relationship with the United States—characterized by the export of raw commodities like coffee, bananas, and bauxite—would be restructured, and an infusion of new American cash would become the basis for export-led development. Funding for the CBI was supplemented by money borrowed individually by each nation from the world's multilateral lending institutions: The International Monetary Fund, the World Bank, the Inter-American Development Bank, and the Caribbean Development Bank. Direct and indirect financial aid were both made conditional on the acceptance of privatization of government services, wage controls, elimination of energy and food subsidies, and rescheduling of the debt. The United States Agency for International Development (USAID) had been in existence since the early post-war period, funding programs to support the infrastructure and social programs of developing countries. With the Reagan administration, its mission changed. Funding was now channeled to apparel-producing Caribbean Basin Initiative countries not through their governments but through their business promotion agencies: FIDE in Honduras; CINDE in Costa Rica; FUSADES in El Salvador, and the IPC in the Dominican Republic (ibid: 118, 129, 132–133).

Meanwhile, US garment and textile interests sensed an opportunity. US textile companies who were losing their US apparel customers to East Asian countries realized that garment factories in the Caribbean basin, using US made cloth, could allow them to compete with Asia. The infrastructure constructed to support the Special Access Program for apparel made possible the development of Export Processing Zones in the Caribbean Basin Initiative countries. Building this infrastructure made the region increasingly attractive as a place to do business. Caribbean Basin Export Processing Zones made investing in the countries easy for transnationals, who could now contract for the low-wage labor of workers in places where infrastructure and private security were already in place. Reagan administration rhetoric, meanwhile, presented export apparel as an "engine of growth" or a "starter industry" (ibid.: 23, 139, 142, 148–150).

Between 1974 and 2005, the Multifiber Agreement placed limits on how many garments could enter developed countries like the US from developing ones. The agreement limited exporting countries to a concrete number of items, which incentivized the production of high-dollar value goods. Now, thanks in part to lobbying efforts by a retail industry association—the same that clamored for NAFTA, and for the preferential tariffs that turned central America into the US' garment district in the 1990s—this system was phased out between 1995 and 2005. When it ended, clothing imports increased astronomically, and the price of clothing tanked. The types of market access engendered in the Caribbean Basin Initiative became the rule, rather than the exception. For half a century, the garment industry had been gaining practice as a global, footloose enterprise, scouring the world for the lowest priced labor. Now, this practice could proceed utterly unconstrained. Thanks to Export Processing Zones, which often provide their own electricity and security guards, companies can search out the places where cheap wages exist even if they are found in violent, unstable countries with unreliable electricity. While quotas had forced exporters to try to pack value into each garment, the new system values sheer volume, with no bottom limit on quality. Clothing prices dropped in half, and American consumers began buying twice as many. This sent water withdrawals for cotton agriculture skyrocketing, not to mention the chemical inputs used in manufacturing cotton. The chemical defoliant Paraquat, developed in the same lab as Agent Orange, which rained down on the jungles of Vietnam, still rains down on fields of Texas cotton, endangering the health of the mostly non-citizen agricultural workforce.

Microfibers and Fast Fashion

Cheap garment labor incentivizes the hyper-production of cheap fabrics, which is achieved by using zones with attenuated environmental protection for bleaching, dying, treating fabric, and in using water in unsustainable ways to grow cotton, leading to desertification on a mass scale. Recently, the ultra-destructive consequences of microfiber production have come to light. In the 1990s, polyester gained popularity once more, thanks to the advent of microfiber. "Micro" was "the fashion message of the 1990s" DuPont representatives announced triumphantly, "with the company's own 'micromattique' poised to take the lead" (Schneider 1994: 5). Under five millimeters in length, and with diameters measured in one thousandths of a millimeter, microfibers are vastly more versatile in producing different fabric 'handles'. However, because the fibers are so tiny, no filter inside washing machines can catch them, and they pass through sewage into treatment plants, most of which also lack filters fine enough to catch them. Treated wastewater is then dumped into rivers or seas, bringing the plastic fibers with it. Once the tiny plastics are in the ocean, there is no way to remove them. There, they enter "the diets of marine animals and accumulate throughout the food chain", writes journalist Brian Resnick. The plastic pieces are "toxic to wildlife on their own, but they can also act like sponges, soaking up other toxins in the water" (Resnick 2019: np). A 2018 study showed microplastics in the stomachs of three quarters of fish caught at mid-ocean depths in the northwest Atlantic. Even animals in the Mariana Trench, where the Pacific Ocean sinks to its deepest reaches, have been found to be ingesting microfibers in the water. Rivers running red with dye are a dramatic symbol of the environmental toll of the garment industry. But the minuscule human-made plastics called microfibers, that are now used to make synthetic fabrics, are everywhere and totally invisible to the naked eye.

Microfibers have been key to the rise of athleisure brands like Lululemon that define youth style. Meanwhile, as the rise of fast fashion companies like Shein have brought the speed and sheer volume of new clothes imports to greater heights, there has been a tendency to blame the young for the destructive consequences. "Will Gen Z ever give up its dangerous love of fast fashion?" asked a recent Guardian headline (Kale 2021: np), while businessoffashion.com offered to explain "Why Fast Fashion Still Has Gen-Z's Heart" (Deeley 2021: np) and Vox added in their defense: "Gen Z doesn't know a world without fast fashion" (Nguyen 2021: np). A pair of Danish researchers even penned a study called "The Fast Fashion Paradox" that looked at "why the participants kept purchasing fast fashion despite their own desires to be more sustainable" (Rønholt and Overgaard 2020). Today's young people don't buy these clothes because of some complicated kink in their psychology, however: They buy them because they are for sale. The reason they are for sale is tariff policy that was architected before these young people were even born, but this profoundly affects the clothes available to them. Someone made these tariff decisions, and it wasn't Zoomers. Of course, the dry stuff of international quota regimes is probably less fun than it is to deplore the depravity of the teens and ponder the "paradox" of their failure to live up to their own values: Wanting clothes, and not wanting the earth to become unlivable in their lifetime. Both of which are relatively modest aspirations.

Questions for Further Consideration

- What political forces shape the way that clothing is manufactured today?
- Whose responsibility is it to help create a more just clothing system?
- What forces would be likely to oppose this movement?
- What strategies might be employed to show consumers the actual cost of cheap clothing?

Further Reading

Rosen, E.I. (December 2, 2002). *Making Sweatshops.* University of California Press.

Resnick, B. (2019). "More than ever, our clothes are made of plastic." *Vox,* January 11. www.vox.com/the-goods/2018/9/19/17800654/clothes-plastic-pollution-polyester-washing-machine

References

Deeley, Rachel. (2021). "Why Fast Fashion Still Has Gen-Z's Heart." October 11. Businessoffashion.com

Guillebaud, J.C. and Depardon, R. (1994). *Return to Vietnam.* trans. John Simmons. Verso.

Kale, S. (2021). "Out of style: Will Gen Z ever give up its dangerous love of fast fashion?" *Vox,* October 6. www.theguardian.com/fashion/2021/oct/06/out-of-style-will-gen-z-ever-give-up-its-dangerous-love-of-fast-fashion

Nguyen, T. (2021) "Gen Z doesn't know a world without fast fashion: Why do we expect teenagers to out-thrift major retailers?", *Vox,* July 19. www.vox.com/the-goods/2021/7/19/22535050/gen-z-relationship-fast-fashion

Resnick, B. (2019). "More than ever, our clothes are made of plastic." *Vox,* January 11. www.vox.com/the-goods/2018/9/19/17800654/clothes-plastic-pollution-polyester-washing-machine

Rønholt, N. and Overgaard, M. (2020). "An Exploratory Study: The Fast Fashion Paradox." May 30. doi:10.13140/RG.2.2.33506.15049.

Rosen, E.I. (2002). *Making Sweatshops: The Globalization of the US Apparel Industry.* 1st ed., University of California Press, 15, 29, 34–36, 39, 56.

Schneider, J. (1994). "In and Out of Polyester", *Anthropology Today,* 10(4): 2–10.

Warr, P.G. (June, 1989). "Export Processing Zones and Trade Policy", *Finance and Development,* 34(26): 34–36.

12 Consuming Tourism

Sonya Graci and Kaitlyn Washbrook

Summary

- Tourism can be the source of environmental and social impacts resulting from emissions that contribute to climate change, loss of biodiversity, water and air pollution, low and seasonal wages, cultural appropriation, and overtourism.
- Tourism can also be a force for good and can contribute to sustainable livelihoods and conservation if a regenerative tourism lens is used for development and management.
- Regenerative tourism is practiced in places like Fogo Island, Canada.

Keywords: Sustainable Tourism; Regenerative Tourism; Sustainable Livelihoods; Environmental Impacts; Ecotourism

Introduction

Tourism as an industry encompasses many smaller industries, such as transportation (airlines, moto-coaches, cruises), accommodation (hotels, hostels, inns, resorts), and ancillary services (attractions, restaurants, entertainment, retail), all of which have their own unique positive and negative impacts on the places where tourism occurs (Camilleri, 2018). Tourism is responsible for carbon emissions in the atmosphere, the depletion of freshwater resources, and degradation of land (Dodds et al, 2010; Koçak et al, 2020). Tourism's impact on communities and cultures of destinations have also become a significant concern; with anti-tourism protests occurring in world-famous destinations like Barcelona and Venice (Milano et al, 2020). There is a recognition in recent years that mass tourism has the potential to degrade a destination rapidly, contributing upwards of 10 percent to global carbon emissions (Bella, 2018; Filho et al, 2023) and leading to biodiversity loss and pollution of resources. Despite these infractions, there is opportunity to change the trajectory of the industry, not only through reducing the negative impacts and creating sustainability, but

DOI: 10.4324/9781003412526-13

by utilizing tourism to revitalize what has been taken from the destination's local culture and environment. Unlike with some consumables, the consumption of tourism does not need to stop completely, but it should be developed with the concept of regeneration in mind. This will lead to tourism being a force for the development of sustainable livelihoods.

Being a tourist, traveling to a destination, and purchasing tourism products are all facets of tourist consumption. Consuming tourism can have negative impacts on the destinations where it occurs, not only in regards to the environment but also the social impact experienced by host communities (Kim et al, 2013). This chapter will discuss the impacts caused by tourism, such as over-tourism, climate change, social impacts, and cultural misrepresentation, then look at the positive direction tourism is moving towards with concepts like sustainable livelihoods, eco-tourism, and regenerative tourism.

Introducing Tourism

The definition of a tourist is broad. A tourist as defined by Leiper as "temporary visitors staying at least 24 hours in the country whose journey can be classified under one of the following headings: A) Leisure, B) Business, C) Family, D) Mission, or E) Meeting" (1979: 393). Before talking about tourism consumption and the impacts of tourism, the basis of tourism and its encompassing definitions must be explored.

Firstly, a destination "is a physical space with or without administrative and/or analytical boundaries in which a visitor can spend an overnight" (United Nations World Tourism Organization [UNWTO]: nd). It is built up of a combination of products and services, and a collection of many smaller destinations can make up a larger destination (ibid.). For instance, the cities that make up a state or province are all destinations, but so is that state or province itself. This understanding helps paint the picture of what it means to discuss the impacts of tourism on a destination. To understand what it means to consume tourism, tourism products must first be defined. According to Smith (1994), tourism products may be conceptualized using the following five elements: A physical place where the product is being consumed, the inclusion of service by a provider, the addition of hospitality (meaning an enhanced service experience), a variety of choice within the experience, and finally, a level of required participation from the consumer. Within these conceptual restraints, booking a hike in the Swiss Alps contains several examples of tourism products. There is the physical location of the mountains, the tour guide as the provider, the inclusion of food and/or storytelling to enhance the experience, the choice between the many mountains to hike in Switzerland, and finally, the tourist needing to walk the hike themselves. The same process may be applied to many other traditionally associated tourism products like airports, hotels, restaurants, tours, attractions, and activities.

There are many types of tourism, some defined by the tourists' motivations for travel, such as VFR (visiting friends and relatives) or voluntourism. Other types are categorized by the tourism products offered, such as nature-based or ecotourism, which is defined as enjoyment of (mostly) undisturbed natural phenomena (Valentine 1992). Tourism may also be discussed in terms of its impact on the destinations, with terms such as over-tourism and regenerative tourism, which will be discussed more later in this chapter. The terms that look at tourism impact are most useful in understanding the positive and negative effects of consuming tourism.

Understanding the Impacts of Tourism

Over-Tourism

Dodds and Butler (2019) define **over-tourism** as an excessive number of tourists that result in negative impacts on a specific destination. Since tourism ranges from an economic necessity to a net-negative, where tourism creates more harm than good, over-tourism solutions are not as simple as putting a stop to travel (ibid). Seraphin et al. (2018) highlights that locals of several tourism destinations no longer see how the benefits of tourism (usually economic) outweigh the costs it has on their livelihood (Rivera et al. 2016). In combination with these definitions, the United Nations World Tourism Organization (UNWTO) highlights that over-tourism is a result of a lack of management and uncontrolled development (Duignan 2019). Dodds (2010) has indicated that Destination Marketing/Management Organizations (DMMOs) must move away from their role as solely marketing agencies and become active in the management of destinations to reduce the negative impacts of tourism. Over-tourism is not just a concept that affects local residents of the destinations, it has long term effects on the attractiveness of the destinations. An example of over-tourism is seen in Barcelona, Spain. Some attribute the origin of the term over-tourism to Barcelona, coming from the Spanish term "turismo-phobia", which translates to tourism-phobia (Milano 2018; Koens et al. 2018). Milano et al. (2020) identify that Barcelona had been plagued by growth-centric policies, which have affected the standard of living amongst local residents. Berzei et al. (2022) note the gradual increase of dissatisfaction amongst Barcelona residents. In 2017, residents ranked tourism as the largest problem in the city, above other issues, such as crime. This illustrates the deep impact over-tourism has on a destination and the degradation of livability and of the environment that is felt by residents. The degrowth activists of Barcelona reject that this problem is merely a 'fear of tourism', but instead an issue of social misjustice that must be rectified (Milano et al 2020). The lack of tourism management and over-tourism has created many issues in destinations around the world, including for the tourists themselves. As concluded by Dodds et al (2010), consumers care about the sustainability of the destinations they visit and degraded natural and social environments affect tourists' enjoyment in a destination.

Climate Change

As tourism emissions continue to grow, current data indicates tourism is responsible for 10 percent of global carbon emissions (Bella 2018; Filho et al 2023). When considering all facets of tourism consumption, it is no longer reasonable to only consider tourism's impact on climate change in terms of tourism transportation, that is; the impact of getting to and from the tourist destination. All aspects of tourism product consumption must be considered. For instance, Koçak et al (2020) suggests that the relationship between tourist arrivals and emissions should include the impact that an increased number of arrivals contributes to the development of tourism infrastructure like accommodations, restaurants, airports, roads, and more. Looking at the issue more narrowly, individual destinations can be greatly affected by the emissions caused by international tourists, such as in small island destinations where between 30 and 80 percent of national emissions come from the international tourists visiting the islands (Lenzen et al, 2018).

Scott (2021) calls for decarbonization in the tourism industry, stating that tourism cannot be considered sustainable while carbon emissions are above scientifically safe targets. Applying a **Resource Use Intensities** (RUI) measure of resources, Gossling and Peeters (2015) note that RUIs are higher in luxury-branded accommodations, cruise ships, aviation, and long-haul travel, indicating that these forms of travel are worse for the environment, and should be avoided where possible. At the time of study, the authors determined that tourism's impact on water, land use, energy, food, and CO2 emissions would double within 25–45 years. This is likely because modern travel's decrease in cost has increased its accessibility regardless of the implications this level of access has for the environment and climate change (Dodds and Butler 2019). Furthermore, Lenzen et al (2018) notes that when considering income levels above $40,000USD, a 10 percent increase in income creates a 13 percent increase in carbon footprint. Scott (2021) argues that climate change is a risk that affects all destinations due to tourism's inherent interconnectedness. From the climate statistics above, and the warnings from researchers such as Scott (2021), it is clear that there needs to be a change in how tourism is developed and how it is consumed.

Community Impacts

Seasonality in tourism can be described as demand and supply fluctuations. These fluctuations have many causes (Corluka 2019; Allcock 1989). There are some destinations that suffer from high variances in their seasonality, such as beach destinations that experience seasons of over-tourism and then seasons with too few tourists (Corluka 2019). Shen et al (2008) note that issues like seasonality can have a significant impact on livelihoods of the local population. In relation to concepts like mass tourism, Corluka (2019) discusses how this growth has exacerbated the impacts that seasonality has on the tourism industry (Yan and Wall 2002). Tourism businesses grow to accommodate the increased demand during peak seasons, then struggle to downsize again during the slower seasons (Corluka 2019). The seasonal nature of tourism has great impacts for local communities, especially community members who rely on income from tourism. Murphy (1985) notes that, for some businesses, the income that comes in during the (sometimes short) peak season must last until the next year's peak season. The volatile changes in demand means unreliable employment (Chung 2009).

Kim et al. (2013) highlights findings that illustrate dire negative impacts on communities, including increased begging, prostitution, gambling, and drug trafficking (Ahmed and Krohn 1992; Andereck et al 2005; Var and Kim 1989). Boissevain (1996) also offers another laundry-list of community impacts such as loss of privacy, cultural destruction, hostility due to perceived exploitation, and commodification. Furthermore, tourism broadens the infrastructure needs of a destination, therefore subjecting residents to more construction and traffic as well as an increased cost of living (Ross 1992; Craik 1995). A new challenge for communities is the rise of Airbnb, with many investors taking advantage of using property for short-term rentals, by evicting tenants to make room for tourists, as argued by Smith (2018).

Cultural Impacts

Mass tourism development does not consider the preservation of culture, but instead considers culture a commodity (Coşkun 2021). This is problematic as local communities whose culture is appropriated for the purpose of tourism see little of the economic benefits from those tourism activities (George 2010). Gertner (2019) notes several ways in which South Pacific Islander culture has been appropriated by tourists and in tourism experiences. Luaus, tiki bars and fire knife dancing, are not a part of Hawaiian traditions yet are sold to be so (McAvoy 2012). Significant impacts arise when tourism development is put ahead of cultural preservation and sensitivity, such as when thousands of Native Hawaiian bones were removed to allow for construction of the Ritz-Carlton Kapalua resort (Landgraf 2019). This happens because the authenticity of the cultural experience is not seen as important to the tourist by tourism decision-makers and therefore economic goals are placed ahead of cultural preservation (Coşkun 2021; Caton and Santos 2009). Further examples of cultural commodification come from the Cham community in Viet Nam, where authorities pressure community members to perform religious dances outside of religiously significant days specifically for tourists, which is against their tradition. Cham elders describe feeling that their religious traditions were trampled on because of this (Quang et al 2022). There is opportunity to establish the same sensitivity awareness in the context of tourism, where cultural appropriation is even more problematic since destinations may be economically reliant on tourism (Gertner 2019).

Tourism of our Future: Eco-Tourism Towards Destination Regeneration

Aiming to Create Sustainable Livelihoods

Tourism can be a tool for the development of sustainable livelihoods, which are described by Chambers and Conway as "[A livelihood] which can cope with and recover from stress and shocks, maintain or enhance its capabilities and assets, and provide sustainable livelihood opportunities for the next generation" (1992: 6). Just as tourism can have negative impacts on a community, there is opportunity to create and participate in tourism that develops sustainable livelihoods for the community. Shen et al (2008) identify tourism as a tool for poverty alleviation, and by utilizing the Sustainable Livelihood Approach, this demonstrates the possibility that tourism can create good in the communities it operates within, when developed and consumed correctly. For example, tourism in rural communities may drive economic development and poverty reduction (Hall 2004; Iorio and Corsale 2010). Ma et al (2021) found that culture can be the basis for long-term sustainable livelihoods. Impoverished, rural communities can benefit when aware of cultural protection and utilizing their cultural resources to build sustainable tourism development (Ma et al 2021). Tao and Wall consider a sustainable livelihood as that which "encourages the adoption of a broad perspective from which to examine the consequences of tourism" (2009: 97). Viewing tourism as a component of sustainable livelihood strategies, especially in rural and marginalized communities, helps us to understand approaches required to make a truly positive impact. The following section will discuss the need for sustainability in tourism.

Moving from Eco-Tourism towards Regenerative Tourism

The International Eco-Tourism Society defines **eco-tourism** as "responsible travel to natural areas that conserve the environment, sustains the wellbeing of the local people and involves interpretation and education" (2015: para.2). The focus on natural areas is problematic as the premise of responsible travel should be incorporated into all aspects of tourism. As far back as the 1990s, researchers note concerns that the eco-tourism label was 'greening' (greenwashing) nature tourism (Orams 1995; Wight 1993). Wall (1997) proposed that eco-tourism was diverting attention away from the problems associated with mass tourism and that the issues plaguing tourism planners are not the small groups of eco-conscious tourists viewing beautiful natural scenery. Though eco-tourism has acted as an important step in acknowledging the need to reduce the environmental impact tourism has, eco-tourism cannot be the future of tourism without sustainable tourism (Wall 1997).

Moving forward, a new mindset has emerged in hopes of a better tourism future. Dredge writes that regenerative tourism "seeks to ensure travel and tourism reinvest in people, places and nature and that it supports the long-term renewal and flourishing of our social-ecological systems" (2022: 271). Regenerative tourism is a holistic view that considers the interconnectedness of a destination's environment, people and visitors. The concept is designed to repay the environment and community (Hussain 2021). The most complete definition of sustainable tourism is presented by Butler (1993, 1999) as, "tourism which is developed and maintained in an area (community, environment) in such a manner and at such a scale that it remains viable over an infinite period" (1993:2). While sustainable tourism has traditionally focused on reducing harm, regenerative tourism is a new focus on creating benefits for destinations (Duxbury et al 2020; Hoxie et al 2012; Reed 2007; Du Plessis 2012). Today, as tourism has unfortunately continued to take from communities, merely developing a sustainable destination is no longer sufficient. Tourism must move towards replenishing and bringing good to the communities and destinations it has degraded.

The following case study on Fogo Island Inn in Newfoundland, Canada exemplifies how tourism can be developed regeneratively to create sustainable livelihoods in a destination.

Case Study: Fogo Island Inn

Fogo Island Inn is a social enterprise located on Fogo Island in Newfoundland, Canada. Fogo Island Inn is an example of tourism being used as a regenerative tool for a destination. One of the Inn's goals since its creation is to maximize its economic benefit for Fogo Island, which differs from traditional business goals of maximizing profit for shareholders (Shorefast, n.d). Fogo Island Inn does not have shareholders to answer to: instead it is owned by the Shorefast Organization, a registered charity that uses both philanthropy and community businesses to fund programs and initiatives that help local communities gain stake in the global economy (ibid.). The Inn reinvests all its surplus revenue into Shorefast (ibid.).

As a social enterprise, Fogo Island Inn developed a transparency tool called the Economic Nutrition Label. This label, based on the Canadian Required Food Nutrition labels, breaks down how each dollar a tourist is charged is spent. The Inn's management team believes that when given all the information, consumers will make the most informed and responsible purchase. It also helps guests understand how their purchase impacts the local community (Fogo Island Inn nd). The Economic

Nutrition Label is used at every business operated by Shorefast, broken down into what the money is paying for and where the money is going (Shorefast, n.d.). This level of transparency builds Fogo Island Inn's trust with travelers and the local community.

For Fogo Island Inn, being a social enterprise means having a 'not-just-for-profit' approach to its business. The Inn utilizes programs like the Community Host Program, where a guest is matched with a member of the community during their stay to create connection and provide an opportunity to learn. This also creates a circular relationship between the Inn and the community (Fogo Island Inn nd). Fogo Island Inn does not only take from the island; it gives back. Through focusing on environment practices when building, and sourcing locally when developing environmentally responsible dining experiences, the Inn is an example of how consciously executed tourism initiatives, with a holistic view of the destination, can be

Economic NutritionCM

fogo island inn

NIGHTLY STAY	WHERE THE MONEY GOES
Labour	**49%**
Food, Room Supplies	**12%**
Commissions, Fees	**5%**
Operations, Admin	**18%**
Sales, Marketing	**4%**
Surplus Reinvested in the community of Fogo Island	**12%**

Economic Benefit Distribution

Fogo Island	65%	Canada	19%
Newfoundland	13%	Rest of the World	3%

ECONOMIC NUTRITION is a contication trademark of Shorefast Foundation, used under license by Shorefast Social Enterprises inc.

Figure 12.1 Economic Nutrition: Fogo Island Inn.

a positive influence on the local community and destination (ibid.). When staying at the Fogo Island Inn, guests are assured that they are making a low impact on the local environment and are also made comfortable knowing their presence is welcome in the community. Every detail of the Inn has been taken into consideration to ensure the product and other outputs are net positive for the community (ibid.). For example, 80 percent of the ingredients used by the Inn's restaurant are harvested, fished, or hunted on the island, and the kitchen uses every edible part of ingredients. As another example, mattresses are made from organic materials and crafted within Canada, while guest toiletries are sourced locally in St. John's, Newfoundland (ibid.). Tourism organizations and tourism businesses are required to consider even the smallest detail when aiming for a regenerative impact. If tourism is to continue its movement away from the damage it has created in the past, it must not only grow from it, but fix it. This is the true intention of regenerative tourism, and it is exemplified beautifully by the Fogo Island Inn, which has given Fogo Island a second life.

Conclusions

Mass tourism is not only about the overwhelming number of tourists visiting the destination, but the immense environmental, economic, social, and cultural impacts perpetuated by that growth mindset. As shown through the case of Fogo Island Inn, by focusing on a regenerative model it is possible for tourism to bring positive effects to destinations. The development of sustainable livelihoods should be central to tourism planning, as it is a preventative measure to the negative community impacts that have become an inevitable result of tourism development for many destinations. It also ensures that there is a focus on the sustainable livelihoods, which create authentic tourism experiences along with protecting the resources that sustain the industry. Tourism is past the point of return in regard to the goals of eco-tourism and sustainability. Whereas these may have been solutions in the past, tourism has now reached a point where regeneration is required to move forward in a responsible and sustainable way. Tourism planners and operators must look at how they can give back what they have taken from destinations. As Fogo Island Inn and the Shorefast Organization have shown, every decision matters when building a tourism business that preserves and regenerates the community it exists in.

Questions for Consideration

- Was there ever a time when you were a tourist and felt like you could have made more environmentally conscious choices? Did you know those options were available to you? How would you make the more regenerative options known to potential travelers?
- Due to the regenerative nature of its business Fogo Island Inn charges upwards of $1,000 for a night's stay. Consider who might be impacted if all

tourism cost this much? Is it okay to "price out" demographics in the name of regeneration of destinations?

- Can you think of a time you saw a "performance" of your own culture in the name of tourism? How did it make you feel? What were the tourists' reactions?

Further Reading

Bellato, L., Frantzeskaki, N., & Nygaard, C. A. (2023). Regenerative tourism: a conceptual framework leveraging theory and practice. *Tourism Geographies, 25*(4), 1026–1046. https://doi.org/10.1080/14616688.2022.2044376

Dodds, R., & Butler, R. (2019). The phenomena of overtourism: a review. [The phenomena of overtourism]. *International Journal of Tourism Cities, 5*(4), 519–528. https://doi.org/10.1108/IJTC-06-2019-0090

Scott, D. (2021). Sustainable tourism and the grand challenge of climate change. *Sustainability, 13*(4), 1966. https://doi.org/10.3390/su13041966

References

Ahmed, Z. U., & Krohn, F. B. (1992). International tourism, marketing and quality of life in the third world: India, a case in point. *Development in Quality of Life Studies in Marketing, 4,* 150–156.

Allcock, J. B. (1989). Seasonality. In Witt, S. F. & Moutinho, L. (eds.), *Tourism Marketing and Management Handbook* (pp. 387–392). London: Prentice Hall.

Andereck, K. L., Valentine, K. M., Knopf, R. C., & Vogt, C. A. (2005). Residents' perceptions of community tourism impacts. *Annals of Tourism Research, 32*(4), 1056–1076. https://doi.org/10.1016/j.annals.2005.03.001

Bella, G., (2018). Estimating the tourism induced environmental Kuznets curve in France, *Journal of Sustainable Tourism, 26*(12), 2043–2052. https://doi.org/10.1080/09669582.2018.1529768

Berzei, E., Schwitzguébel, A. C. & Torres-Delgado, A. (2022). From success to unrest: the social impacts of tourism in Barcelona. *International Journal of Tourism Cities, 8*(3), 675–702. https://doi.org/10.1108/IJTC-05-2021-0076

Boissevain, J. (Ed.) (1996). Coping with tourists: European reactions to mass tourism, Vol. 1. New York, NY: Berghahn Books.

Butler, R. W. (1993). Tourism – an evolutionary perspective. In Nelson, J., G., Butler, R., W., & Wall, G. (eds.), *Tourism and Sustainable Development: Monitoring, Planning, Managing* (pp. 27–44). Waterloo, Ontario: University of Waterloo (Department of Geography Publication 37).

Butler, R. W. (1999). Sustainable tourism: a state-of-the-art review, *Tourism Geographies, 1*(1), 7–25. https://doi.org/10.1080/14616688990872129

Camilleri, M. A. (2018). The tourism industry: an overview. In *Travel Marketing, Tourism Economics and the Airline Product* (Chapter 1, pp. 3–27). Cham, Switzerland: Springer Nature. https://doi.org/10.1007/978-3-319-49849-2_1

Caton, K., & Santos, C. A. (2009). Images of the other: selling study abroad in a postcolonial world. *Journal of Travel Research, 48*(2), 191–204. https://doi.org/10.1177/0047287509332309

Chambers, R., & Conway, G.R. (1992). Sustainable rural livelihoods: practical concepts for the 21st century. *IDS Discussion Paper – Institute of Development Studies*. ISBN: 0 903715 58 9

Chung, J. Y. (2009), Seasonality in tourism: a review. *e-Review of Tourism Research (eRTR), 7*(5), 82–96.

Corluka, G. (2019). Tourism seasonality–an overview. *Journal of Business Paradigms, 4*(1), 21–43.

Coşkun, G. (2021), Authentic experience in tourism and commodification. *Journal of Tourism Leisure and Hospitality, 3*(2), 95–102. https://doi.org/10.48119/toleho.867086

Craik, J. (1995). Are there cultural limits to tourism?. *Journal of Sustainable Tourism, 3*(2), 87–98.

Dodds, R. (2010). Destination marketing organizations and climate change—the need for leadership and education. *Sustainability, 2*(11), 3449–3464. https://doi.org/10.3390/su2113449

Dodds, R., & Butler, R. (2019). The phenomena of overtourism: a review. [The phenomena of overtourism]. *International Journal of Tourism Cities, 5*(4), 519–528. https://doi.org/10.1108/IJTC-06-2019-0090

Dodds, R., Graci, S. R., & Holmes, M. (2010). Does the tourist care? A comparison of tourists in Koh Phi Phi, Thailand and Gili Trawangan, Indonesia. *Journal of Sustainable Tourism, 18*(2), 207–222. https://doi.org/10.1080/09669580903215162

Dredge, D. (2022). Regenerative tourism: transforming mindsets, systems and practices. *Journal of Tourism Futures, 8*(3), 269–281. https://doi.org/10.1108/JTF-01-2022-0015

Du Plessis, C. (2012). Towards a regenerative paradigm for the built environment. *Building Research & Information,* 40(1), 7–22. https://doi.org/10.1080/09613218.2012.628548

Duignan, M. (2019). *'Overtourism'? Understanding and managing urban tourism growth beyond perceptions: Cambridge case study: strategies and tactics to tackle overtourism* (pp. 34–39). United Nations World Tourism Organisation (UNWTO). https://doi.org/10.18111/9789284420070

Duxbury, N., Bakas, F. E., Vinagre de Castro, T., & Silva, S. (2020). Creative tourism development models towards sustainable and regenerative tourism. *Sustainability, 13*(1), 2. https://doi.org/10.3390/su13010002

Filho, W.,L., Ng, A.W., Sharifi, A. et al. (2023). Global tourism, climate change and energy sustainability: assessing carbon reduction mitigating measures from the aviation industry. *Sustainability Science 18*, 983–996. https://doi.org/10.1007/s11625-022-01207-x

George, E. (2010). Intangible cultural heritage, ownership, copyrights, and tourism. *International Journal of Culture, Tourism and Hospitality Research, 4*(4), 376–388. https://doi.org/10.1108/17506181011081541

Gertner, R. K. (2019). The impact of cultural appropriation on destination image, tourism, and hospitality. *Thunderbird International Business Review, 61*(6), 873–877. https://doi.org/10.1002/tie.22068

Gössling, S., & Peeters, P. (2015). Assessing tourism's global environmental impact 1900–2050. *Journal of Sustainable Tourism, 23*(5), 639–659. https://doi.org/10.1080/09669582.2015.1008500

Hall, D. (2004). Rural tourism development in southeastern Europe: Transition and the search for sustainability. *International Journal of Tourism Research, 6*(3), 165–176. https://doi.org/10.1002/jtr.482

Hoxie, C., Berkebile, R., & Todd, J. A. (2012). Stimulating regenerative development through community dialogue. *Building Research & Information, 40*(1), 65–80. https://doi.org/10.1080/09613218.2011.628546

Hussain, A. (2021). A future of tourism industry: conscious travel, destination recovery and regenerative tourism. *Journal of Sustainability and Resilience, 1*(1), 5. https://digitalcommons.usf.edu/jsr/vol1/iss1/5

Iorio, M., & Corsale, A. (2010). Rural tourism and livelihood strategies in Romania. *Journal of Rural Studies, 26*(2), 152–162. https://doi.org/10.1016/j.jrurstud.2009.10.006

Kim, K., Uysal, M., & Sirgy, M. J. (2013). How does tourism in a community impact the quality of life of community residents?. *Tourism Management, 36*, 527–540. https://doi.org/10.1016/j.tourman.2012.09.005

Koçak, E., Ulucak, R., & Ulucak, Z. Ş. (2020). The impact of tourism developments on CO2 emissions: an advanced panel data estimation. *Tourism Management Perspectives, 33*, 100611. https://doi.org/10.1016/j.tmp.2019.100611

Koens, K., Postma, A., & Papp B., (2018) Is overtourism overused? Understanding the impact of tourism in a city context. *Sustainability, 10*(12), 4384. https://doi.org/10.3390/su10124384

Landgraf, K., (2019). Ponoiwi. In Aikau, H., K., & Gonzalez, V., V. (Eds.), *Detours: A Decolonial Guide to Hawai'i*. United Kingdom: Duke University Press. https://doi.org/10.1215/9781478007203

Leiper, N. (1979). The framework of tourism: towards a definition of tourism, tourist, and the tourist industry. *Annals of Tourism Research, 6*(4), 390–407. https://doi.org/10.1016/0160-7383(79)90003-3

Lenzen, M., Sun, YY., Faturay, F. et al. (2018) The carbon footprint of global tourism. *Nature Climate Change 8*, 522–528. https://doi.org/10.1038/s41558-018-0141-x

Ma, X., Wang, R., Dai, M., & Ou, Y. (2021). The influence of culture on the sustainable livelihoods of households in rural tourism destinations. *Journal of Sustainable Tourism, 29*(8), 1235–1252. https://doi.org/10.1080/09669582.2020.1826497

McAvoy, A. (2012, October 14). Hawaii takes aim at inauthentic island icons. USA Today. www.usatoday.com/story/travel/destinations/2012/10/14/hawaii-tourism-grass-skirts-tiki-bars/1624825/

Milano, C. (2018). Overtourism, social unrest and tourismphobia. a controversial debate. *PASOS: Revista de Turismo y Patrimonio Cultural, 16*(3), 551–564. https://doi.org/10.25145/j.pasos.2018.16.041

Milano, C., Novelli, M., & Cheer, J. M. (2020). Overtourism and degrowth: a social movements perspective. In Fletcher, R., Mas, I., M., Romero, A., B., Blazquez-Salom, M. (Eds.), *Tourism and Degrowth* (pp. 113–131). Routledge.

Murphy, P. (1985). Tourism: a community approach. Methuen: New York and London. *Tourism Review, 6*(2), 9–10.

Orams, M. B. (1995). Towards a more desirable form of ecotourism. *Tourism management, 16*(1), 3–8. https://doi.org/10.1016/0261-5177(94)00001-Q

Quang, T. D., Noseworthy, W. B., & Paulson, D. (2022). Rising tensions: heritage-tourism development and the commodification of "Authentic" culture among the

Cham community of Vietnam. *Cogent Social Sciences, 8*(1), 2116161. https://doi.org/10.1080/23311886.2022.2116161
Reed, B. (2007). Shifting from 'sustainability 'to regeneration. *Building Research & Information, 35*(6), 674–680. https://doi.org/10.1080/09613210701475753
Rivera, M., Croes, R., & Lee, S. H. (2016). Tourism development and happiness: a residents' perspective. *Journal of Destination Marketing & Management, 5*(1), 5–15. https://doi.org/10.1016/j.jdmm.2015.04.002
Ross, G. F. (1992). Resident perceptions of the impact of tourism on an Australian city. *Journal of Travel Research, 30*(3), 13–17. https://doi.org/10.1177/004728 75920300030
Scott, D. (2021). Sustainable tourism and the grand challenge of climate change. *Sustainability, 13*(4), 1966. https://doi.org/10.3390/su13041966
Seraphin, H., Sheeran, P., & Pilato, M. (2018). Over-tourism and the fall of Venice as a destination. *Journal of Destination Marketing & Management, 9*, 374–376. https://doi.org/10.1016/j.jdmm.2018.01.011
Shen, F., Hughey, K. F., & Simmons, D. G. (2008). Connecting the sustainable livelihoods approach and tourism: a review of the literature. *Journal of Hospitality and Tourism Management, 15*(1), 19–31. https://doi.org/10.1375/jhtm.15.19
Shorefast. (n.d). *Our Work*. https://shorefast.org/our-work/
Smith, D. (2018). Renting diversity: Airbnb as the modern form of housing discrimination. *DePaul Law Review, 67*(3), 581–606. https://via.library.depaul.edu/law-rev iew/vol67/iss3/6
Smith, S. L. (1994). The tourism product. *Annals of Tourism Research, 21*(3), 582–595. https://doi.org/10.1016/0160-7383(94)90121-X
Tao, T. C., & Wall, G. (2009). Tourism as a sustainable livelihood strategy. *Tourism management, 30*(1), 90–98. https://doi.org/10.1016/j.tourman.2008.03.009
TIES Announces Ecotourism Principles Revision. (January, 2015). The International Ecotourism Society. https://ecotourism.org/news/ties-announces-ecotourism-pri nciples-revision/
Valentine, P. (1992). Review: nature-based tourism. In Weiler, B., & Hall, M., C., (Eds.), *Special Interest Tourism* (pp.105–127). Belhaven Press.
Var, T., & Kim, Y. (1989). Measurement and findings on the tourism impact. unpublished paper, College Station (TX, USA), Texas A&M University, Department of Recreation, Park and Tourism Sciences.
Wall, G. (1997). Is ecotourism sustainable?. *Environmental Management, 21*(4), 483–491. https://doi.org/10.1007/s002679900044
Wight, P. (1993). Ecotourism: ethics or eco-sell?. *Journal of Travel Research, 31*(3), 3–9. https://doi.org/10.1177/004728759303100301
Yan, M., & Wall, G. (2002). Disaggregating visitor flows: the example of China. *Tourism Analysis, 7*(3-4), 191–205. https://doi.org/10.3727/108354203108750049

13 Consuming Green

Marta Massi and Terry Beckman

Summary

- Consumers purchase green products for a variety of reasons. They may be seeking personal benefits, such as improved health from consuming organic foods, or they may derive a sense of altruistic satisfaction from contributing to societal well-being.
- Despite their expressed interest in green products, many consumers do not follow through with purchases. Remarkably, research has yet to fully explain the eco-gap between green consumer attitudes and behaviors, often resulting in a disconnect between intentions and the actual purchase of green products.
- This chapter identifies the key barriers to green consumption and provides a framework with solutions that managers can employ to promote green consumption.

Keywords: Eco-Gap; Green Consumption Barriers; Green Consumers; Greenwashing; Green Marketing

Introduction

In an era marked by escalating ecological and societal challenges, the call for green products and sustainable choices has never been louder among consumers (Reddy et al., 2023). The surge in consumer interest extends to a wide array of eco-conscious products, spanning from organic foods to energy-efficient appliances, electric vehicles, and sustainable clothing (First Insight, 2022). A compelling testament to this shift can be found in the Deloitte's ConsumerSignals report (Pieters et al., 2023), which revealed that approximately 46 percent of consumers across the 23 surveyed nations made green purchases in April 2023. Furthermore, this trend transcends generational boundaries, as Baby Boomers to Gen Z cohorts declare a willingness to invest

DOI: 10.4324/9781003412526-14

more in green products, with 90 percent of Gen X consumers open to paying at least a 10 percent premium for sustainable options (First Insight, 2022).

In response to this surging demand, businesses have introduced an array of green products accompanied by advertising campaigns aimed at influencing consumer choices (Reddy et al., 2023). Nevertheless, a significant challenge persists: marketers often lack a profound understanding of the intricate drivers shaping consumers' green purchasing decisions (First Insight, 2022).

Consumers embrace **green products** for a myriad of reasons, ranging from personal advantages, such as improved health, to altruistic satisfaction derived from contributing to societal well-being (Mahasuweerachai and Suttikun, 2022). These motivations encompass adherence to social norms, fairness principles, the warm glow of benefiting others, ethical values, political engagement, and social signaling (First Insight, 2022). Moreover, green product choices are often rooted in the belief that individual actions can have a meaningful impact on environmental issues (Darnall et al., 2012). Intriguingly, these motivations often extend beyond traditional environmental concerns or altruism, encompassing desires for safety, exclusivity, affiliation, sophistication, authenticity, novelty, and opinion leadership (Massi and Ottobrini, 2020; Xu et al., 2020). In general, green consumption has been linked to self-identity and the extended self (Belk, 1988; White et al., 2019).

Despite the extensive literature exploring the motivations behind green product purchases (Zhang and Dong, 2020), there has been a notable gap in addressing the barriers hindering green consumption (Tan et al., 2016; White et al., 2019). Indeed, despite consumers' expressed interest, their uptake of green products often falls short of expectations, with green products accounting for just 17.3 percent of purchases compared to "conventionally marketed" purchases in 2022 (Kronthal-Sacco and Whelan, 2023).

This chapter addresses the barriers hindering **green consumption**, contributing to the "eco-gap", which reflects the disparity between consumer values and actual purchasing behavior (ElHaffar et al., 2020). Our objective is to categorize these barriers and offer insights into potential solutions that policymakers and businesses can harness to craft effective green marketing strategies. This chapter unfolds in two parts: first, it reviews existing literature on green consumers and the barriers they face, and second, it presents a spectrum of potential solutions. The ultimate aim is to empower policymakers, businesses, and consumers with a comprehensive understanding of the complex landscape of green consumption and actionable strategies to drive sustainable choices.

The Green Consumer

A **green consumer** is defined as one who considers their "impact on the physical environment when making product purchases" (Gleim et al., 2013: 45). Green consumers are demographically diverse, spanning various age groups, income levels, and cultural backgrounds (Mehraj et al., 2023). They are aware of environmental issues, such as climate change, deforestation, and resource depletion, and strive to reduce their ecological footprint, thus making efforts to purchase environmentally friendly or sustainable products and services (Gleim et al., 2013).

Being well informed about environmental matters, green consumers actively seek information about the products they buy, including manufacturing processes, sourcing, and lifecycle impacts (Wu and Chiang, 2023). Their knowledge often leads to skepticism toward environmental claims. With the rise of greenwashing, they tend to critically assess marketing claims, researching and verifying the environmental claims made by brands. However, when they find brands that align with their values, they often demonstrate strong brand loyalty and become brand advocates (Amoako et al., 2021).

Green consumption is not a binary concept but rather a spectrum. Individuals may exhibit these characteristics to varying degrees, and their motivations and actions can evolve over time, influenced by new information, changing circumstances, and evolving personal values. This chapter will outline the factors that counteract such motivations and present barriers to green consumption.

Barriers to Green Consumption

The existence of barriers to green consumption arises from a complex interplay of factors, originating from both individual consumer characteristics and broader systemic issues (Kollmuss and Agyeman, 2002). These barriers underscore the complexity involved in promoting green consumption and highlight the necessity for multifaceted approaches, encompassing education, policy changes, economic incentives, and cultural shifts to overcome them (Kollmuss and Agyeman, 2002). Research has indicated that these barriers to green consumption fall into four main categories: economic, informational, psychological, and sociocultural (Gleim et al., 2013; Kollmuss and Agyeman, 2002; Malodia and Bhatt, 2019). Figure 13.1 provides a visual representation of these barriers along with their corresponding solutions.

Economic Barriers

Economic barriers significantly influence consumer decision-making and behavior (Kollmuss and Agyeman, 2002). The higher price of green products compared to their counterparts presents a notable obstacle to green consumption, impacting consumer preferences (Grankvist et al., 2004). Often, green products require more costly materials and production processes, thus justifying higher prices (Majeed et al., 2021). In addition, the prevailing economic system, which is largely focused on mass production and consumption, frequently does not align with sustainability principles, leading to higher prices for green products (Velenturf and Purnell, 2021). Based on the

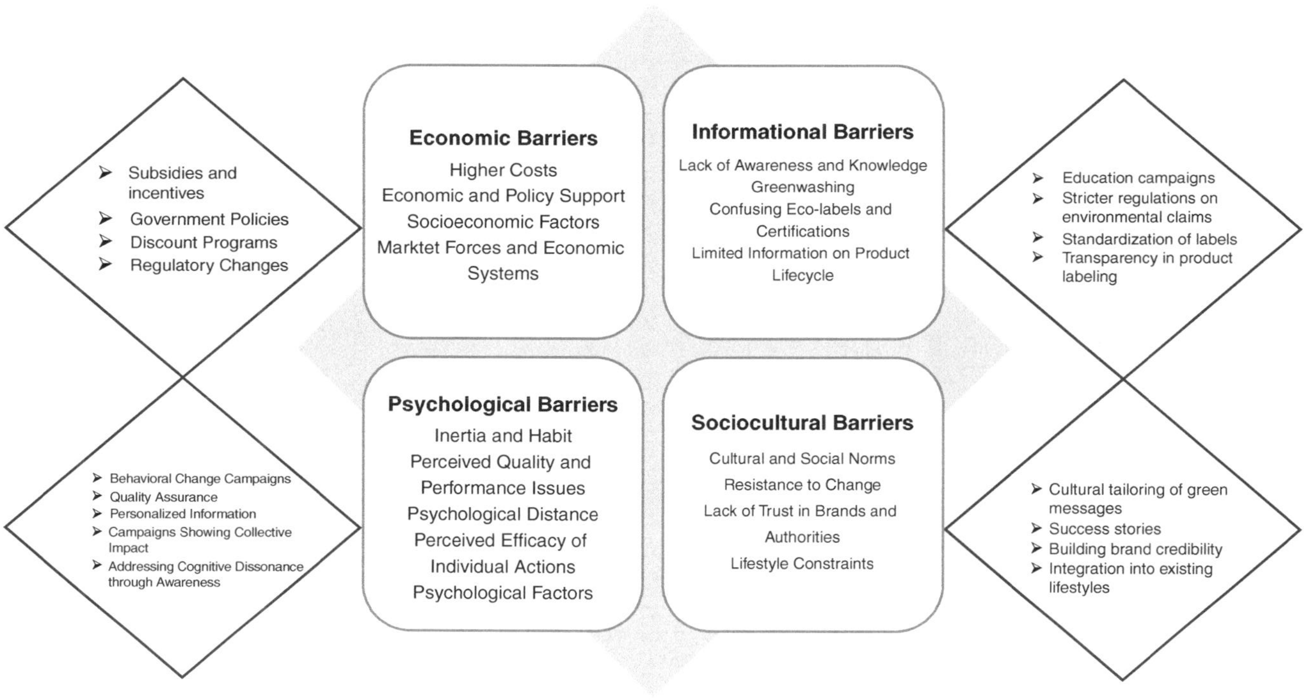

Figure 13.1 Barriers to Green Consumption: Challenges and Solutions.

Sustainable Market Share Index (Kronthal-Sacco and Whelan, 2023), green products are priced 27.6 percent higher than their conventionally marketed counterparts. This disparity in price can pose a considerable challenge, especially for lower and middle-income consumers, who might find these products unaffordable (Hough and Contarini, 2023). Socioeconomic factors play a role in determining the purchase of green products, with individuals in lower-income categories frequently giving precedence to their immediate and practical requirements over environmental concerns (Hough and Contarini, 2023). However, younger generations, such as Gen Z, are more willing to pay a premium for green products (First Insight, 2022). The premium price of green products is often justified based on factors such as the use of sustainable materials, eco-friendly production processes, and the lower economies of scale associated with their production (Yang et al., 2021). Moreover, the absence of supportive economic policies and incentives for green products in many countries further hinders green consumption (Tseng et al., 2013). Economic measures such as subsidies, tax breaks, or financial incentives play a vital role in making green products more accessible and affordable (Galarraga et al., 2011).

The prevailing market and economic systems, which frequently prioritize profitability and efficiency, can also work against green products. This focus can restrict the availability and development of such products, as environmental sustainability is sometimes compromised for economic gain (Jolink and Niesten, 2015). In many markets, green products are not as readily available as conventional products, making them less accessible to consumers (Walia et al., 2020). The limited availability of green products in certain categories, often offering fewer choices than conventional products, can deter consumers who are unwilling to compromise features, quality, or preferences (Walia et al., 2020).

Overcoming the economic barriers to green consumption necessitates a multifaceted approach that addresses both supply and demand aspects. On the supply side, developing subsidies and tax incentives for producers of green products can lower production costs, making these products more competitive in the market (Yi et al., 2022). On the demand side, educating consumers about the long-term economic and environmental benefits of green products is crucial (Sari et al., 2021).

Furthermore, promoting research and development in sustainable technologies is essential. Advancements in this area can lead to reductions in production costs, making green products more affordable, which can result in the introduction of discount programs for low-income consumers and a wider range of products to suit different budgets (Maksimovic, 2018). Finally, encouraging changes in market and economic systems to prioritize sustainability is key. This could involve regulatory changes and the promotion of corporate social responsibility initiatives.

Informational Barriers

Informational barriers significantly impede green consumption due not only to a lack of awareness and knowledge of consumers but also to information overload (White et al., 2019). As Young et al. (2010) noted, many consumers are not adequately informed about the environmental impact of their consumption choices or the advantages of green products. This knowledge gap can lead to diminished interest in or motivation to adopt sustainable consumption practices (Young et al., 2010). Gleim et al. (2013) further emphasized this issue, pointing out that many consumers are not aware of the true environmental impacts of their purchases or the benefits of green consumption and often struggle to discern genuinely green products from those that are not due to misleading or complex information.

Misleading environmental information, or **greenwashing**, further complicates this scenario. Delmas and Burbano (2011) described how firms often engage in greenwashing by making misleading or overstated claims about their products' environmental attributes. This misinformation can mislead consumers into supporting unsustainable practices and erode trust in genuinely sustainable products. A notable example is the "Volkswagen Dieselgate" case.

Case Study: Volkswagen Dieselgate

Volkswagen, a prominent brand in the automotive industry, has actively engaged in Corporate Social Responsibility (CSR) efforts, including establishing a CSR-focused communications team and embracing sustainability reporting (Zhang et al., 2021). Despite these efforts, the company faced a major setback in 2015 with the "Volkswagen Dieselgate" scandal, when it was found using "defeat devices" in its diesel engines, altering emissions data to falsely meet environmental standards during tests, while the vehicles emitted pollutants well above legal limits in normal conditions. This act of portraying diesel vehicles as greener than they were led to accusations of greenwashing (Siano et al., 2017). The scandal resulted in several legal and financial consequences for Volkswagen, including criminal charges, substantial fines, and extensive compensation settlements. By making false claims about the environmental attributes of their products, companies can create an informational barrier for consumers. This misinformation may, indeed, lead consumers to unwittingly support unsustainable practices, and it can also undermine trust in products that are genuinely sustainable.

The abundance of confusing eco-labels and certifications can also exacerbate this challenge (D'Souza et al., 2007). The plethora of labels and certifications, originally intended to decrease information asymmetry, can paradoxically overwhelm consumers, making it challenging for them to make informed choices regarding green products (Chen et al., 2023). In addition, the lack of comprehensive information on the product lifecycle presents another significant barrier. Consumers often lack detailed information about the complete lifecycle of products, including aspects of production, usage, and disposal (Diaz et al., 2021). This lack of transparency hinders their ability to assess the full environmental impact of products.

Overcoming the informational barriers hindering green consumption requires the implementation of several strategic initiatives. First, educational campaigns and initiatives play a pivotal role in enhancing consumer awareness and knowledge (Sari et al., 2021). By informing consumers about the benefits of green products and their positive environmental impact, these campaigns can stimulate interest and encourage sustainable purchasing decisions. Second, the enforcement of stricter regulations and standards for environmental claims is essential to combat greenwashing (Yang et al., 2020). Such measures ensure that consumers receive accurate and reliable information, fostering trust and confidence in green products. Third, simplifying and standardizing eco-labels is crucial (Ní Choisdealbha and Lunn, 2020). This approach would help make eco-labels more understandable and meaningful, aiding consumers in making informed choices without confusion or ambiguity.

In addition, increasing transparency in product labelling is vital (Reimers and Hoffmann, 2019). Providing detailed information about price and environmental impact throughout a product's lifecycle, from production to disposal, enables consumers to grasp the full extent of their consumption choices.

By effectively addressing these informational barriers through a combination of education, regulation, and transparency, consumers can be better equipped to make informed and sustainable choices, which is essential for the promotion of green consumption.

Psychological Barriers

Overcoming psychological barriers to green consumption is a multifaceted challenge that is deeply rooted in inertia, habit, perceived product quality, psychological distance, and the perceived efficacy of individual actions. Inertia and habit play a crucial role, as established routines and the comfort of familiar brands often impede the shift toward more sustainable choices. Psychological reactance can arise in green consumption, where consumers might feel that their freedom to choose is constrained, thus inadvertently increasing their desire for non-green products (Hinsch et al., 2021). This resistance to change is not only about convenience but also involves a deep-seated adherence to established lifestyles, as noted by Whitmarsh and O'Neill (2010) in their exploration of how personal identity and habits influence environmental behavior. Adding to this complexity are perceived quality and performance issues. As Gleim et al. (2013) pointed out, many consumers believe that green products are less effective or of lower quality than traditional products, a perception that significantly hinders their willingness to try and purchase these products.

Psychological distance further complicates matters. The abstract nature of environmental issues often diminishes the urgency and relevance of adopting green behaviors (Gifford and Nilsson, 2014). This detachment makes the consequences of non-sustainable consumption seem less immediate, thus reducing the motivation for change. Finally, the perceived efficacy of individual actions, or lack thereof, plays a role. As highlighted by Truelove et al. (2014), many individuals believe their actions have a negligible environmental impact, leading to apathy and reduced motivation to engage in green consumption.

Addressing the psychological barriers to green consumption necessitates a comprehensive approach that includes conducting behavioral change campaigns, enhancing perceived effectiveness, making environmental impacts more tangible, and empowering individual action. Conducting behavioral change campaigns that leverage social marketing techniques can be instrumental in altering established habits and fostering the trial of green products (Ottman, 2017). These campaigns can utilize a mix of educational content, motivational messages, and incentives to shift consumer attitudes and behaviors toward sustainability. Enhancing the perceived effectiveness of green products is another crucial strategy. By demonstrating their quality and performance through trials and guarantees and showcasing positive customer testimonials, consumer confidence in these products can be bolstered.

In addition, making the environmental impacts of products more tangible is essential. This can be achieved by using vivid messaging and relatable local examples, thereby reducing the psychological distance, and making the consequences of environmental issues feel more immediate and personal. Empowering individual actions is also key. Highlighting the collective impact of individual efforts and fostering community initiatives can significantly strengthen the belief in the efficacy of personal actions toward environmental sustainability.

By implementing these strategies through targeted communication, educational efforts, and community engagement, it is possible to overcome psychological barriers and significantly enhance participation in green consumption behaviors, steering society toward a more sustainable future.

Sociocultural Barriers

Sociocultural barriers to green consumption encompass factors such as cultural attitudes, social norms, resistance to change, brand trust, and lifestyle constraints, all of which significantly shape consumer behavior (Wiederhold and Martinez, 2018). Cultural and social norms have a substantial influence on consumer preferences (Tan et al., 2016). In some cultures or communities where environmental responsibility is not emphasized, green practices may not be prevalent, often deterring individuals from green consumption due to the desire to conform to social expectations. In addition, resistance to change, a common sociocultural barrier identified by Steg and Vlek (2009), shows why people often prefer familiar products and brands, even if they are less environmentally friendly, due to their comfort with the status quo.

Moreover, distrust in companies and regulatory authorities (Connolly and Prothero, 2008) can lead to skepticism about the sustainability of products, exacerbated by past instances of misleading claims and greenwashing. Lifestyle constraints also play a crucial role in green consumption. Daily routines and local infrastructure, such as the availability of recycling facilities, can significantly impact the integration of green products into consumers' lives (Jackson, 2005).

Overcoming sociocultural barriers to green consumption requires a thoughtful and targeted approach that respects and leverages the diversity of cultural and social contexts. Key strategies include community engagement and cultural tailoring, where sustainability initiatives are developed to resonate with specific cultural values and social norms. This approach ensures that green messages are relevant and impactful within different communities. In addition, harnessing the power of social marketing, influencers can play a crucial role in establishing new social norms around green consumption. Influencers and social marketing campaigns can effectively shift perceptions and encourage wider adoption of sustainable practices.

Building brand credibility and trust is another essential strategy. Companies need to focus on transparency, honesty, and ethical practices, which are fundamental in building consumer trust and overcoming skepticism about the sustainability of products. This involves clear and honest communication about product origins, manufacturing processes, and environmental impacts. Adapting to lifestyle needs is also critical for promoting green consumption. This strategy entails offering green products and solutions that can be easily integrated into existing lifestyles, enhancing the convenience and practicality of choosing sustainable options. Improving the accessibility of these products ensures that they are viable choices for a broader range of consumers, regardless of their current lifestyles or habits.

Conclusions

In this chapter, we embarked on a journey through the intricate landscape of green consumption, uncovering a rich tapestry of economic, informational, psychological, and sociocultural barriers that shape consumer choices, nurturing the so-called "eco-gap" (ElHaffar et al., 2020). These barriers interweave and influence one another, creating a complex web that policymakers, businesses, and consumers must navigate to foster green consumption habits. Only through a coordinated effort involving individuals, communities, businesses, and governments can these barriers be effectively overcome to promote widespread green consumption. The framework presented (Figure 13.1) not only helps in categorizing the barriers but also provides a structured approach for developing strategies to overcome them.

Policymakers play a crucial role in fostering green consumption. To promote green choices among consumers, they should consider implementing a range of incentives and regulations. These include offering tax breaks or subsidies for green product manufacturers to lower production costs, thus reducing the price gap with conventional products. Furthermore, policymakers can enforce stricter regulations on environmental claims and eco-labelling to combat greenwashing. Moreover, promoting research and development in sustainable technologies can drive down production costs, leading to more affordable green products.

Businesses should align their strategies with the growing demand for green products. To attract green consumers, companies can prioritize transparency, honesty, and ethical practices in their operations. Clear communication about product origins, manufacturing processes, and environmental impacts builds consumer trust. Collaborating with social media influencers and leveraging social marketing campaigns can help create new social norms around green consumption.

Finally, consumers can make a significant impact by adopting green consumption practices. It is essential for individuals to stay informed about the benefits of green products and critically assess marketing claims to avoid falling victim to greenwashing. Consumers can prioritize purchasing green products that align with their personal values and sustainability goals, even if they come at a slightly higher price. They can also explore the potential for collective action and community initiatives to amplify the impact of individual choices. Moreover, consumers can influence their social circles by advocating for sustainable practices and sharing positive experiences with green products.

Questions for Consideration

- Do the rise and availability of artificial intelligence tools provide a way for consumers to learn about green products and better detect instances of greenwashing, or can artificial intelligence guide consumers toward green products and help them avoid non-green products?
- Could social media influencers make an impact on the area of green consumption?
- Much of the onus of green consumption is put on consumers, policymakers, and green producers but the role of other producers is often omitted. There are indirect costs to production that regulators could allocate to companies, ensuring a neutral impact on the environment. This could reduce the gap in prices between non-green and green products. Would this gap reduction be enough to encourage green consumption in a significant way?
- In the area of communication, is it possible to use labelling similar to the warnings that appear on cigarette packages, but instead of showing graphic

images of cancer on a human body, environmental impact images such as dead animals (e.g. orangutans) that result from the up- or down-stream impacts of non-green production processes can be shown?
- Is there a tipping point to persuade consumers to buy green products?

Further Reading

Berger, J. (2019). Signaling can increase consumers' willingness to pay for green products: Theoretical model and experimental evidence. *Journal of Consumer Behaviour, 18*(3), 233–246.

Emekci, S. (2019). Green consumption behaviours of consumers within the scope of TPB. *Journal of Consumer Marketing, 36*(3), 410–417.

Hamouda, M., and Aissaoui, A. (2023). Rooting for the green: Consumers and brand love. *Journal of Business Strategy, 45*(4), 275–281.

Nittala, R., and Moturu, V. R. (2023). Role of pro-environmental post-purchase behavior in green consumer behavior. *Vilakshan-XIMB Journal of Management, 20*(1), 82–97.

Nygaard, A., and Silkoset, R. (2023). Sustainable development and greenwashing: How blockchain technology information can empower green consumers. *Business Strategy and the Environment, 32*(6), 3801–3813.

Pop, R. A., Săplăcan, Z., and Alt, M. A. (2020). Social media goes green—The impact of social media on green cosmetics purchase motivation and intention. *Information, 11*(9), 447.

References

Amoako, G. K., Doe, J. K., and Dzogbenuku, R. K. (2021). Perceived firm ethicality and brand loyalty: The mediating role of corporate social responsibility and perceived green marketing. *Society and Business Review, 16*(3), 398–419.

Belk, R. W. (1988). Possessions and the extended self. *Journal of Consumer Research, 15*(2), 139–168.

Chen, J., Lai, J., Chen, X., and Gao, Z. (2023). Effects of shared characteristics between eco-labels: A case for organic and local food. *International Journal of Consumer Studies, 47*(1), 285–298.

Connolly, J., and Prothero, A. (2008). Green consumption: Life-politics, risk and contradictions. *Journal of Consumer Culture, 8*(1), 117–145.

Darnall, N., Ponting, C., and Vazquez-Brust, D. A. (2012). *Why consumers buy green.* Springer Netherlands.

Delmas, M. A., and Burbano, V. C. (2011). The drivers of greenwashing. *California Management Review, 54*(1), 64–87.

Diaz, A., Schöggl, J. P., Reyes, T., and Baumgartner, R. J. (2021). Sustainable product development in a circular economy: Implications for products, actors, decision-making support and lifecycle information management. *Sustainable Production and Consumption, 26*, 1031–1045.

D'Souza, C., Taghian, M., Lamb, P., and Peretiatko, R. (2007). Green decisions: Demographics and consumer understanding of environmental labels. *International Journal of Consumer Studies, 31*(4), 371–376.

ElHaffar, G., Durif, F., and Dubé, L. (2020). Towards closing the attitude-intention-behavior gap in green consumption: A narrative review of the literature and an overview of future research directions. *Journal of Cleaner Production, 275*, 122556.

First Insight. (2022). *The sustainability disconnect between consumers and retail executives.* www.firstinsight.com/white-papers-posts/the-sustainability-disconnect-between-consumers-and-retail-executives

Galarraga, I., González-Eguino, M., and Markandya, A. (2011). The role of environmental taxation. *Fiscal Policy and the Environment, 21*(3), 164–182.

Gifford, R., and Nilsson, A. (2014). Personal and social factors that influence pro-environmental concern and behaviour: A review. *International Journal of Psychology, 49*(3), 141–157.

Gleim, M. R., Smith, J. S., Andrews, D., and Cronin Jr, J. J. (2013). Against the green: A multi-method examination of the barriers to green consumption. *Journal of Retailing, 89*(1), 44–61.

Grankvist, G., Dahlstrand, U., and Biel, A. (2004). The impact of environmental labelling on consumer preference: Negative vs. positive labels. *Journal of Consumer Policy, 27*(2), 213–230.

Hinsch, C., Tang, Y., and Lund, D. J. (2021). Compulsion and reactance: Why do some green consumers fail to follow through with planned environmental behaviors?. *Psychology and Marketing, 38*(12), 2209–2226.

Hough, G., and Contarini, A. (2023). Can low-income consumers choose food from sustainable production methods?. *Current Opinion in Food Science*, 51, 101035.

Jackson, T. (2005). *Motivating sustainable consumption: A review of evidence on consumer behaviour and behavioural change.* Sustainable Development Research Network.

Jolink, A., and Niesten, E. (2015). Sustainable development and business models of entrepreneurs in the organic food industry. *Business Strategy and the Environment, 24*(6), 386–401.

Kollmuss, A., and Agyeman, J. (2002). Mind the gap: Why do people act environmentally and what are the barriers to pro-environmental behavior?. *Environmental Education Research, 8*(3), 239–260.

Kronthal-Sacco R., and Whelan T. (2023). *Sustainable market share index.* www.stern.nyu.edu/sites/default/files/2023-09/Final%202022%20CSB%20Report%20for%20website.pdf

Mahasuweerachai, P., and Suttikun, C. (2022). The effect of green self-identity on perceived image, warm glow and willingness to purchase: A new generation's perspective towards eco-friendly restaurants. *Sustainability, 14*(17), 10539.

Majeed, T., Wahid, M. A., Alam, M. N., Mehta, Y., and Siddiquee, A. N. (2021). Friction stir welding: A sustainable manufacturing process. *Materials Today: Proceedings, 46*, 6558–6563.

Maksimovic, M. (2018). Greening the future: Green Internet of Things (G-IoT) as a key technological enabler of sustainable development. In Dey, N., Hassanien, A., Bhatt, C., Ashour, A., Satapathy, S. (eds.), *Internet of Things and Big Data Analytics Toward Next-Generation Intelligence* (Vol. 30, pp. 283–313). Springer.

Malodia, S., and Bhatt, A. S. (2019). Why should I switch off: understanding the barriers to sustainable consumption?. *Vision, 23*(2), 134–143.

Massi, M., and Ottobrini, C. F. (2020). Are businesses washing consumerism with green Ideology?: The green marketing oxymoron. In Kaufmann, H. R, and Panni,

M. F. A. K. (Eds.) *Handbook of research on contemporary consumerism* (pp. 92–109). IGI Global.

Mehraj, D., Qureshi, I. H., Singh, G., Nazir, N. A., Basheer, S., and Nissa, V. U. (2023). Green marketing practices and green consumer behavior: Demographic differences among young consumers. *Business Strategy and Development*, *6*(4), 571–585.

Ní Choisdealbha, Á., and Lunn, P. D. (2020). Green and simple: Disclosures on eco-labels interact with situational constraints in consumer choice. *Journal of Consumer Policy*, *43*(4), 699–722.

Ottman, J. (2017). *The new rules of green marketing: Strategies, tools, and inspiration for sustainable branding*. Routledge.

Pieters, L., Cascone, J., Rogers, S., and Pankratz, D. (2023, May 31). Green products come of age: Expectations of sustainable products are rising, but consumers are likely to reward brands that deliver. Deloitte Insights. https://www2.deloitte.com/us/en/insights/industry/retail-distribution/consumer-behavior-trends-state-of-the-consumer-tracker/sustainable-products-customer-expectations.html

Reddy, K. P., Chandu, V., Srilakshmi, S., Thagaram, E., Sahyaja, C., and Osei, B. (2023). Consumers perception on green marketing towards eco-friendly fast moving consumer goods. *International Journal of Engineering Business Management*, *15*, 18479790231170962.

Reimers, H., and Hoffmann, S. (2019). Transparent price labelling for sustainable products. *Marketing: ZFP–Journal of Research and Management*, *41*(H. 2), 21–36.

Sari, H., Firmanzah, F., Harahap, A. A., and Siahaan, B. C. (2021). The role of customer education: A repeated cross-sectional study. *Journal of Science and Technology Policy Management*, *12*(2), 193–214.

Siano, A., Vollero, A., Conte, F., and Amabile, S. (2017). "More than words": Expanding the taxonomy of greenwashing after the Volkswagen scandal. *Journal of Business Research*, *71*, 27–37.

Steg, L., and Vlek, C. (2009). Encouraging pro-environmental behaviour: An integrative review and research agenda. *Journal of Environmental Psychology*, *29*(3), 309–317.

Tan, L. P., Johnstone, M. L., and Yang, L. (2016). Barriers to green consumption behaviours: The roles of consumers' green perceptions. *Australasian Marketing Journal*, *24*(4), 288–299.

Truelove, H. B., Carrico, A. R., Weber, E. U., Raimi, K. T., and Vandenbergh, M. P. (2014). Positive and negative spillover of pro-environmental behavior: An integrative review and theoretical framework. *Global Environmental Change*, *29*, 127–138.

Tseng, M. L., Tan, R. R., and Siriban-Manalang, A. B. (2013). Sustainable consumption and production for Asia: Sustainability through green design and practice. *Journal of Cleaner Production*, *40*, 1–5.

Velenturf, A. P., and Purnell, P. (2021). Principles for a sustainable circular economy. *Sustainable Production and Consumption*, *27*, 1437–1457.

Walia, S. B., Kumar, H., and Negi, N. (2020). Impact of brand consciousness, perceived quality of products, price sensitivity and product availability on purchase intention towards "green" products. *International Journal of Technology Management and Sustainable Development*, *19*(1), 107–118.

White, K., Hardisty, D. J., and Habib, R. (2019). The elusive green consumer. *Harvard Business Review*, *11*(1), 124–133.

Whitmarsh, L., and O'Neill, S. (2010). Green identity, green living? The role of pro-environmental self-identity in determining consistency across diverse pro-environmental behaviours. *Journal of Environmental Psychology*, *30*(3), 305–314.

Wiederhold, M., and Martinez, L. F. (2018). Ethical consumer behaviour in Germany: The attitude-behaviour gap in the green apparel industry. *International Journal of Consumer Studies*, *42*(4), 419–429.

Wu, S. W., and Chiang, P. Y. (2023). Exploring the mediating effects of the theory of planned behavior on the relationships between environmental awareness, green advocacy, and green self-efficacy on the green word-of-mouth intention. *Sustainability*, *15*(16), 12127.

Xu, X., Hua, Y., Wang, S., and Xu, G. (2020). Determinants of consumer's intention to purchase authentic green furniture. *Resources, Conservation and Recycling*, *156*, 104721.

Yang, M., Chen, H., Long, R., Wang, Y., Hou, C., and Liu, B. (2021). Will the public pay for green products? Based on analysis of the influencing factors for Chinese's public willingness to pay a price premium for green products. *Environmental Science and Pollution Research*, *28*(43), 61408–61422.

Yang, Z., Nguyen, T. T. H., Nguyen, H. N., Nguyen, T. T. N., and Cao, T. T. (2020). Greenwashing behaviours: Causes, taxonomy and consequences based on a systematic literature review. *Journal of Business Economics and Management*, *21*(5), 1486–1507.

Yi, Y., Wang, Y., Fu, C., and Li, Y. (2022). Taxes or subsidies to promote investment in green technologies for a supply chain considering consumer preferences for green products. *Computers and Industrial Engineering*, *171*, 108371.

Young, W., Hwang, K., McDonald, S., and Oates, C. J. (2010). Sustainable consumption: Green consumer behaviour when purchasing products. *Sustainable Development*, *18*(1), 20–31.

Zhang, M., Atwal, G., and Kaiser, M. (2021). Corporate social irresponsibility and stakeholder ecosystems: The case of Volkswagen Dieselgate scandal. *Strategic Change*, *30*(1), 79–85.

Zhang, X., and Dong, F. (2020). Why do consumers make green purchase decisions? Insights from a systematic review. *International Journal of Environmental Research and Public Health*, *17*(18), 6607.

14 Consuming Preparedness

Myra J. Hird and Jacob Riha

Summary

- Preppers are people who plan for an imagined future by accumulating skills and things.
- Preppers focus on insulating themselves from future disaster rather than helping their communities.
- Preppers influence the very conditions that they then feel compelled to respond to as they intensify over-consumption (and therefore, over-production).
- Prepping is a contemporary reiteration of western consumer/trashing culture, which feeds the global neoliberal capitalist system responsible for the very apocalyptic conditions to which preppers believe they must respond.

Keywords: Preppers; Preventers; Neoliberal Capitalism; Accumulation; Inverted Quarantine; Consumers; Problem of Amplification

Introduction

Preppers are individuals who plan for an imagined apocalyptic future by accumulating survivalist skills and things.[1] Preppers distinguish themselves from 'hoarders' based on their purposeful stockpiling of things anticipated to be vital to surviving short- or long-term disaster. Not only do preppers eschew initiatives that seek to *prevent* an imagined future apocalypse, as **preventers** do, but as this chapter will detail, preppers influence the very conditions that they then feel compelled to respond to as they intensify the hegemony of over-consumption (and its rather more silent yet far bigger twin, over-production). As such, this chapter argues that the increasingly popular phenomenon of prepping is a contemporary reiteration of western consumer/trashing culture, which feeds the global neoliberal capitalist system responsible for the very

DOI: 10.4324/9781003412526-15

apocalyptic conditions to which preppers believe they must respond (see Hird and Riha 2021 for an extended version of this argument).

Si vis pacem, para bellum (If You Want Peace, Prepare for War)

During its run, the US reality TV show Doomsday Preppers featured weekly snapshots of individuals preparing for either cataclysmic natural or human-made disasters. Numerous films, some based on novels, depict human-made environmental disasters (The Day After Tomorrow, Children of Men, Mad Max, The Road, On the Beach, Threads, Miracle Mile, and Dr Strangelove); natural disasters (Sunshine and Melancholia); zombie apocalypse (World War Z); global alien invasion (War of the Worlds, Edge of Tomorrow, and Signs); robot ascension (The Terminator and I, Robot); or – yes, global viral infection (The Seventh Seal, The Omega Man, 12 Monkeys, Outbreak, and Contagion) or some combination of these. Of course, the mainstreaming of disaster and apocalypse stretches much further back in time than these films. The so-called 'first doom boom' occurred during the Cold War, as Americans in particular (but also Soviets – see Brown 2013) worried about nuclear war and its aftermath. Further back still, the Christian New Testament's 'Book of Revelation', also known as the 'Apocalypse of John', details the 'apokalypsis' or unveiling – the reckoning of all humanity with the forces of good and evil. We find variations on the end-of-days theme in other major religions such as Islam (The Hour), Judaism (Day of the Lord, War of Gog and Magog), and Hinduism (Vishnu's return to earth in the form of Kulki to destroy the forces of evil). Max Brooks, author of *The Zombie Survival Guide: Complete Protection from the Living Dead*, nicely enjoins the contemporary agnostic with the ancient religious: "If you believe you can accomplish everything by "cramming" at the eleventh hour, by all means, don't lift a finger now. But you may think twice about beginning to build your ark once it has already started raining" (2003: 159).

As Indigenous scholars and activists (ex. Watt-Cloutier 2015; Hoover 2017), environmental racism researchers (ex. Nixon 2011; Adeola 2012) and, more recently, supra-national organizations such as the Intergovernmental Panel on Climate Change (IPCC 2020) have pointed out, real apocalyptic conditions arrived hundreds of years ago for millions. The UNHCR, for instance, 'estimates that there are over 65.6 million forcibly displaced people worldwide, of whom approximately two-thirds are internally displaced and therefore unprotected by international law…[with another] 10 million stateless individuals' (UNHCR 2016 in Alexander and Sanchez 2020: 11). One third of the global human population have no electricity. Moreover, it is clear that those most responsible for climate change are not living with its already-here effects: the poorest 45 percent of human beings are responsible for just 7 percent of anthropogenic carbon emissions while the richest 7 percent create 50 percent of the world's carbon emissions (Malm and Hornborg 2014).

These past and present unnamed millions are not preppers; they are living with chronic disasters that have shifted into permanently degraded living conditions now, and not in some anticipated future (Foster 2014; Klein 2008; Mills 2018; Robbins and Moore 2013). Preppers fear a diverse range of impending disasters, from solar flares that wipe out electrical grids to terrorist attacks to peak-oil to cataclysmic floods, that more closely resemble something out of a movie rather than the already-here apocalyptic living conditions of the world's abject (Ginn 2015; Kristeva 1980; Agamben 1995; Schneider-Mayerson 2013). A series of polls taken pre-COVID-19, and summarized by Michael Mills, shows that US residents, in particular, have a host of anxieties: "[O]ver 40% of Americans fear losing a loved one to terrorism … international conflict (47.5%), economic collapse (44.4%), cyber-attacks (39.1%), a collapse of the electrical grid (35.7%) and biological warfare (41.8%)" (2018: 3). Research estimates that (pre-COVID-19) there were between three to five million Americans who identified with the prepping movement (ibid). Of course, these are vague estimates because a critical feature of the prepper is that they prepare for disaster in secret in order to prevent other people from stealing their things, a point we return to later in the chapter.

And while media and researchers report prepping as a phenomenon found in a range of countries and cultures in the globalized north, the most popular representation of the prepper is the white middle-class American man, woman and/or family because the United States is most strongly associated with the quintessential 'personality trait' of preppers: hyper-consumerism with an emphasis on buying guns and ammunition. Indeed, prepping is a consumer bonanza. There are the lazy-person's ready-made non-perishable prepping staples: for instance, TheReadyStore.com sells the READY pre-2000 Food Storage Supply Kit for a 27-year life span for US$3,683.25. Filtration and cleaning supplies may be purchased from the Berkey Light System for US$200–300. Wise Food Storage sells a one-year supply of food for two people for US$2,595 and Costco's Chef's Banquet All-Purpose Readiness Kit sells a 20-year supply of 600 meals for one person for US$149.99. Caro shipping containers may also be purchased for US$1,000 each in order to store all of these purchased products.

For the more committed prepper, there is a cornucopia of 'essential' products to purchase. Bug-out gear includes predictable things like generators, candles and hand-crank emergency radios, knives, guns, and ammunition but also less obvious things like gold and silver. The list is, by design, endless. As Gwendolyn Foster highlights, "there is a lot of money to be made out [of] prepping" (2014: 16). To wit, the revenue for some dehydrated and preserved food companies increased by as much as 708 percent in 2007/8 (Murphy 2013). There are also books to be bought: *A Complete Beginner's Guide to Prepping* (Tactical.com nd), *The Prepping Guide: SHTF Plans* (Brown nd), *The Prepper's Water Survival Guide* (Luther 2015), *When Technology Fails: A Manual for Self-Reliance, Sustainability, and Surviving the Long Emergency* (Stein 2008), *The Prepper's Blueprint* (Pennington and Luther 2014), *When*

All Hell Breaks Loose: Stuff You Need to Survive When Disaster Strikes (Lundin 2007), and many more. All in all, and before the COVID-19 pandemic, prepping was a US$500 million per year industry (Kelly 2016). This sum doesn't include Larry Hall's Survival Condo bunker, which alone cost some US$20 million (Garrett 2020). And since preppers live in a constant state of preparation, they lament that it is only their finances and space that constrain further consumption, leading preppers to use whatever space is available until, eventually, those who can afford it move to bigger houses, purchase bigger secret bunkers and/or more storage containers.

All of this consumption takes place within the context of a global **neo-liberal capitalist** system dependent on ever-increasing extraction, manufacturing, distribution, retail, consumption and, inevitably, waste. And managing all of this waste is big business: not only is haulage and disposal a multibillion-dollar industry but so is the remediation of superfund and other contaminated waste legacy sites (Hird 2021; Beckett and Keeling 2019). Indeed, the global production of waste and its contamination of human bodies, wildlife, land and water, itself constitutes one of the key dystopian futures that preppers seek to shield themselves and their loved ones from. And thus, prepping through hyper consumption accelerates the very environmental condition that they are preparing themselves for: environmental degradation through accelerating industrial and military extraction and production, and its corollary, increasingly toxic and contaminating waste polluting the environment. Like the Terminator who creates the conditions of its own existence, preppers contribute to the environmental apocalypse they are preparing for.

Case Study: The COVID-19 Pandemic

During the COVID-19 pandemic, people across the world displayed stockpiling behaviours that differed in amount and product types from their usual shopping habits (Vigdor 2020). Sales of household cleaning and disinfectant products dramatically increased since the World Health Organization declared a global health emergency. According to Statistics Canada, for instance, year-over-year sales growth of hand sanitizer, masks and various cleaning supplies reached as high as 639 percent, 404 percent and 180 percent, respectively; while paper towels and toilet paper increased by 288 percent during the same period (2020; Bedford 2020).

In the United States, the same pattern occurred: panic-induced purchasing increased sales of aerosol disinfectants (385 percent), multipurpose cleaners (148 percent) and tissue products (60 percent) (Conway 2020). Similar stockpiling of grocery items saw household spending in Canada increase by roughly 46 percent in the spring of 2020 – led most notably by rice (239 percent), dried pasta (205 percent), canned vegetables (180 percent) and flour (179 percent) (Statistics Canada 2020). Alongside this, fresh produce sales decreased by 15 percent while pre-packaged foods and frozen items – wrapped in plastics packaging – surged by 31 percent (Roe, Bender and Qi 2020). The coronavirus also caused a surge in firearm sales: gun sales in the United States rose from 80,000 per day to more than 176,000 per day (Collins and Yaffe-Bellany 2020).

In some areas, like New York City, residential solid waste generation increased by 5 to 30 percent, with the total volume of waste in the United States peaking nationally at 20 percent higher than normal in April 2020 (ibid.). Singapore discarded an additional 1,470 tons of plastics waste from takeout packaging alone during just an eight-week period of lockdown measures (UNCTAD 2020). Add to this an overwhelming production of medical waste, and those parts of the world hit hardest by Covid-19 saw an unprecedented increase in waste by upwards of 445 percent (Kulkarni and Anantharama 2020; Sarkodie and Owusu 2020). Illegal dumping increased by an estimated 300 percent during lockdown (Sarkodie and Owusu, 2020). Historical data tell us that more than 75 percent of COVID-related waste will end up mismanaged, filling landfills and city streets and floating in oceans for decades to come (Forster et al 2020; UNCTAD 2020).

Figure 14.1 Consuming During the COVID-19 Pandemic. Photo by Myra Hird and used with Permission.

"I've Already Been in this Movie"

In *Shopping Our Way to Safety: How We Changed from Protecting the Environment to Protecting Ourselves*, Andrew Szasz persuasively argues that the relationship between individualism, capitalism, and consumerism effects a pronounced and insidious consequence – the decline of collective action, or what he calls "political anaesthesia" (2007: 195). Szasz's starting point is the well-traversed risk theory literature (Beck 1992) that argues that modernity is characterized by a significant increase in people's understanding that they live (and die) with not simply an increase in both the numbers and diversity of potentially harmful hazards, but also an appreciation that risks are inherent to our technologically dependent and driven society:

> [I]ndoor air is more toxic than outdoor air. That is because many household cleaning products and many contemporary home furnishings – carpets, drapes, the fabrics that cover sofas and easy chairs, furniture made of particle board – outgas toxic volatile organic chemicals. Ok, we will go outside – only to inhale diesel exhaust, particulates suspended in the air, molecules of toxic chemicals wafting from factory smokestacks.
>
> (Szasz 2007: 1)

For Ulrich Beck and other risk theory scholars, risk is perceived, filtered and made sense of through neoliberal capitalism, which emphasizes a market economy, enhanced privatization, an overall decrease in government control in favour of industry control and a general entrepreneurial approach to profit maximization (Crooks 1993; Foote and Mazzolini 2012). **Neoliberal capitalism** has successfully transformed citizens into individuals, and individuals into consumers. And it is as **consumers** that we are supposed to make sense of environmental risk:

> [T] he brutal fact of ontological insecurity always has an ultimate addressee: the recipient of the residual risk of the world risk society is the individual. Whatever propels risk and makes it incalculable, whatever provokes the institutional crisis at the level of the governing regime and the markets, shifts the ultimate decision-making responsibility onto the individuals, who are ultimately left to their own devices with their partial and biased knowledge, with undecidability and multiple layers of uncertainty. This is undoubtedly a powerful source of right-wing radicalism and fundamentalism.
>
> (Beck 2007: 195)

Of the myriad forms that individual responses to environmental risk might take, it is primarily in the 'modality of consumer' within neoliberal capitalist societies (Szasz 2007: 4). As such, much preparedness takes the form of consuming (and ultimately wasting) products. Some products, as we have seen, are specifically marketed as disaster preparation (such as high-end bunkers for billionaires) while far more products – indeed everything that can be purchased – are now marketed as 'general preparedness' for an unknowable future.

Thus, within the neoliberal capitalist system, attenuating environmental risk is to be achieved through relentless individual consumption. Each purchase is directed at protecting the individual consumer and their family rather than their community or society as a whole. We witness the enthusiasm, passion and time, attention and energy that consumers devote to determining the 'best' bottled water or the 'best' organic underarm deodorant in the numerous posts on Facebook, Reddit and other online forums devoted to consumer lifestyles. Millions of privileged individual acts of consumption that attempt to insulate the individual and their loved ones against environmental risk leave behind an increasing number of individuals, households, and communities that struggle with issues of safe drinking water, air quality, non-toxic food, and so on:

> An affluent minority – a savvy and influential minority whose political influence is disproportionately greater than their numbers – buys out of the toxic environment, believes it has taken care of the problem for themselves, and loses further interest in that particular toxic issue. Support for more substantive reform weakens. At best, as with organic foods, the situation will tend toward the creation of a permanent dual market, the larger of which consists of products manufactured in a toxic work environment and that contain toxic ingredients, and whose production and consumption continues to discharge these substances into the environment.
>
> (Szasz 2007: 208)

Companies such as Airinum have rushed in to profit from the new COVID-19 'mask mania' by selling designer masks for US$99 or more. From Airinum's website, we learn that:

> [w] e take around 20,000 breaths every day and air is essential for our survival. When we breathe poor quality air, it can severely damage our health and contribute to asthma, respiratory diseases, cancer, strokes and even death. In fact, 7 million people die annually as a result of poor air quality, a number far too high. Whether you need protection from toxic air pollution, itchy pollen, to stay away from bacteria or simply want to be at your very best, the Urban Air Mask will empower you to breathe cleaner and healthy air.
>
> (Airinum nd)

Airinum explicitly acknowledges (indeed highlights) the effect of air pollution in killing seven million people per year. But the solution is not to improve air quality – to take the lead in producing less, lobbying governments, supporting affected communities – but to increase consumption – what industry calls 'empowering' the individual privileged enough to afford their designer masks.

And, familiarly, the privileged few respond accordingly within the neoliberal capitalist script, as these testimonials on Airinum's website attest:

> I was so pleased with these respirators, they fit perfectly, look great, and actually do the job. After wearing it for about an hour, I decided to take it off, thinking that the bushfire smoke had dissipated. However, as I began to remove the mask, I quickly realized this was not the case, rather the mask had filtered out the smoke so well that it made me think the air was clear. (David M.)
>
> I wear the mask when walking through the centre of London for half an hour, two times a day. The mask fits well and keeps my nose and mouth covered. It does it's job, I can't smell the pollution or cigarette smoke – which I was really happy with as I have a strong sense of smell! The filter feels substantial, I feel protected from the polluted environment in built-up areas. (Emma M.)

David need not question the association between climate change and Australia, British Columbia or California's forest fires and Emma need not question why London's air is so polluted; they opt out of these concerns by insulating themselves from risk by buying designer masks. Indeed, Gwyneth Paltrow, whose company Goop is valued at US$250 million, sports an Urban Air Mask from the comfort of her private jet in her Instagram post to which she claims to have "already been in this movie", referring to her role in the virus pandemic film Contagion (in Press Association 2020). Paltrow, the Kardashians, other celebrities and elites like the Walton family – who own Walmart, which sells prepping kits – all endorse prepping. During the COVID-19 pandemic, those wealthy enough opted to use their private planes or charter jets for 'evacuation flights' out of infected areas and into vacations: 'Avoid coronavirus by flying private. ...Request a quote today!' advertises Southern Jet. Others opted to spend time on their yachts or rented islands (feat. Kim Kardashian's private island birthday party in October 2020) to isolate themselves from infected shoreline communities. "It totally makes sense", the president of B&B Yacht Charter Jennifer Saia exclaimed, whose family spent its spring vacation on a yacht in the Bahamas instead of their regular villa in Italy: "You're keeping your family contained in a very small, should-be-clean environment. And going from your car to your F.B.O. [private jet terminal] to your private jet right onto the tarmac. And from there, right onto your yacht, and not having to deal with the public" (quoted in Williams and Bromwich 2020: np).

Risk and privilege are relative: middle-class suburbanites may not control the economic system that, say, defines and decides acceptable levels of DDT administered on crop lands in Somalia (although they may), but they do have the economic power to move themselves and their families to more environmentally safe enclaves, and to further insulate themselves through product purchases that are prohibitively expensive for most people.

Thus, prepping constitutes an increase – often exponentially – in consumption and what Peter Dauvergne (2008) terms its 'shadow': increasing extraction and manufacturing producing environmental degradation, which significantly includes waste. As Szasz points out with regard to the consumption of bottled water: "To make a bottle full of (more or less) clean water, mountain springs are turned into industrial sites, plastic polymers have to be produced, energy used, hazardous wastes and postconsumer, "solid" wastes generated. The production process transforms nature, pollutes nature. Clean consumption is compatible with, even requires, dirty production" (2007: 197).

Thus, ever increasing consumption encourages individuals to believe that they are protected while masking (as double-entendre) the intended and unintended consequences of profit-driven production and consumption in terms of rights-diminished, increasingly unsafe and impoverished labour, community economic, political and cultural devastation, (increasingly toxic) waste generation and so on. As such, prepping to protect ourselves and our loved ones contributes to the very disasters that this behaviour seeks to avoid.

Conclusions

Since the Cold War, the neoliberal capitalist leitmotif to environmental disaster and degradation is 'blame and shop; shop and blame'. Patriarch Filaret, head of the Ukrainian Orthodox Church of the Kyiv Patriarchate, publicly stated that the Covid-19 pandemic was "God's punishment for the sins of men and sinfulness of humanity...First of all, I mean same-sex marriage. This is the cause of the coronavirus" (Villareal 2020: np). After Filaret tested positive for COVID-19, his church defended him, stating, "As the head of the church and as a man, the Patriarch has the freedom to express his views, which are based on morality" and asked the public to "pray for His Holiness Patriarch Filaret, so that the All-Merciful and Almighty Lord God will heal the Patriarch" (ibid). Former President Donald Trump and his supporters blamed China and the World Health Organization for the "China virus" while the Chinese government blamed the US army for the virus (Winter 2020). And as this chapter demonstrates, along with the familiar blame-game, we insulated ourselves from each other:

> Community, empathy and logic are not easy to merchandise; they are not profitable to corporations who like to keep us divided and conquered. There is a lot of money to be made out [of] prepping. Paranoia sells. Guns and ammo and other prepping gear such as underground bunkers and security, food and water, and so on is an extremely lucrative marketplace.
>
> (Foster 2014: 16)

Insidiously, these individual acts of consumption (multiplied by millions of people, repeated billions of times), are integral to how neoliberal capitalism defines and structures morality, or our relationship to both our immediate and distant communities:

> In combination with neoliberalism, the individual becomes his own 'moral entrepreneur' and thus holds the fate of civilization in his (sic) hands. The result is a new 'categorical imperative': act as though the fate of the world depends on your action. Separate your waste, ride a bicycle, use solar energy, etc. The key contradiction which is both obscured and revealed here is that the individual is condemned to individualization and self-responsibility, even vis-a-vis global threats, despite the fact that he (sic) is severed from the decision contexts which escape his (sic) influence.
>
> (Beck 2007: 169)

Immediately after the 9/11 attacks, President George W. Bush advised citizens to go out and shop (Leonard 2010). After the first COVID-19 wave, France's government told its citizens to "go out and start spending" (The Local 2020: np). Not only are we encouraged to believe that increased consumption will resolve global problems such as disease and terrorist attacks but this individualization of responsibility produces the **problem of amplification**, whereby the extractive and manufacturing industries produce far more waste in producing the products we buy (or that remain stockpiled in warehouses or dumped in open dumps, landfills or incinerators if we do not buy) and individuals voluntarily shoulder the burden of responsibility for the ensuing environmental degradation, including waste (Hird 2022). Increases in extraction, production, and distribution (far more than consuming) brings peak oil, toxic waste, and other global environmental crises closer. One of prepping's significant ironies is that instead of leading to independence from the neoliberal capitalist industrial complex, prepping depends upon it. Indeed, neoliberal capitalism and the industrial manufacturing complex created prepping, and thus cannot be called upon to resolve ever-increasing production and consumption.

Former President Trump's 2020 election rhetoric rehashed the neoliberal capitalist accusation familiar since America's participation in the Cold War: that any emphasis on community is 'socialist and anti-American' (Foster 2014: 16). Yet, we also see a lively counter-narrative in grass-roots movements, such as Black Lives Matter and Idle No More, that are clearly demonstrating that millions of people do not have access to the (privileged) individual response of self-insulation from harm and are instead building and supporting community-level solutions. Various alternative futures, from economic steady-state theories, de-growth initiatives (see Chapter 15), transition towns, citizen libraries to anti-capitalist youth movements, challenge individual-level neoliberal capitalist responses that are accelerating environmental degradation and disaster (Bodenheimer and Leidenberger 2020; Kallis and March 2015; Libroiron 2014). Even some preppers resist their portrayal in the media as hyper consumers. Indeed, as Mills found, prepper concerns are 'overwhelmingly non-apocalyptic' and 'that any worst-case disaster was… going to be temporary' (2018: 6). Out of the 39 preppers in Mills's ethnographic study, all of them stockpiled food for only a few months, and only one couple had a bunker.

Still others identify themselves as **preventers** rather than preppers. For example, preventers put their energies into adopting renewable energy systems such as solar panels and windmills, as well as building environmental resiliency through permaculture and other Indigenous practices. Preventers reuse, refurbish and repurpose materials, frequenting junkyards and yard sales rather than Costco and Amazon. So, whereas preppers largely practice what Szasz terms 'inverted quarantine', aiming to isolate themselves from environmental disaster through heightened consumption, preventers set their intentions on challenging the conditions that are leading to disaster.

Questions for Consideration

- How do preppers justify hyper-consumption?
- What media (tv, films) depict preventers rather than preppers?
- What do preppers do with all of their consumer goods when the apocalypse does not arrive?

Note

1 Myra Hird thanks Samm Medeiros for her early assistance in reviewing the literature on preppers.

Further Reading

Foster, G.A. (2014). *Hoarders, Doomsday Preppers, and the Culture of Apocalypse.* New York: Palgrave Macmillan.

Hird, M.J. (2022). *A Public Sociology of Waste.* Bristol: Bristol University Press.

Mills, M.F. (2018). 'Preparing for the unknown...unknowns: "Doomsday" prepping and disaster risk anxiety in the United States', *Journal of Risk Research*, 22(10): 1267–1279.

References

Adeola, F.O. (2012). *Industrial Disasters, Toxic Waste, and Community Impact: Health Effects and Environmental Justice Struggles around the Globe.* London: Lexington Books.

Agamben, G. (1995). *Homo Sacer: Sovereign Power and Bare Life.* Trans. Daniel Heller-oazen. Stanford, CA: Stanford University Press

Airinum. (nd). [online], Available from: www.airi num.com/ [Accessed 15 May 2021].

Alexander, C. and Sanchez, A. (2020). *Indeterminacy: Waste, Value, and the Imagination.* New York: Berghahn Books.

Beck, U. (1992). *Risk Society: Towards a New Modernity*. London: SAGE.
Beck, U. (2007). *World at Risk*. Cambridge: Polity Press.
Beckett, C. and Keeling, A. (2019). 'Rethinking remediation: Mine reclamation, environmental justice, and relations of care', *Local Environment*, 24(3): 216–30.
Bedford, E. (2020). 'Canadian sales growth of personal care and cleaning products due to coronavirus 2020', *Statista*, [online], Available from: www.statista.com/statistics/1110 802/coronavirus-growth-in-personal-care-and-cleaning-product- alescanada/ [Accessed 4 May 2021].
Bodenheimer, M. and Leidenberger, J. (2020) 'COVID- 19 as a window of opportunity for sustainability transitions? Narratives and communication strategies beyond the pandemic', *Sustainability: Science, Practice and Policy*, 16(1): 61–6.
Brooks, M. (2003). *The Zombie Survival Guide: Complete Protection from the Living Dead*. New York: Three Rivers Press.
Brown, B. (nd). 'The prepping guide, SHTF plans', *The Prepping Guide*, [online], Available from: https://thepreppingguide.com/about/ [Accessed 26 October 2020].
Brown, K. (2013). *Plutopia: Nuclear Families, Atomic Cities, and the Great Soviet and American Plutonium Disasters*. Oxford: Oxford University Press.
Collins, K. and Yaffe-Bellany, D. (2020). 'About 2 million guns were sold in the U.S. as virus fears spread', *New York Times*, [online], 1 April, Available from: www.nytimes.com/interactive/2020/04/01/business/coronavirus-gun-sales.html [Accessed 6 May 2021].
Conway, J. (2020). 'Cleaning product sales growth from the coronavirus in the U.S. in March 2020', *Statista*, [online], 6 January, Available from: www.statista.com/statistics/1104333/cleaning-product-sales-growth-from-coronavirus-us/ [Accessed 6 May 2021].
Crooks, H. (1993). *Giants of Garbage: The Rise of the Global Waste Industry and the Politics of Pollution Control*. Toronto: James Lorimer & Company.
Dauvergne, P. (2008). *The Shadows of Consumption: Consequences for the Global Environment*. Cambridge, MA: MIT Press.
Foote, S. and Mazzolini, E. (eds.) (2012). *Histories of the Dustheap: Waste, Material Cultures, Social Justice*. Cambridge, MA: MIT Press.
Forster, P.M., Forster, H.I., Evans, M.J., Gidden, M.J., Jones, C.D., C.A., Lamboll, R.D., Le Quéré C., Rogelj, J., Rosen, D., Schleussner, C.-F., Richardson, T.B., Smith, C.J. and Turnock, S.T. (2020). 'Current and future global climate impacts resulting from COVID- 19', *Nature Climate Change*, 10: 913–19.
Foster, G.A. (2014). *Hoarders, Doomsday Preppers, and the Culture of Apocalypse*. New York: Palgrave Macmillan.
Garrett, R. (2021). 'Doomsday preppers and the architecture of dread', *Geoforum*, 127: 401–411.
Ginn, F. (2015). 'When horses won't eat: Apocalypse and the Anthropocene', *Annals of the Association of American Geographers*, 105(2): 351–359.
Hird, M.J. (2021). *Canada's Waste Flows*. Montréal: McGill- Queen's University Press.
Hird, M.J. (2022). *A Public Sociology of Waste*. Bristol: Bristol University Press.
Hird, M.J. and Riha, J. (2021). 'Prepping for the [insert here] apocalypse and wasting the future' in Z. Gille and J. Lepawsky (eds.) *Handbook of Waste Studies*. New York and London: Routledge, pp. 305–321.
Hoover, E. (2017). *The River Is in Us: Fighting Toxics in a Mohawk Community*. Minneapolis: University of Minnesota Press.

Intergovernmental Panel on Climate Change (IPCC). (2020). 'Climate change and land', [online], Available from: www.ipcc.ch/site/assets/uploads/sites/4/2020/02/SPM_Updated-Jan20.pdf [Accessed 21 May 2021].

Kallis, G. and March, H. (2015). 'Imaginaries of hope: The utopianism of degrowth', *Annals of the Association of American Geographers*, 105(2): 360–368.

Kelly, C. (2016). 'The man-pocalypse: Doomsday preppers and the rituals of apocalyptic manhood'. *Text Performance Quarterly*, 36(2–3): 95–114.

Klein, N. (2008). *The Shock Doctrine: The Rise of Disaster Capitalism*. Toronto: Vintage Canada.

Kristeva, J. (1980/2). *Powers of Horror: An Essay on Abjection*. New York: Columbia University Press.

Kulkarni, B.N. and Anantharama, V. (2020). 'Repercussions of COVID-19 pandemic on municipal solid waste management: Challenges and opportunities', *Science of the Total Environment*, 743: 2–8.

Leonard, A. (2010). *The Story of Stuff*. New York: Simon & Schuster.

Liboiron, M. (2014). 'Solutions to waste and the problem of scalar mismatches', *Discard Studies*, [online], 10 February, Available from: https://discardstudies.com/2014/02/10/solutions-to-waste-and-the-problem-of-scalar-mismatches/ [Accessed 6 May 2020].

Local, The. (2020). 'French told to "go out and start shopping" to relaunch economy', [online], 29 May, Available from: www.thelocal.fr/20200529/french-old-go-out-and-start-spending-to-relaunch-the-economoy?fbclid=IwAR1H1SNc227Sm3LdJ65L4-sPbhkh YBWN8h53TPuC9LuUChB-K3tvSHUmvbQ [Accessed 6 May 2021].

Lundin, C. (2007) *When All Hell Breaks Loose: Stuff You Need to Survive When Disaster Strikes*. Kaysville, UT: Gibbs Smith.

Luther, D. (2015). *The Prepper's Water Survival Guide*. Berkeley: Ulysses Press.

Malm, A. and Hornborg, A. (2014). 'The geology of mankind? A critique of the Anthropocene narrative', *Anthropocene Review*, 1(1): 62–69.

Mills, M.F. (2018). 'Preparing for the unknown...unknowns: "Doomsday prepping and disaster risk anxiety in the United States', *Journal of Risk Research*, 22(10): 1267–1279.

Murphy, T. (2013). 'Preppers are getting ready for the Barackalypse', *Mother Jones News*, [online], January/ February issue, Available from: www.motherjones.com/politics/2012/12/preppers-survivalist-doomsday-obama/[Accessed 6 May 2021].

Nixon, R. (2011). *Slow Violence and the Environmentalism of the Poor*. Cambridge, MA: Harvard University Press.

Pennington, T. and Luther, D. (2014). *The Prepper's Blueprint*, np. London, UK: CreateSpace Independent Publishing Platform.

Press Association (2020). 'I've been in this movie': Gwyneth Paltrow takes coronavirus precautions', *The Guardian*, 26 February. www.theguardian.com/film/2020/feb/26/gwyneth-paltrow-coronavirus-contagion. Accessed 5 August 2024.

Roe, B.E. Bender, K. and Qi, D. (2020). 'The Impact of COVID-19 on Consumer Food Waste', *Applied Economic Perspectives and Policy*, 3(1): 401–411

Robbins, P. and Moore, S.A. (2013). 'Ecological anxiety disorder: Diagnosing the politics of the Anthropocene', *Cultural Geographies*, 20(1): 3–19.

Sarkodie, S.A. and Owusu, P.A. (2020). 'Impact of meteorological factors on COVID-19 pandemic: Evidence from top 20 countries with confirmed cases', *Environmental Research*, 191: 1–7.

Schneider-Mayerson, M. (2013). 'Disaster movies and the "peak oil" movement: Does popular culture encourage eco- apocalyptic beliefs in the United States?', *Journal for the Study of Religion, Nature and Culture*, 7(3): 289–314.

Statistics Canada. (2020). 'Canadian consumers prepare for COVID-19', [online], Available from: www150.statcan.gc.ca/n1/en/pub/62f0014m/62f0014m2020004-eng.pdf?st=tk2_Wyh_ [Accessed 9 March 2021].

Stein, M. (2008). *When Technology Fails: A Manual for Self- Reliance, Sustainability and Surviving the Long Emergency*. White River Junction: Chelsea Green Publishing.

Szasz, A. (2007). *Shopping Our Way to Safety: How We Changed from Protecting the Environment to Protecting Ourselves*. Minneapolis: University of Minnesota Press.

Tactical.com. (nd). 'A complete beginner's guide to prepping', [online], Available from: www.tactical.com/complete-beginners-guide-to-prepping/ [Accessed 26 October 2020].

UNCTAD. (2020). 'Growing plastic pollution in wake of COVID- 19: How trade policy can help', [online], 27 July, Available from: https://unctad.org/news/growing-plastic-pollution-wake-covid-19-how-trade-policy-can-help [Accessed 6 May 2021].

Vigdor, N. (2020). 'A hoarder's huge stockpile of masks and gloves will now go to doctors and nurses, F.B.I. says', *New York Times*, 2 April, Available from: www.nytimes.com/2020/04/02/nyregion/brooklyn-coronavirus-price-gouging.html [Accessed 24 May 2021].

Villareal, D. (2020). 'Ukrainian church leader who blamed COVID-19 on gay marriage tests positive for virus', *NBC News*, [online], 8 September, Available from: www.nbcn ws.com/feature/nbc- ut/ukrainian-church-leader- ho-blamed-covid-19-gay-marriage-tests-1239 528 [Accessed 6 May 2021].

Watt-Cloutier, S. (2015). *The Right to Be Cold: One Woman's Story of Protecting Her Culture, the Arctic and the Whole Planet*. Toronto: Penguin.

Williams, A. and Bromwich, J.E. (2020). 'The rich are preparing for the coronavirus differently', *New York Times*, [online], 5 March, Available from: www.nytimes.com/2020/03/05/style/the-rich-are-preparing-for-coronavirus-differently.html [Accessed 7 October 2020].

Winter, L. (2020). 'Chinese officials blame US Army for coronavirus', *The Scientist*, [online], 13 March, Available from: www.the-scientist.com/news-opinion/chinese-officials-blame-us-army-for-coronavirus-67267 [Accessed 6 May 2021].

15 Consuming Less

Myra J. Hird and Gabriella Dee

Summary

- In order to live within our planet's carrying capacity, we must consume less.
- Most people are consuming within planetary limits, while a few million people are very significantly over-consuming.
- Consuming cannot be meaningfully separated from producing.
- Consumers with the income and time resources may make purchasing decisions that are less detrimental to the environment.
- People may effectively contribute to community, non-governmental organizations and other efforts to pressure governments and industry to produce both fewer, and more eco-friendly, products.

Keywords: Consuming; Social Injustice; Producing; Individual Responsibility; Corporate Responsibility

Introduction

This edited collection provides insights into the environmental costs of consuming many things: land, food, water, plastics, clothing, electronics, fossil fuels, and more. The chapters detail consumption's environmental impacts, such as carbon emissions and contaminants, that have detrimental effects on human health and the environment. What the chapters also significantly argue is that these negative environmental and human health effects should not be separated from social justice issues.

Consuming Land details the environmental costs that extractive projects – which entail significant land use – have, not only on the land itself but on the Indigenous communities who live on, and near, this land. The chapter highlights the consequences that different understandings of land have on negotiation processes between local communities and resource extraction companies and corporations. For Brazil's Yudjá/Juruna people, land has its

DOI: 10.4324/9781003412526-16

own rights, and is fundamentally interconnected with its people, necessitating an ongoing sacred and respectful relationship. The Yudjá/Juruna people – generation after generation – understand that their flourishing depends on the health of land, waters and air on which they depend. For the mining companies and national government, land and water are commodities: products to be extracted and marketed for profit. The tensions between these two oppositional worldviews results in serious ongoing clashes that in some cases has resulted in the loss of human life, as well as environmental devastation (Wilkes and Hird 2019).

Consuming Water, similarly explores the tensions between Indigenous communities in Australia and for-profit companies that understand water in oppositional ways. Through an examination of agricultural markets, cities, mobility, and leisure, the chapter analyzes how companies market and commodify water as integral to contemporary Australian settler colonial identity. By contrast, Indigenous peoples in Australia understand water as having its own rights and proclivities, and that people's dependence on water necessitates a respectful relationship that neither commodifies nor over-consumes water beyond capacity.

In Consuming Fossil Fuels, Nick Graham details how the fossil fuel industry is responsible for a significant proportion of the global increases in carbon dioxide emissions. The chapter analyzes how fossil fuels have become deeply embedded in contemporary consumer society, literally fueling the staggering increase in the production of products, their global circulation, and consumption. The chapter argues not only that we must transition to renewable energy (sun, water, wind), but that this transition must take place much more rapidly than current plans.

Consuming Energy complements the previous chapter in highlighting the negative environmental costs of consuming energy at ever-increasing rates. The abundance of fossil fuel energy, heavy government subsidies and a 'buy-now; pay-later' capitalist approach all interconnect to significantly contribute to the global climate crisis we now face. Consuming Energy argues that profound changes to what, how, and how much we consume requires understanding the linkages between consumption and energy.

Consuming Food also focuses on the social injustice 'baked' into contemporary neoliberal capitalist food production and consumption. Elaine Power examines how the industrial capitalist food system produces an abundance of food relatively inexpensively, which appears to serve the literal appetites of a relative minority of the global population, but actually serves the profit interests of a small group of transnational corporations that monopolize the food production system. The chapter focuses on the growing trend in downloading food waste onto food-insecure individuals and communities, and reveals how this reinforces existing inequities, and indeed perpetuates the environmental and other problems endemic to our current food production, distribution, and consumption system.

Much of the food we buy at grocery stores is wrapped in plastics. Consuming Plastics connects plastics to their origin: fossil fuels. The chapter examines the environmental and human health unsustainability of ever-increasing plastics production and consumption. It points to local, regional, national, and supra-national initiatives that are identifying ambitious – yet for the most part promissory – targets to better regulate and manage plastics production, consumption and waste.

Consuming Electronics similarly connects electronics consumption to social justice issues by examining the extraction of rare earth and other materials necessary to build smartphones and watches, laptops, cars, airplanes, and all of the other electronics that proliferate in affluent societies. Patrick Brodie also highlights the economies of obsolescence and waste, driving the ever-increasing accumulation of e-waste. The chapter examines how extraction, production, consumption, and waste is afforded by networks of imperial capitalism, and the social injustice endemic to the system.

The overarching social injustice of textile production is the subject of Sofi Thanhauser's ethnography of clothes production in Vietnam, China, and other textile-manufacturing nations. Focusing on the establishment of the Export Processing Zone, Consuming Fashion details how poorer countries exploit their (mainly female) labor force through low pay, lax and/or unenforced health and safety standards and practices, and tax concessions to large fashion companies that flood the market with consumer products that are discarded at an ever-increasing pace. The chapter connects with the examination of fossil fuels, energy, and plastics, pointing out that the rapid expansion and utilization of synthetic fibers is exacerbating the environmental and human health impacts of textiles.

Consuming Pets offers the interesting and largely unremarked negative impacts of pet food on the environment. The chapter focuses on the environmental impacts of meat as a key ingredient in most pet food (particularly dogs and cats), and the impact of meat-production industry on carbon emissions, soil degradation, and other environmental crises. The chapter considers other pet-food ingredient options that less negatively impact the environment, as well as disrupt the killing of animals to feed other animals.

Consuming Waste examines contemporary government and industry initiatives to consume waste in order to decrease waste. The increasing popularity of energy-from-waste facilities offers the promise of both a largely untapped source of energy (garbage), diverting waste from landfills, and 'disappearing' waste itself by burning it. The chapter examines how energy-from-waste, as an energy regime, purports to contribute to the Circular Economy, but in fact perpetuates the current industrial capitalist linear economy that contributes to profound negative effects on the environment and human health.

Consuming Preparedness examines another facet of consumption: the enigmatic attainment of preparedness. In this chapter, Myra Hird and Jacob

Riha demonstrate how neoliberal capitalism has encouraged consumption for the purpose of being prepared for environmental, human health, and other calamities. By relentlessly highlighting potential risk, companies market anything and everything – from toilet paper to bunkers – that purport to shield consumers from harm. The chapter argues that consumption in the name of preparedness is contributing to the very environmental collapse (through increased resource extraction, manufacturing, consumption, and waste) that people are consuming to avoid.

The Consuming Eco/Tourism and Consuming Green chapters explore some consumers' desire to buy products and services that have a less negative environmental and human health impact, as well as a greater social justice and equity added value. Consuming Eco/Tourism examines the significant impact that all major facets of tourism – from travel, accommodation, food, and myriad services – has on local environments, labor, and community wellbeing. It notes that some areas (such as Venice, Italy) have been so 'over-visited' that local governments are instituting either tourist bans or restrictions. Other tourist destinations are attempting to work with visitors to help them to better understand the impact that their tourism has on local resources, livelihoods, and environments, and to devise ways to minimize the negative impacts and increase positive impacts.

Lara Houston continues the examination of electronics consumption by focusing on two electronic products – mobile phones and digital sensors – and their negative environmental footprint. Like the other chapters, Consuming Knowledge offers insights into how some individuals and community initiatives are finding non-capitalist (i.e. less environmentally harmful) ways of consuming, or indeed ways of prolonging product 'life' in order to consume less. This chapter considers the Right to Repair movement in several countries around the world that focuses on supporting people in repairing their own electronics and other manufactured products rather than discarding them when they break down. Increasingly, regulations are requiring electronics companies to make product manuals available (at least to professional repairers). Repairing products keeps these products in use for longer periods of time, and thus delays their disposal as well as the purchase of new products. And there is an added-value in people learning how to repair their things, as well as the social benefits of community-building.

Consuming Green again focuses on the increased consumer recognition of the negative environmental and human health impacts of consumption, and the relatively recent invention of 'green' products on the market. The chapter outlines the challenges to consuming products that tend to cost more but promise to incur less negative impact on the environment. These challenges range from higher cost to the phenomenon of 'greenwashing' whereby companies make false or misleading claims about the environmental impact of their products.

Consuming Differently

Currently, consuming green, repair shops and other initiatives tend to target consuming and consumerism at the individual level. As the Introduction examines, the resource extraction, manufacturing, and retail industries very successfully market consuming as key to individual choice, efficiency, and freedom. Indeed, consuming is *emblematic* of freedom in western countries. Now, an increasing number of individuals are recognizing the connections between consumption and environmental degradation, including the climate crisis. Individuals and households with the money, time, and other resources are making lifestyle choices (types of vehicles driven, amount of energy used in the home, length of showers, diet and so on) that decrease their carbon footprint and are otherwise less harmful to the environment. In other words, for the most part, sustainable living in industrialized high-income countries typically means individuals altering their consumption habits. When these alterations lead to decreased consumption, then environmental benefits include decreases in energy use and waste, as well as the potential psychological benefits to individuals that they are making a positive impact on the environment.

Since capitalism is predicated on ever-increasing consumption, we would anticipate that our global political-economic system will seek ways of enveloping attempts to decrease consumption within its system. And, indeed, capitalism does this by harnessing neoliberalism's focus on individual responsibility and entrepreneurship. For example, the Zero Waste Movement focuses on approaches such as product eco-design, using innovative technologies to produce products within a closed-loop supply chain, and ascertaining the environmental impact of any given product through Life Cycle Analysis (Song et al.2015). The main objective of Zero Waste is to divert as much generated waste as possible. However, Zero Waste 'lifestyle influencers' and community organizations tend to focus more on 'green consuming' and recycling rather than consuming less.

Indeed, in an effort to live Zero Waste lifestyles, people are often encouraged to consume *more*: household goods such as metal and glass storage containers for bulk goods, reusable containers, brushes made from wood and natural fibers etc. As such, the Zero Waste movement has actually created a new marketing *niche*. Granted, the movement does advocate shopping at refilleries or other places that offer goods in bulk, thus reducing packaging, and shopping at thrift stores. But Zero Waste's major focus is to divert waste away from landfill, and not in consuming less per se. We might say that the Zero Waste movement favors consuming differently over consuming less. Simply reclassifying waste as recycling or compost does not require (or even encourage) decreased consumption, but is rather a way of 'hiding behind' diversion rather than tackling the challenge of reducing the production of products. We need to keep in mind that Zero Waste individual behaviors and/or group initiatives are largely dependent upon recycling, which comes with considerable environmental costs (Hird 2022). Indeed, Samantha MacBride identifies recycling as 'busyness': a 'sense that progress is being made' even though the facts show that it is not (2012: 171).

As we saw in the Introduction and throughout the chapters in this book, even when individuals attempt to consume responsibly, they are often forced to consume items due to the planned obsolescence of those purchased items. A well-made item will last a lifetime and only be purchased once – great for the consumer, not so great for the manufacturer and capitalist profit (it is more profitable for some people to buy the same product repeatedly than for more people to buy a product only once). Thus, as well as sophisticated marketing strategies, and the constant introduction of 'new' products (since its first version served in 1886, Coca-Cola has created over 100 different variations on this single beverage product), manufacturers rely on planned obsolescence to increase consumption. The light bulb is the first documented case of planned obsolescence (Rivera and Lallmahomed, 2016). Even though filament technology in the 1920s produced bulbs that could last 2500 h, producers cooperated to impose a 1000 h limit on bulb lifetimes in order to increase the need for lightbulbs, resulting in increased producer profit.

Like attempts to reduce individual and household consumption, people are increasingly pushing back against planned obsolescence. And governments are paying attention. For instance, in 2018 the Italian Competition Authority fined both Apple and Samsung for unfairly promoting software updates that seriously impaired the functioning of customer cellular devices (Busch et al., 2018). In an attempt to reduce e-waste, the EU passed an amendment in 2022 that all cellular devices released after 2024 have to be equipped with universal charging ports (Fourneaux, 2024). Progress is also being made to provide consumers with a greater right to repair goods. In 2023, the government of France earmarked €154m in a five-year fund to financially incentivize people to repair their clothes and shoes (Willsher, 2023). This initiative aims to provide a repair bonus (people will be able to claim back between €6-€25 for the cost of repairs), support workers and retailers who offer repairs, create new jobs, reduce waste in the fashion industry, and to promote a more Circular Economy. In the same month, Canada's province of Québec passed Bill 29: An Act to Protect Consumers from Planned Obsolescence and to Promote the Durability, Repairability and Maintenance of Goods. The increasing appearance of Right to Repair legislation means that consumers will have greater control over their consumption of goods, and more services will be available to them.

Case Study: Adopting Regulations to Help Decrease Consumption

In the 1990s, the European Union (EU) instituted a consumer-friendly labeling system to better inform consumers about the energy efficiency of consumer equipment or vehicles. This labeling system was accompanied with strict regulations surrounding energy efficiency, and incentivized manufacturers to create and sell more efficient products at a lower cost; thereby helping consumers to reduce their energy consumption (Fourneaux, 2024). In 2018, an EU impact assessment found that 63% of participating EU citizens were dissatisfied with the need to purchase a new mobile phone charger when purchasing a new mobile phone, 76% felt inconvenienced, and 63% favored the EU regulating companies to create a common electronic device charger for devices such as mobile phones (ibid.). This same assessment found that mobile phone chargers were responsible for 11,000 tons of e-waste. If phone chargers were standardized and unbundled from purchased phones, the amount of e-waste that chargers generate on a yearly basis could be greatly reduced. Ahmed et al. (2021) found that strong regulations have the best chance of reducing energy consumption (Ahmed et al. 2021). This research suggests that stronger, enforceable regulations to curve consumption could have a large positive effect on global sustainability.

As with Right to Repair initiatives, what's known as the Sharing Economy aims to reduce consumption. Many large cities already have bicycle share programs, in which consumers can pay a fee to ride a bicycle, thereby reducing the number of bicycles that are privately owned (Murphy and Usher, 2015). Car-sharing in many European countries is successfully increasing the use of shared electric vehicles, reducing the cost of mobility to users, reducing the number of privately owned cars, and reducing greenhouse gas emissions (Roblek et al. 2021). The Sharing Economy is also increasingly applying to food serviceware. In mid 2024, Canada's capital city of Ottawa will be piloting a first-of-its-kind collaborative program with major grocers. This program will give consumers the opportunity to purchase selected products in free reusable containers, which they can then return to 'smart' tracking bins for collection, sanitization and redistribution by the grocery service partner. It is hoped that this pilot program, if successful, can be expanded to include more retailers (such as restaurants that offer meals to go) as well as expand over a greater geographic area (Circular Innovation Council, 2024). On a smaller though similar scale, the tourist city of Banff, Alberta is currently piloting a reusable cup program to reduce the number of disposable coffee cups thrown out on a daily basis (Rhode, 2024).

Extracting, Producing, and Retailing

While individual and household behavior focused on reducing consumption are beneficial to the environment, we need to understand these actions in their broader context. For example, at least one study found that bicycle share users are mostly middle- and upper-class males, suggesting inequity in the ability of

Figure 15.1 Of all the Rs (Reduce, Reuse, Recycle, Refurbish, Redesign, etc.), Reduction is Key to Impacting Our Consumption Rate. Based on the Universal Recycling Logo.

consumers to access the program (Murphy and Usher 2015). In other words, individuals and households who are able to make choices to consume less and/or consume in ways that are less detrimental to the environment are more likely to be people who have the financial means and resources. At least one parent must have sufficient leisure time to shop 'green'. According to the US Department of Agriculture (2009), about 2.3 million people (just over 2% of all households in the United States) live in 'food deserts': these millions of people lack access to healthy food options such as fruits and vegetables, and affordable food. What people do have access to tends to be more take-out fast-food that is more highly packaged, creating more waste.

Consumers with the financial and leisure means to choose what they buy *and to over-consume* represent, as the Introduction notes, about 20% of the global population. This means that about 80% of people do not have the financial means to either over-consume or choose what they consume; most people are not sufficiently income-secure to exercise the privilege of buying more expensive green products.

And though reuse programs, such as cup-sharing and returnable food containers do reduce the use of resources needed to produce these products, the tradeoff is a greater use of water and energy (for washing) and transportation of reusable containers from the return bins to the sanitation facility and back to the distribution centers and grocery stores. If the sanitation centers are not local, significant carbon emissions costs can be incurred. It is crucial, when setting such programs up, that all environmental costs are evaluated to ensure that overall consumption is truly being reduced.

All of this brings us to the critical question that receives less media and public attention: the role of resource extraction, manufacturing, and retail industries in detrimental human health and environmental impacts. Put another way, there is a stark unevenness to the focus on individuals and households to shoulder the responsibility for the staggering amount of pollution and waste. What about the producers of all of the myriad products available to consume? As Francois Jarrige and Thomas Le Roux observe, "the decoupling of sites of production – subjected to direct pollution – from sanitized sites of consumption rendered almost imperceptible to the public the increase in emissions of toxic substances in the environment" (2020: 237).

We need to consider what motivates producers to create products with known and unknown contaminants. What regulatory and policy incentives (carrots) and penalties (sticks) might we develop to hold industry responsible for the products they produce, and all of the marketing that encourages, incites, shames, flatters, and otherwise increases the consumption of their products? How do we encourage producers to build product waste and contamination into their product production projections? All of these amount to one overarching question: How do we get producers to take more responsibility for consumption?

Under public pressure, governments are increasingly turning to Extended Producer Responsibility (EPR) regulations. EPR shifts responsibility for any given product's life-cycle on to the companies that manufacture these products. In 2022, the European Union proposed the EU Packaging Regulation that, if passed, will make all packaging recyclable by 2030, restrict unnecessary packaging, and promote reusable and refillable packaging solutions. The Regulation will also create mandatory rates of recycled content that producers have to include in new plastic packaging, with the target being to reduce packaging waste by 15% per capita per Member State by 2040 compared to 2018 levels (European Commission, 2022). The EU's Waste from Electrical and Electronic Equipment (WEEE) Directive and EU Battery Directive focus on specific products and their waste.

In response, some companies are investigating ways to eco-design product packaging and are otherwise moving towards less packaging, refill, and return options. But not all companies are readily shouldering responsibility for the products they produce. In a study of 1,925 large-cap firms, Yu et al. (2020) found that a lack of standardization in disclosure rules of sustainability data and no global governing body to ensure accuracy of reporting by companies about their efforts to be more environmentally conscious resulted in more than half of the companies engaging in greenwashing. The Center for International Environmental Law (2024) found the following concerning information: at the recent Fourth Session (INC-4) of the UN's Environment Programme meetings whose purpose is to develop an international and legally binding document on plastic pollution, there were 196 lobbyists for the fossil fuel and chemical industry. This number of lobbyists is three times greater than the 58 independent scientists from the Scientists' Coalition for an Effective Plastic Treaty, and seven times greater than the 28 representatives of the Indigenous Peoples Caucus. The fossil fuel and chemical industry had more lobbyists at the INC-4 meetings than the smallest 87 country delegations *combined*. And the fossil fuel and chemical industry lobbying was successful: after a full week of meetings, the INC-4 failed to include any provisions for the reduction of plastic or polymer production.

This is one example of a long-standing pattern whereby companies market themselves as environmentally conscious on their websites and through other advertising means, while at the same time actively resist taking responsibility for the environmental costs of their products' life cycles. Katharine Owens and Katie Conlon put it like this: "If you walked into your bathroom to find your tub overflowing with water, would you first begin mopping up the water on the ground, or would you turn off the tap?" (2021: 5). These researchers join a growing chorus of scholars and environmental groups advocating the brand names (Coca-Cola and so on) take financial and environmental responsibility for the environmental pollution their products create (see for ex. BreakFreeFromPlastic 2023; Cowger et. al. 2024; Charles, Kimman and Saran 2021).

Conclusions

People with the means to make choices about what they consume are likely to be able to consume less. These same people have reported that they are willing to pay more for environmentally friendly products and may be more likely to purchase products from firms they consider to be socially responsible (de Freitas Netto et al., 2020). Some people may also have the means to consume differently, consuming products whose life cycle has a less negative environmental footprint than other products. People with the means – the upper and middle classes of any given country – are also more likely to draw the attention of their government representatives, who court their vote at each election cycle. This means that people who are concerned about the environmental impacts of producing and consuming products may join their voices and signatures to environmental initiatives that call for greater industry and government responsibility in eliminating and better managing pollution and human health concerns. By creating binding regulations, as is being done in the EU, those same consumers can have greater confidence that the products they are purchasing are indeed more environmentally sound and being produced more sustainably than alternative products. That is, we need to take action to reduce consumption whenever we can, try to consume differently within our means, and join forces with others to advocate for a less contaminated and more social just planetary system.

Questions for Consideration

- What changes might you make to your daily living that would decrease the amount you consume?
- Of all of the things that you consume, what things are essential to living and what things are not? Why?

- How might individuals join local communities (for instance, university clubs) to decrease consumption within the places that we study (universities, high schools) and work?
- How might consumers better understand the relationships between the things we buy and the environmental costs of extracting the materials for producing and distributing these things?

Further Reading

Heidbreder, L.M., Bablok, I., Drews, S. and Menzel, C. (2019) Tackling the plastic problem: A review on perceptions, behaviors, and interventions. *Science of the Total Environment*, 668: 1077–1093.

Jackson, T. (2005) Live better by consuming less? Is there a "double dividend" in sustainable consumption? *Journal of Industrial Ecology*, 9(1-2): 19–36.

McGouran, C. and Prothero, A. (2016) Enacted voluntary simplicity – Exploring the consequences of requesting consumers to intentionally consume less. *European Journal of Marketing*, 50: 189–212.

Senbel, M., McDaniels, T., and Dowlatabadi, H. (2003) The ecological footprint: A non-monetary metric of human consumption applied to North America. *Global Environmental Change*, 13(2): 83–100.

References

Ahmed, Z., Ahmad, M., Rjoub, H., Kalugina, O.A. and Hussain, N. (2021) Economic growth, renewable energy consumption, and ecological footprint: Exploring the role of environmental regulations and democracy in sustainable development. *Sustainable Development*, 30: 595–605.

BreakFreeFromPlastic. (2023) *Branded 6: Brand Audit Report.* Accessed on April 30, 2024: https://brandaudit.breakfreefromplastic.org/brand-audit-2023/

Busch, C., De Franceschi, A., Durovic, M., Zuzak, J., Mak, V., Morais Carvalho, J., Nemeth, K., Podszun, R. and Riefa, C. (2018) Planned obsolescence challenging the effectiveness of consumer law and the achievement of a sustainable economy: The Apple and Samsung cases. *Journal of European Consumer and Market Law*, 7: 217–264.

Center for International Environmental Law. (2024) Fossil fuel Lobbyists outnumber national delegations, scientists, and indigenous peoples at plastics treaty negotiations. www.ciel.org/news/fossil-fuel-and-chemical-industry-influence-inc4/

Charles, D., Kimman, L., and Saran, N. (2021) *The Plastic Waste Makers Index: Revealing the Source of the Single-Use Plastics Crisis.* Minderoo Foundation.

Circular Innovation Council. (January 17, 2024) Circular Innovation Council collaborates with Canada's biggest grocers to design an innovative reuse program. Accessed on April 30, 2024: www.globenewswire.com/news-release/2024/01/17/2811057/0/en/Circular-Innovation-Council-Collaborates-with-Canada-s-Biggest-Grocers-to-Design-an-Innovative-Reuse-Program.html

Cowger, W. et.al. (2024) Global producer responsibility for plastic pollution. *Sciences Advances*, 10: 1–7.

De Freitas Netto, S.V., Sobral, M.F.F., Ribeiro, A.R.B. and da Luz Soares, G.R. (2020) Concepts and forms of greenwashing: A systematic review. *Environmental Sciences Europe*, 32: 1–12.

European Commission (na). (30 November 2022) *European Green Deal: Putting an end to wasteful packaging, boosting reuse and recycling.* Press release. Accessed on 7 May, 2024: https://ec.europa.eu/commission/presscorner/detail/en/ip_22_7155

Fourneaux, A. (2024) The European Union's new USB-C standardization amendment: What does it mean for innovation within the consumer technology industry? *Northwestern Journal of International Law and Business*, 44(1): 149–171.

Hird, M.J. (2022) *A Public Sociology of Waste.* Bristol University Press.

Jarrige, F. and Le Roux, T. (2020) *The Contamination of the Earth: A History of Pollutants in the Industrial Age.* MIT Press.

MacBride, S. (2012) *Recycling Reconsidered: The Present Failure and Future Promise of Environmental Action in the United States.* The MIT Press.

Murphy, E. and Usher, J. (2015) The role of bicycle-sharing in the city: Analysis of the Irish experience. *International Journal of Sustainable Transportation*, 9(2): 116–125.

Owens, K.A. and Conlon, K. (2021) Mopping up or turning off the tap? Environmental injustice and the ethics of plastic pollution. *Frontiers in Marine Science*, 8:713385.

Rhode, M. (April 19, 2024) 'Banff Borrows': How the town is combatting single-use waste. *Calgary Herald.* Accessed on April 30, 2024: https://calgaryherald.com/news/local-news/banff-borrows-how-the-town-is-combatting-single-use-waste

Rivera, J.L. and Lallmahomed, A. (2016) Environmental implications of planned obsolescence and product lifetime: A literature review. *International Journal of Sustainable Engineering*, 9(2): 119–129.

Roblek, V., Meško, M. and Podbregar, I. (2021) Impact of car sharing on urban sustainability. *Sustainability*, 13(2): 905.

Song, Q., Li, J., and Zeng, X. (2015) Minimizing the increased solid waste through zero waste strategy. *Journal of Cleaner Production*, 104: 199–210.

United States Department of Agriculture Economic Research Service. (2009) Access to affordable and nutritious food: Measuring and understanding food deserts and their consequences. www.ers.usda.gov/webdocs/publications/42711/12716_ap036_1_.pdf?v=41055

Wilkes, J. and Hird, M.J. (May 29, 2019) Colonial ideologies of waste: Implications for land and life. *EuropeNowJournal*, np. www.europenowjournal.org/2019/05/06/confronting-waste/

Willsher, K. (12 July, 2023). Stitch in time: France to help pay for clothes to be mended to cut waste. *The Guardian.* Accessed on July 28, 2023: www.theguardian.com/environment/2023/jul/12/stitch-in-time-france-to-help-pay-for-clothes-to-be-mended-to-cut-waste

Yu, E.P., Luu, B.V. and Chen, C. (2020) Greenwashing in environmental, social and governance disclosures. *Research in International Business and Finance*, 52: 101192.

Index

Note: Page locators in *italics* represents figures.